The Blackwell Great Minds series gives readers a strong sense of the fundamental views of the great western thinkers and captures the relevance of these figures to the way we think and live today.

Forthcoming

blackwell great minds

kierkegaard

M. Jamie Ferreira

WILEY-BLACKWELL

A John Wiley & Sons, Ltd., Publication

This edition first published 2009
© 2009 M. Jamie Ferreira

Blackwell Publishing was acquired by John Wiley & Sons in February 2007.
Blackwell's publishing program has been merged with Wiley's global Scientific,
Technical, and Medical business to form Wiley-Blackwell.

Registered Office
John Wiley & Sons Ltd, The Atrium, Southern Gate, Chichester, West Sussex,
PO19 8SQ, United Kingdom

Editorial Offices
350 Main Street, Malden, MA 02148-5020, USA
9600 Garsington Road, Oxford, OX4 2DQ, UK
The Atrium, Southern Gate, Chichester, West Sussex, PO19 8SQ, UK

For details of our global editorial offices, for customer services, and for
information about how to apply for permission to reuse the copyright material
in this book please see our website at www.wiley.com/wiley-blackwell.

The right of M. Jamie Ferreira to be identified as the author of this work has been
asserted in accordance with the Copyright, Designs and Patents Act 1988.

All rights reserved. No part of this publication may be reproduced, stored in a
retrieval system, or transmitted, in any form or by any means, electronic,
mechanical, photocopying, recording or otherwise, except as permitted by the UK
Copyright, Designs and Patents Act 1988, without the prior permission of the
publisher.

Wiley also publishes its books in a variety of electronic formats. Some content
that appears in print may not be available in electronic books.

Designations used by companies to distinguish their products are often claimed as
trademarks. All brand names and product names used in this book are trade names,
service marks, trademarks or registered trademarks of their respective owners. The
publisher is not associated with any product or vendor mentioned in this book. This
publication is designed to provide accurate and authoritative information in regard to
the subject matter covered. It is sold on the understanding that the publisher is not
engaged in rendering professional services. If professional advice or other expert
assistance is required, the services of a competent professional should be sought.

Library of Congress Cataloging-in-Publication Data

Ferreira, M. Jamie.
  Kierkegaard / M. Jamie Ferreira.
    p. cm. — (Blackwell great minds)
  Includes bibliographical references and index.
  ISBN 978-1-4051-4277-9 (hardcover : alk. paper) — ISBN 978-1-4051-4278-6
(pbk. : alk. paper) 1. Kierkegaard, Søren, 1813–1855. I. Title.
  B4377.F47 2009
  198'.9—dc22
  [B]
                                                                2008027410

A catalogue record for this book is available from the British Library.

Set in 9.5/12pt Trump Mediaeval by Graphicraft Limited, Hong Kong
Printed in Singapore by Utopia Press Pte Ltd

1 2009

Contents

Preface

In one sense, this book is my answer to all those people over the years who have asked me why I find reading Kierkegaard so fascinating. Although it is not a conventional introduction (and I appreciate the support of my editor, Nick Bellorini, for allowing me this freedom), it is intended to benefit the various kinds of audiences served by this series – namely, students reading Kierkegaard in classes, as well as scholars in other areas who want a brief but serious introduction to Kierkegaard. Perhaps even Kierkegaard scholars might find something of value in it, since we usually specialize in some, but not all, of his writings. But my fondest hope is that this book will be of interest to people who have always wanted to read something of Kierkegaard's but have felt daunted by the prospect, or people who have tried to read a particular work and given up. I want to help people to read these texts even if they do not intend to become Kierkegaard scholars, even if they are not particularly excited about keeping up with the latest debates in the secondary literature, even if they don't already know what the phrase "incommensurability with actuality" means.

My book is directly geared to helping readers who want to pick up a given book of Kierkegaard's. While it is no doubt true that overviews and analyses of themes drawn synthetically from all of Kierkegaard's writings are valuable, and that examinations of him as philosopher, or as religious thinker, or as humorist, etc., do a great service to readers by highlighting a particular dimension of his thought,[1] there is a sense in which they keep readers at a secondary remove from the primary texts. That is, on their own terms such introductions to Kierkegaard do not attempt to do justice to the particular, distinctive performance that goes on in each of Kierkegaard's texts. Readers may still need help approaching any given text; they may need a better sense of what to expect, and they may need extra help once they have started to read. At the same time, because it covers the entire length of Kierkegaard's authorship, this introduction reveals a development in the way certain themes are repeated with a difference, even while it highlights the consistency of Kierkegaard's general concerns. Moreover, it addresses the authorship in its distinctive structure, as a kind of double helix in which the pseudonymous works and the upbuilding or religious discourses are examined in the light of each other.

An "introduction" is, I have discovered, the hardest thing to write, not only because one always wants to say something more by way of qualification, but also because it is a genre that depends in different ways on everything I have ever read about Kierkegaard, and the citations and bibliography would be endless. In lieu of that, I dedicate this book to all the professional scholars and students in my seminars with whom I have learned to read Kierkegaard. A special word of thanks is owed to the Søren Kierkegaard Research Center in Copenhagen and the Kierkegaard Library at St Olaf College (Northfield, Minnesota) for generously offering a nurturing environment for writing parts of this book, and to George, Walter, and the two Emilys for making my life easier.

I am grateful to Princeton University Press for permission to reproduce text.

note

1 For example: George Pattison, *The Philosophy of Kierkegaard* (Chesham [UK]: Acumen Publishing, 2005); David J. Gouwens, *Kierkegaard as Religious Thinker* (Cambridge: Cambridge University Press, 1996); John Lippitt, *Humour and Irony in Kierkegaard's Thought* (Basingstoke [UK]: Macmillan, 2000).

Abbreviations

C	*The Crisis and a Crisis in the Life of an Actress*, trans. Howard V. Hong and Edna H. Hong (Princeton, NJ: Princeton University Press, 1997)
CA	*The Concept of Anxiety*, trans. Reidar Thomte in collaboration with Albert B. Anderson (Princeton, NJ: Princeton University Press, 1980)
CD	*Christian Discourses*, trans. Howard V. Hong and Edna H. Hong (Princeton, NJ: Princeton University Press, 1997)
CI	*The Concept of Irony*, trans. Howard V. Hong and Edna H. Hong (Princeton: Princeton University Press, 1989)
CUP	*Concluding Unscientific Postscript to "Philosophical Fragments,"* vol. 1, trans. Howard V. Hong and Edna H. Hong (Princeton, NJ: Princeton University Press, 1992)
EO1,2	*Either – Or*, 2 vols., trans. Howard V. Hong and Edna H. Hong (Princeton, NJ: Princeton University Press, 1987)
EPW	*Early Polemical Writings*, ed. and trans. Julia Watkin (Princeton, NJ: Princeton University Press, 1990)
EUD	*Eighteen Upbuilding Discourses*, trans. Howard V. Hong and Edna H. Hong (Princeton, NJ: Princeton University Press, 1990)
FPOSL	"From the Papers of One Still Living," in *Early Polemical Writings*, ed. and trans. Julia Watkin (Princeton, NJ: Princeton University Press, 1990)
FSE	*For Self-Examination*, trans. Howard V. Hong and Edna H. Hong (Princeton, NJ: Princeton University Press, 1990)
FT	*Fear and Trembling*, trans. Howard V. Hong and Edna H. Hong (Princeton, NJ: Princeton University Press, 1983)
IKC	International Kierkegaard Commentary Series, ed. Robert L. Perkins (Macon, GA: Mercer University Press, 1984–)
JC	*Johannes Climacus*, trans. Howard V. Hong and Edna H. Hong (Princeton, NJ: Princeton University Press, 1985)
JFY	*Judge for Yourself!* trans. Howard V. Hong and Edna H. Hong (Princeton, NJ: Princeton University Press, 1990)

JP	*Søren Kierkegaard's Journals and Papers*, 4 vols., ed. and trans. Howard V. Hong and Edna H. Hong, assisted by Gregor Malantschuk (Bloomington and London: Indiana University Press, 1967–1978)
KSY	*Kierkegaard Studies: Yearbook*, eds. Niels Jørgen Cappelørn and Hermann Deuser (Berlin and New York: Walter de Gruyter, 1996–)
LD	*Letters and Documents*, trans. Hendrik Rosenmeier (Princeton, NJ: Princeton University Press, 1978)
OMWA	"On My Work as an Author," in *The Point of View*, trans. Howard V. Hong and Edna H. Hong (Princeton, NJ: Princeton University Press, 1998)
PC	*Practice in Christianity*, trans. Howard V. Hong and Edna H. Hong (Princeton, NJ: Princeton University Press, 1991)
PF	*Philosophical Fragments*, trans. Howard V. Hong and Edna H. Hong (Princeton, NJ: Princeton University Press, 1985)
PV	*The Point of View For My Work as an Author*, in *The Point of View*, trans. Howard V. Hong and Edna H. Hong (Princeton, NJ: Princeton University Press, 1998)
R	*Repetition*, trans. Howard V. Hong and Edna H. Hong (Princeton, NJ: Princeton University Press, 1983)
SLW	*Stages on Life's Way*, trans. Howard V. Hong and Edna H. Hong (Princeton, NJ: Princeton University Press, 1988)
SUD	*The Sickness unto Death*, trans. Howard V. Hong and Edna H. Hong (Princeton, NJ: Princeton University Press, 1980)
TA	*Two Ages: The Age of Revolution and the Present Age. A Literary Review*, trans. Howard V. Hong and Edna H. Hong (Princeton, NJ: Princeton University Press, 1978)
TDIO	*Three Discourses on Imagined Occasions*, trans. Howard V. Hong and Edna H. Hong (Princeton, NJ: Princeton University Press, 1993)
TM	*"The Moment" and Late Writings*, trans. Howard V. Hong and Edna H. Hong (Princeton, NJ: Princeton University Press, 1998)
UDVS	*Upbuilding Discourses in Various Spirits*, trans. Howard V. Hong and Edna H. Hong (Princeton, NJ: Princeton University Press, 1993)
WA	*Without Authority*, trans. Howard V. Hong and Edna H. Hong (Princeton, NJ: Princeton University Press, 1997)
WL	*Works of Love*, trans. Howard V. Hong and Edna H. Hong (Princeton, NJ: Princeton University Press, 1995)

chapter 1

Introduction: Reading Kierkegaard

Søren Aabye Kierkegaard (1813–1855) left behind a most unusual literary legacy. It is different from that of other great minds who left us intellectual projects that were in the traditional form of essays or treatises that could be straightforwardly mined for philosophical and theological insights and arguments. However difficult it might be to present the thought of people like Kant or Hegel, even acknowledging the scholarly differences of opinion that inevitably exist, the work of Kierkegaard is difficult to present for very different reasons. Given the remarkable variety of genres in which he writes, the counterpart to such traditional exposition and critique is the challenge of orienting and guiding readers in the activity of reading Kierkegaard's works.

Robert Frost once wrote that "a poetic philosopher or philosophical poet" was his "favorite kind of both,"[1] and Ludwig Wittgenstein suggested that "Philosophy ought really to be written only as a *poetic composition.*"[2] It is interesting, therefore, to note that Kierkegaard presented himself not as a traditional philosopher or religious thinker, but as a kind of "poet" and as someone who was "in love" with his pen.[3] This is not incompatible with offering sound philosophical, religious, or psychological insights, but it does mean that we will have to be prepared to read his works a little differently. Kierkegaard's own description of the genres of his works is a sign that this is the case. We find, for example, a "Dialectical Lyric," "A Venture in Experimenting Psychology," "A Fragment of Philosophy," "A Mimical-Pathetical-Dialectical Compilation, an Existential Contribution," as well as *Works of Love* and "Discourses for Communion." Readers need to be alerted to certain facts about the writing, as well as to certain assumptions and strategies that inform the writing. I hope to present introductory accounts of the texts that will provide both encouragement for readers to turn to the originals and guidance for them when they do. I do not intend my brief introductions to spare readers the need of reading the texts.

In what follows I want to introduce Kierkegaard's thought, not by telling what he thought, but rather by showing *how* he thought. I want to consider how his texts are provocative performances or performative provocations. Although it might be said that every text is a performance of sorts, this is especially important in Kierkegaard's case since his work covers a variety of genres. A fruitful reading of these texts requires that we are sensitive to the "how" of the performance. I want to introduce readers to what I love about reading Kierkegaard by providing examples of the sorts of activities he engages in, and by providing enough of his own inimitable language and style to tempt readers to read (or re-read) the originals carefully.

Let me suggest the following reasons for picking up Kierkegaard's writings, knowing that the reader will have to judge for herself as the book proceeds. I read Kierkegaard for his *passionate* performances, as well as for the passionate ways he puts passion in question. That is, I read him for the ways in which he embodies a resistance to one-sidedness and to closure (he calls this his "dialectical" aspect). He does this by using literary strategies and techniques to unsettle us, to perplex us, to cause us to rethink things; he is always asking provocative questions and using unexpected inversions and comparisons, to make us uncomfortable in our security, to defamiliarize us with something we think we are familiar with already, to make problematical the totality, the system, the closed, the finished, the completed, and the finalized. He uses pictures that provoke the reader to do some work. He will paint a picture – then ask what is wrong with the picture. He will repeatedly ask us to imagine strange situations, saying what if someone who wanted to achieve X were to do Y, what would you think? He constantly invites the reader to do the work of making judgments or coming up with alternatives. His writings encourage us to appreciate the tension-filled nature of life.

Kierkegaard's works are full of challenges, posed through satire, sarcasm, and humor; there are passionate polemics. But there is always a complementary or underlying *compassion*. I think all his books could have the subtitle he gave to one of them, "For Upbuilding and Awakening." They are designed to build up or encourage, as well as awaken or provoke. In other words, they are designed to be appropriated by the reader. But that is precisely what makes it difficult for me to introduce them. Most of the time, I feel I am in a difficulty similar to that noted by one of Kierkegaard's pseudonymous authors, Johannes Climacus, who considers the task of trying to paint a mythological figure in the armor that makes him invisible – as he says, "the point is the invisibility" (CUP, 174). How do you suggest that something is invisible? What features of its surroundings or background will need to be brought out in order to evoke the invisibility? One cannot simply paint the armor, and one cannot refuse to paint at all, leaving a blank space. All of Kierkegaard's writings illustrate to some degree the problem of indirection he points to. And while Kierkegaard is usually quite artful in his indirection, it is difficult for me not to reduce it as I present it.

Every scholar who has ever worked on Kierkegaard's writings probably has felt pangs of conscience at the thought that he/she may be doing exactly the kind of analysis that Kierkegaard ridiculed or condemned. The only way to keep on going is to remind oneself that Kierkegaard appreciated the Socratic art of maieutics and it is possible to see what we scholars do as maieutic work – as being an occasion for others in the way that Kierkegaard is himself an occasion for us all. There is a kind of authority that is impossible to claim with respect to the study of these works.

I hope to provide enough analysis and commentary to indicate the fruitful perplexity that readers should expect to encounter, and to suggest why this can be a good thing rather than a frustrating thing. As will become increasingly apparent, we are faced with an authorship in which there is much ambiguity, many unresolved questions, no pat answers, no "results" we can easily summarize – a bit like life, actually. We should ask what these texts *do*. That is, we should shift the question from "What did the author want to do?" to "What did the author do?" or "What do these texts do?" Only then can we ask ourselves what we think of what they do.

This project is torn, however, between two impulses. On the one hand, I want the reader to discover these works for herself – to confront them (the title, the author and/or editor, the introductory guidance, and the text itself) as if for the first time. I want to show the reader how themes emerge in the writings themselves, *as* they emerge, rather than impose at the outset a list of the themes to be explored. And I want to treat each work as a particular. The problem with simply doing all that, however, is that the reader needs a little orientation up front about why she should bother to read Kierkegaard at all, and that involves suggesting how the reading may prove valuable. The reader also needs some preliminary sense of how the particulars fit into the whole, and what are the already existing practices of, and debates about, reading Kierkegaard. So there is a tension between what I need to say up front and what I try to save for the reader to discover for herself. What we have are texts that can be edifying, or entertaining, or shocking – and in some cases all three. The most I can do is prepare, orient, and guide the reader.

I The Visual Introduction

The first, and in one sense the most important, piece of guidance that can be given to a reader concerns the most unusual feature of Kierkegaard's writing – namely, the variety of forms it takes. The best short "intro-duction to Kierkegaard" is found in the visual picture of his writings provided by a listing of all the works he authored, along with their dates (see the appendix at the end of this chapter). The titles and dates and "signatures" by themselves already reveal a great deal about why his writings have always had passionate readers – whether uncritical devo-tees, critical students, or intrigued analysts. It is a unique body of writings. Apart from the obviously intriguing names to which the books are attributed (Constantin Constantius, Johannes de Silentio, Johannes Climacus, Vigilius Haufniensis, Nicolaus Notabene, Anti-Climacus, H. H., Inter et Inter, and S. Kierkegaard) or with which they are asso-ciated (Victor Eremita, Hilarius Bookbinder, and S. Kierkegaard), there are provocative titles, like *Either – Or* and *Concluding Unscientific Postscript*.

Moreover, Kierkegaard's works can be sorted out into two columns ordered by date of publication. It is apparent from this that he wrote from beginning to end of his career two parallel sets of quite different kinds of writings, publishing them alongside each other. That is, one set of texts was written under a variety of ingenious pseudonyms, and a second set, predominantly "discourses" ("upbuilding"[4] or "Christian") was written in his own name (S. Kierkegaard), so that at any given point he would be writing/publishing one of the pseudonymous texts at about the same time as he was writing/publishing one of the upbuilding or Christian writings under his own signature. Often the corresponding sets would come out within weeks or months of each other, and once it happened on the very same day. If we look at the parallel lines of signed and pseudonymous works, we see a body of writings that appears to have been written and published very self-consciously. The arrangement does not look accidental; it looks like an authorship that, if not deliberately crafted according to a plan from the outset, at least was deliberately arranged in certain ways as it went along. The parallel lines of author-ship are a reconstruction, to be sure, but that they can be so recon-structed shows that the resulting writings were not produced arbitrarily. By working with both sets of texts at the same time I hope to introduce readers to Kierkegaard's writings in a way that ensures that they never forget this distinctive feature of his authorship.

Many people, especially those interested in his philosophical and religious thought, have studied Kierkegaard under the aspect of one of his famous pseudonyms, for example, Johannes Climacus. Others have been less aware of the pseudonymous aspect of his writing and have concentrated on one of his famous books, like *Fear and Trembling* or *The Sickness unto Death*, uncritically attributing to "Kierkegaard" responses to questions about the relation between ethics and religion or about the existential transformation of the self. And so, there has been a huge literature on "Kierkegaardian" themes like subjectivity, the "leap" to faith, anxiety, the teleological suspension of the ethical in the name of religion, and the relations between esthetic, ethical, and religious ways of living. Others, fewer but the numbers are growing, have studied the "upbuilding discourses" and the "Christian discourses" written in his own name. To readers who are only familiar with the pseudonymous works these discourses will be a revelation. The "upbuilding" discourses, in particular, have been accorded a special importance recently: it has been argued that "upbuilding, or edification, is the central theme of Kierkegaard's authorship"[5] and that the upbuilding discourses provide a "privileged viewpoint on the authorship as a whole."[6] To my knowledge no one has published a book-length study of the entire parallel track of writings in their relation to one another,[7] and yet this product with two different kinds of writing in tandem over a career makes Kierkegaard absolutely unique in the history of thought.

The character of the uniqueness that I am claiming for Kierkegaard should be clarified. In assessing this dual or parallel collection of works, I acknowledge that Kierkegaard was not writing in a literary vacuum – his writings show a mastery of Danish literature and an extensive knowledge of contemporary German literature. Pseudonymity and satire, for example, are found in the Danish and German contexts familiar to Kierkegaard, but his use of it was a pervasive and continuing dimension of his writings throughout his life as an author. Although he builds on the earlier examples of certain genres and approaches, he outdistances each of these individual authors in his variety and consistent use of certain literary techniques.[8] For this reason, the peculiar duality of his authorship has no rival.

This is not to claim that what he did is more important than what other thinkers have done, and it is certainly not to claim that he was equally successful in all he did – it is simply to be unapologetically astonished by what he did. Even in Nietzsche's case, where the departures from traditional form and style are evident – provocative and flamboyant aphorisms as well as vitriolic diatribes – the elements of his authorship are at least presented in his own name (including *Thus Spoke Zarathustra* which has lots of clever deconstruction going on that puts in question any easy identification of Zarathustra with Nietzsche). Something a little more similar to the case of Kierkegaard may be found in David Hume's *Dialogues Concerning Natural Religion*, which has generated a lot of literature about which of the three dialogue partners (Philo, Cleanthes, or Demea) stands for Hume. In this case, it is pretty clear that they are all Hume in some sense, and all not Hume in another sense – each of the characters created by Hume voices views that Hume can be otherwise documented as holding or rejecting. That is, in the case of both Hume and Nietzsche we can assess correspondences between the views of their creations and their own straightforwardly presented views, but it is not clear that there is ever a comparable straightforwardly presented Kierkegaard.

What else do we learn from the visual representation in the appendix to this chapter? First, each set is distinctive: there is the explicit pseudonymity of one set of writings whereas the other set in the parallel listing is signed S. Kierkegaard. The bulk of this latter set consists of what Kierkegaard generically titled "discourses." If we unpack these volumes of "discourses," we will find about 87 religious discourses – either "upbuilding" or "Christian." This signed track of writing shows clearly that Kierkegaard did not become interested in religion at some late stage of writing. The "discourse" differs markedly as a genre from the pseudonymous writings. Although it might be possible to raid these discourses for irony and satire and parody, it seems implausible to think that they are repositories of these literary strategies in the same way as the pseudonymous writings are. Most of them explicitly address New Testament passages, and some begin with a prayer; indeed, they look so much like traditional sermons that Kierkegaard almost invariably insists in their prefaces that they are not sermons, since he lacks the authority for that. Moreover, of the 87 discourses, Kierkegaard delivered four of them in church services. Seven are subtitled "Christian Discourses," and 28 others are explicitly assembled under the rubric "Christian Discourses." One volume of 15 "deliberations, in the form of discourses" addresses the divine commandment to love the neighbor. The visual representation in the appendix shows that there are writings *about religion* from the beginning, and more importantly that there was *religious writing* from the beginning. Even if the author S. Kierkegaard were to be distinguishable from the man Søren Aabye Kierkegaard, these writings are in a different class from the pseudonyms, even the most Christian of the pseudonyms.

It is worth noting that under the rubric of writings signed by S. Kierkegaard, we find not only such religious discourses but also quite a different genre of writing that has attracted attention to Kierkegaard. These are the writings that have generally been associated with what has been called Kierkegaard's "attack on Christendom."[9] The challenge Kierkegaard issued in 1851 (*For Self-Examination*) was eventually followed by his assault in the more public media. During the last years of his life (1854–5), he produced 21 newspaper articles and then 10 more volumes of his own pamphlet series supported by public subscription. These late writings express a very polemical (at times vitriolic) response to the established (state) church in Denmark, but their content is not new. As we shall see, the outrage expressed in these writings is of a piece with Kierkegaard's earlier frustration with what he took to be a dangerous misunderstanding of Christianity.

I do not call attention to the different kinds of writing to separate them, as if they are parallel tracks that never touch or influence each other. It is not as if a university professor adopts a pen name and writes detective novels that have no relation to the academic research she publishes; even in such a case, if both strands began at the same time and continued over a career, it would be hard to imagine that the writings did not mutually influence each other in some way. In the case of Kierkegaard, the pseudonymous and signed writings interweave through each other in interesting ways: a given theme initially explored in a pseudonymous work may then be developed in the discourses or sometimes the other way round.

This visual picture of the writing also provides a different vantagepoint on Kierkegaard's religious discourses – for example, the current presentation of the first 18 upbuilding discourses in a single volume allows one to compare the discourses with each other, but it fails to give the reader any sense of their original publication by Kierkegaard in separate small groups of two, three, or four discourses, and obscures the relation between the individual sets of discourses and the other works Kierkegaard was writing at about the same time. The visual picture gives a better sense of the chronological relation between the sets of discourses and the pseudonymous works.

Finally, another important benefit of presenting these contemporaneous strands together is that it introduces the reader to the vexing question of the pseudonymous authorship which scholars wrestle with, but does so in a way that shows that it is not simply an eccentric technical issue but rather affects the very heart of one's understanding of Kierkegaard's thought. Kierkegaard left us a very mixed bag of writings, with an intriguing array of signatures. Kierkegaard wrote a book and signed it "S. Kierkegaard." Kierkegaard wrote another book and signed it "Johannes de Silentio." Kierkegaard wrote yet another book and signed it "Anti-Climacus, edited by S. Kierkegaard." If we clearly distinguish the pseudonymous presentations of ethics from the religious presentations of ethics, this will prevent even a beginner from making certain mistakes – e.g., conflating "Kierkegaard's ethic" not only with the ethic proposed by Judge William in *Either – Or*, but also with the ethic proposed in *Fear and Trembling* by Johannes de Silentio.

The question whether there is a unity to all of Kierkegaard's writings interests many readers, but the visual picture leaves open the question of whether (as he claimed in his retrospective account of his activity as an author) all his writings, including the pseudonymous ones, were "in the service of Christianity."[10] That question cannot be decided on the basis of the visual representation.

II The Contemporary Discussion –
Kierkegaard the Writer

Although I want to avoid prejudging these texts for the reader, it is probably helpful to preface the examination of the texts with a brief acknowledgement of the contemporary situation in which Kierkegaard scholarship finds itself. An introduction to Kierkegaard's writings done today can avail itself of a marked renaissance in Kierkegaard scholarship during the last few decades. The new directions in Kierkegaard research have benefited from three relatively recent developments. The first was the completion in 2000 of a critical edition begun in 1978 of all the major works in English, which made the writings accessible to a larger audience.[11] The second development was the concentrated attention to the original Danish manuscripts themselves. Much painstaking research into the Danish Royal Library's collection of Kierkegaard's manuscripts – research into the sketches, drafts, printer's copies, and proofs – began in 1994 and continues in a new Danish edition of Kierkegaard's writings, *Søren Kierkegaards Skrifter*, spearheaded in Copenhagen by the Søren Kierkegaard Research Center.[12] While English non-scholars will not be going to this Danish edition, several general benefits to Kierkegaard scholarship have accrued from this research.

The explanatory notes to the Danish edition document the complex dialogue that Kierkegaard had with other authors, theological, philosophical, and literary, as well as with the current events of his day – they reveal the entire intellectual and political background to his writing. For example, it has become clearer that the occasions for much of Kierkegaard's philosophical diatribes were Danish Hegelians, rather than the German philosopher Hegel as such. That is, although Kierkegaard did read some Hegel, he is best understood as responding to people who were inspired by Hegel.[13] Moreover, the researchers for the new *Skrifter* edition have uncovered much detail that is relevant to the dating and composition of the various writings; this shows us that Kierkegaard was often working on several texts at once, going back and forth between them.[14] For those who are interested in the person of Kierkegaard the writer, this research also tells a fascinating story of the quirkiness of Kierkegaard's own writing: his remorseless revisions, his last-minute changes, his micro-management of typographical printing details. Over the years then we have been getting a clearer picture of Kierkegaard the writer – often finicky, sometimes vain, and always passionate.

One important implication of this research has to do with the crafting of the texts of the authorship. Attention to the various versions of the Danish originals shows that Kierkegaard often changed his mind about how to sign his works. He sometimes began a work under his own name, changing it to a pseudonym only at the last minute before it went to the printers. Sometimes he went through several variations whose scratching out we can still see in the originals. As a result, we need to acknowledge that the presence of pseudonyms should nuance any appreciation of the authorship, but we also need to be careful not to take the pseudonyms flatfootedly either. For example, if one knows nothing of the pseudonymous nature of the authorship, one will likely take *Philosophical Fragments* to present "Kierkegaard's" position on the issues discussed. When one becomes aware that the author, Johannes Climacus, is one of Kierkegaard's many pseudonymous creations, it is tempting to conclude that now we should read it differently and that we know exactly how to do that. For example, since Johannes Climacus tells us (in his *Postscript* to *Philosophical Fragments*) that he is not a Christian, we should be very wary of thinking that Johannes Climacus gets the portrayal of Christianity (indirect as it may be) right. That is, one will be suspicious about how to take Climacus's claims. Then, lo and behold, one sees a physical copy of the *Philosophical Fragments* signed by S. Kierkegaard; researchers have discovered the draft from the day before it went to the printers, at which time it still had Kierkegaard's name as author. One seems to come full circle by learning that only at the last minute before sending it to the publisher did Kierkegaard change it to be authored by Johannes Climacus. It is not clear why he made the change, but the shift in signature does suggest that he did not begin by first creating the pseudonymous author and then writing the book in that distinctive (non-Christian) voice. And this is true of other works.[15]

However, this does not at all mean that whether he used a pseudonym was unimportant to him. Pseudonymity signals to the reader that the text is a calculated pedagogical project, with authorial distance, so pseudonymity is crucial to the ways in which Kierkegaard oriented his readers. Moreover, we should not give up our hermeneutics of suspicion when reading the *Fragments* – there are still numerous literary devices and twists going on in the text that need to be appreciated, regardless of the signature. There are levels and levels of appreciation of the strategy of pseudonymity. In this same vein, we know that Kierkegaard expressed regret that he had published under a pseudonym, Anti-Climacus, a text that he later wished he could put under his own name (as he had originally had it in the final draft). Finally, we have evidence that Kierkegaard toyed with the idea of many pseudonyms that he never actually used – he seems to have just liked the sound of some of the names. My discussion will show the dangers of any naïve failure to pay attention to the pseudonyms, but at the same time it will challenge simplistic assumptions about the pseudonyms, as well as qualify post-modern interpretations in which even "S. Kierkegaard" is taken to be a pseudonym. All of this research may seem irrelevant to people who care only about "the ideas" in the books and don't care whose name is signed to them, but pseudonymity is a literary strategy, and if we cease to care about the literary strategies in the texts, we will fail to understand the ideas in the text.

Although I have been concentrating on highlighting the dual strands of Kierkegaard's authorship – the signed and the pseudonymous – it is important to note that his writing includes not only these works, but also a large amount of journal and notebook material, as well as some correspondence. The new Danish edition of Kierkegaard's writings explicitly intended to treat the writing as a unity, to include them all in a single edition, in acknowledgement of the fact that this "extra" material found in the manuscripts was not of a unique private status. Kierkegaard fully expected that some day some of that too would be available to the public – he was, in a sense, always writing for others. This does not mean that all the writings are leveled to a single common denominator – it is still important to make distinctions between the kinds of writing – but it does suggest that there is no special cache of writings that give privileged authoritative access to Kierkegaard's private intentions and motives. There is no doubt that these writings are valuable for research if used rightly; there is much in them that is fascinating and curious, as well as informative and provocative, and I recommend them highly to inter-ested readers.[16] I will not, however, be relying on them; even when the "extra" material is written with others in mind, I think it best not to unduly complicate things by trying to integrate this material into an introduction.

This leads us to the third development in Kierkegaard studies. We currently have a climate in which work on Kierkegaard has benefited from a couple of decades of literary attention. That is, the study of Kierkegaard's texts has been enriched by the attention given them by people who have not only philosophical and religious interests, but also (sometimes especially) literary interests. Recent analyses have demon-strated the pervasive use of literary strategies like irony, humor, and indirect communication, as well as a deeper appreciation of the strategy of pseudonymity.

One of the strengths of the literary approaches to Kierkegaard's writ-ings is that they have shifted the ground away from naïve readings. The attempt to read Kierkegaard's mind (to determine authorial intention through appeal to biography or to journal entries) should be rightly set aside. The practice of reading pseudonymous works without sensitiv-ity to the presence of satire, parody, irony, and humor, should also be guarded against. But there is a danger that focusing attention on literary strategies can draw us out of our literary innocence in such a way that we substitute literary suspicion for literary sensitivity, and thereby limit our reading options. For example, sometimes the literary approach leads people to ask whether Kierkegaard's writings were all put on for show – of cleverness, or wit, or one-upmanship, or revenge. It leads people to posit an illegitimate dichotomy, asking whether a work is "really" about his broken engagement (his shame about his father, the need to justify himself), *or* whether it is "really" about religion. The question then would be what to make of the writings that have given so much edification to people, changed their lives, awakened them, so to speak, to the importance of paradox, passion, despair, and the infinite. But acknowledging Kierkegaard's literary concerns does not preclude taking his works seriously. One danger of a hermeneutic of suspicion is that it can obscure the ways in which a writer's various experiences, interests, and concerns can coincide in the space of his artistry.

There are, indeed, two kinds of writings – pseudonymous and signed – but both are done by a master literary craftsman. It is not possible to separate Kierkegaard's literary works from his religious/philosophical works – he was literary "all the way down," even in his religious and philosophical writings. Therefore, I want to explore the ways in which his literary sensibilities go hand in hand with all the dimensions of his life and issue in a complex overdetermination of his writing. By over-determination I mean simply that there is not necessarily one single thing going on at any given time, not one single motivation informing a given text. We are embodied, contextualized human beings who cannot neatly compartmentalize the various dimensions of our life, so it is not surprising that more than a single motivation or a single concern would inform a given piece of writing.

Let me use a suggestion made by Kierkegaard himself to illus-trate what this "overdetermination" might mean. The general idea that one's various life concerns can be expressed in one's literary pursuits is found in the first work Kierkegaard ever published – *From the Papers of One Still Living* (1838), a review of Hans Christian Andersen's novel, *Only a Fiddler*. That review clearly raises the question of the relation between the quality of an author's life and the quality of an author's writing. It asks: What is true poetry, the poetically true? What is good writing? What is genius? What is art? Kierkegaard makes a striking contrast between two ways of writing, two different uses of one's life experiences: in "the poetically true," one's experiences (living to the "first power") are "transubstantiated" (living to the "second power"); he contrasts this with the case where one's experiences are "undigested," "unappropriated," "unfiltered" (FPOSL, 84). The view that life is appro-priated experience contests both the rationalism and the romanticism of Kierkegaard's day: in order to be appropriated, there must be both immediacy and reflection, and whereas rationalism lacks the indispens-able immediacy, romanticism lacks the equally indispensable reflection on immediacy.

Kierkegaard's critique of Andersen's esthetic failures reveals his view of the inseparability of the esthetic and the authentic – the true esthetic is not vain or self-centered. Kierkegaard's accusations are revealing. He suggests that "instead of carrying through his reflection, he [Andersen] on the contrary encloses himself in a very small space of it," a space which prevents development because it cyclically repeats itself (FPOSL, 74). True artistry, on the contrary, is suffering life through to the second power. In short, Kierkegaard's view of the demands of literary art and its relation to life seems to be one way of making sense of the concept of "esthetic earnestness" that he uses in a letter to his friend Emil Boesen: "I have far too much sense of and reverence for what stirs in a human being not to guard it with just as much esthetic as ethical earnestness."[17]

If we take seriously the notion of "transubstantiation" of lived experience in literature, we will find it difficult to continue simplistically raising the question of "either/or" too often addressed to Kierkegaard's writings. The question whether Kierkegaard was exercising his literary craft *rather than* exploring a religious or philosophical or personal concern does not make sense. The fact that Kierkegaard was a self-conscious author, a literarily minded author, is not incompatible with his being an author who had religious or philosophical or psychological aims. We need to do justice to Kierkegaard's wide variety of concerns and interests: I propose that we call them religious/theological, philosophical, psychological, literary, and personal. It should be clear that I am using the word "literary" to point to two different things – on the one hand, to point to a literary approach, and on the other hand, to point to literary interests. Kierkegaard had literary ambitions – he wanted to be accepted in Danish literary circles; he was disgruntled about not being part of the reigning literary alliances. He wanted to be known as a great writer. But at a different level, at the level of his approach to his writing, even this interest in literary reputation was "transubstantiated" into literature. The category of "personal" here covers things like his relation to his family, and to his fiancée – his private life. Although one could say that things like cultivating a literary reputation and reacting to the goings-on in the competing literary circles of his day were also personal, still these are different from the most important personal relationships he had. But even if we can distinguish these categories conceptually, they are not separate in practice – all his concerns had a bearing on each other in some sense. And ultimately, all his experiences coincided within the space of his artistry; his life was inflected in literary art.

Let me suggest the following heuristic device for thinking about the overdetermination or multivalence in the texts – namely, concentric circles. Immanuel Kant used the image of concentric circles in his book, *Religion Within the Limits of Reason Alone*, to explain the relation between natural and revealed religion. Kant suggested that we "regard [revelation] as the *wider* sphere of faith, which includes within itself the second [historical] as a *narrower* one (not like two circles external to one another, but like concentric circles)."[18] This image is also found in one of Kierkegaard's earliest works, *Either – Or*. The image of "concentric circles" conveys the notion of several thoughts with the same center. The image specifically rules out the idea of overlapping circles (as in Venn diagrams). Concentric circles have the same center. The circles may be larger or smaller, with different ranges, different ramifications and implications, but they all have the same center. In the case of Kierkegaard's authorship, I am suggesting that the center of the circles is the author's life experience. This includes his appropriated experience of learning about the experiences of others. This rich center of life experience is composed of events and acts that involve his ongoing relation with God, his ongoing self-education, his attempts to deal with the literary establishment in Copenhagen, his philosophical questionings, etc. A single event or act can have various descriptions – it might be described as a religious ordeal, a personal heartbreak, a psychological problem, or material providing philosophical insight. All of these could be described as events or acts that need to be coped with through a literary re-appropriation or "transubstantiation."

The image of concentric circles is one way of reminding ourselves that, as an author, Kierkegaard expressed all his dimensions – religious, philosophical, psychological, literary, and personal. Individual texts may express some of Kierkegaard's concerns more prominently than others – for example, the text *Prefaces* seems a literary *tour de force*, while a text like *Fear and Trembling* (the text most people will probably be familiar with) has many layers of things deeper than mere amusement. But most of the works reveal that the author had religious, philosophical, and existential needs (to be loved, to be accepted by the literary elite, to find meaning in life). At heart he was, as he says of himself, "a kind of poet" – a writer whose every experience had to be raised to the level of artistic expression. He found himself in his writing – in all his dimensions. The hypothesis that he was educated by his activity of writing provides a very fruitful way of understanding the multivalence of the authorship in terms of concentric circles.

Since my project is to guide or orient the reader, my introduction should probably stop here. The meaning of the overdetermination of the authorship will become clearer as we see the differing degrees to which all the concerns of Kierkegaard's life are represented in the individual texts. Moreover, all of Kierkegaard's writing calls for individual engagement by the reader, so rather than give you what Kierkegaard would call "results," i.e., an *a priori* rehearsal of various Kierkegaardian themes and tensions and strategies, I turn in the following chapters to the texts themselves. I think the "taste and see" introduction is the best, with its examples of wit, irony, psychological insight, philosophical distinctions, graphic narrative, religious sensitivity, and ethical earnestness. Our reading of the performances in each text will allow Kierkegaard's themes, tensions, and strategies to emerge at the relevant places in the authorship.

The chapters that immediately follow will address those texts that officially begin Kierkegaard's authorship. The year 1843 was a decisive one for the 30-year-old Kierkegaard – in that single year he published three full-length literary works (under three different pseudonyms) and three volumes of religious discourses (under his own signature). But perhaps it is more accurate to say that what preceded 1843 was decisive for him. What formed the man who spouted what he himself termed a veritable "torrent" or "showerbath" of writing?

A brief look at the public facts.[19] Baptized and confirmed in the state church, Kierkegaard was brought up in a religious household. His university studies were initially philosophical and literary. He did some early writing that revealed his literary aspirations and his polemical style, and he published a book-length review of a novel by Hans Christian Andersen in 1838; in that same year his father died. He shifted his focus and began two years of theological studies and examinations culminating in his graduate degree in theology in 1840, with a dissertation entitled "On the Concept of Irony" as part of his Magister Artium (later officially made into a Doctor of Philosophy). He then spent two semesters in the Royal Pastoral Seminary (1840–41) and received his certificate to preach, giving a sermon in Holmens Church, January 12, 1841, on the Scriptural verse "For me to live is Christ and to die is gain." At the age of 27 he became engaged to a 16-year-old girl, Regine Olsen (September 1840), and after a little more than a year he broke off the engagement (October 1841). He immediately left Copenhagen and attended philosophical lectures in Berlin. He came back to Copenhagen in 1842 with a large amount of writing in hand, and then came all the publications of 1843.

Many commentators highlight the broken engagement when they treat Kierkegaard's writings, especially his early writings. There is no doubt that this was a formative experience for him, and it would be surprising if these early texts were not marked by his decision and its aftermath. In the market town of Copenhagen this personal event was not private – it was common knowledge and it was apparently a rather shocking thing at the time to break a publically announced engagement. But it would be naïve to think that this is all these writings are about. Even this briefest of looks at the years preceding 1843 shows that Kierkegaard had strong philosophical, theological, and literary interests, and that he had suffered other personal losses, not the least of which was the loss of his father, to whom he dedicated the religious discourses of 1843 (and many thereafter). We, as readers, cannot read Kierkegaard's mind – nor should we try. But it would be strange if these losses did not mark his early writing as least as much as the famous "engagement crisis." He was exploring personal religious questions and making decisions about theological plans in the years before and during the writing of these works. There is every reason to think that everything he knew and did provided the material of the concentric circles of his literary appropriation of his life.

Let us turn now to *Either – Or* and the two discourses that accompanied it. After deriving some lessons in reading Kierkegaard from these performances, we will turn to the other writings of 1843.

notes

1 Robert Frost, "On Emerson," in *Selected Prose of Robert Frost*, ed. Hyde Cox and Edward Connery Lathem (New York: Holt, Rinehart, and Winston, Inc., 1959), p. 112.

2 *Culture and Value*, trans. Peter Winch (Oxford: Blackwell, 1998), p. 24.

3 Preface to *Two Discourses at the Communion on Fridays* (1851); LD, p. 209, letter to Kierkegaard's cousin Julie Thomsen, February 1847.

4 These may be more familiar in their earlier English translation as "edifying" discourses.

5 IKC, vol. 5, p. 1.

6 George Pattison, *Kierkegaard's Upbuilding Discourses: Philosophy, Literature, and Theology* (London and New York: Routledge, 2002), p. 35.

7 One of my graduate students, Glenn Kirkconnell, did this for the early part of the authorship (*Either – Or* to *Philosophical Fragments*) in his 2002 dissertation, recently published as *Kierkegaard on Ethics and Religion* (New York: Continuum International Publishing Group, 2008).

8 For example, Kierkegaard far exceeds the literary stylings of a master to whom he repeatedly appealed – the unusual eighteenth-century German thinker, Johann Georg Hamann (1730–1788), whose eccentric use of wit and occasional pseudonymity Kierkegaard deeply appreciated.

9 Although Kierkegaard never wrote a book entitled *Attack upon "Christendom,"* these writings were collected under that title by Walter Lowrie in 1956, so English-speaking readers may be familiar with them in that format.

10 PV, p. 24.

11 Howard V. Hong and Edna H. Hong, trans. (Princeton University Press, 1978–2000).

12 *Søren Kierkegaards Skrifter*, ed. Niels Jørgen Cappelørn, Joakim Garff, Anne Mette Hansen, and Johnny Kundrup (Copenhagen: Gads Forlag, 1997–). Published by Søren Kierkegaard Forskningscenteret.

13 Jon Stewart, *Kierkegaard's Relations to Hegel Reconsidered* (Cambridge: Cambridge University Press, 2003).

14 I depend heavily on the documentation found in the *Kierkegaard Studies Yearbooks* devoted to each text, put out by the Kierkegaard Research Center at the University of Copenhagen.

15 This was true of *Philosophical Fragments, The Concept of Anxiety, The Sickness unto Death*, and even *Practice in Christianity*.

16 *Søren Kierkegaard's Journals and Papers* presents some of this material in English, arranged by topics; a new critical edition of the journals and notebooks is currently being prepared for Princeton University Press, headed by Bruce Kirmmse, which will draw on more of the original materials and employ a chronological format.

17 LD, p. 121, letter to Emil Boesen, January 16, 1842.

18 *Religion Within the Limits of Reason Alone*, trans. Theodore M. Greene and Hoyt H. Hudson (New York: Harper Torchbooks, 1960), preface to the 2nd edn., p. 11.

19 Several important biographies should be noted: Walter Lowrie, *A Short Life of Kierkegaard* (Princeton, NJ: Princeton University Press, 1944); Alastair Hannay, *Kierkegaard: A Biography* (Cambridge: Cambridge University Press, 2001); Joakim Garff, *Søren Kierkegaard: A Biography*, trans. Bruce Kirmmse (Princeton, NJ: Princeton University Press, 2005).

Appendix

The Writings of Søren Kierkegaard

Pseudonymous	Signed
Either – Or – February 1843	*Two Upbuilding Discourses* – May 1843
Repetition – October 16, 1843	*Three Upbuilding Discourses* – October 16, 1843
Fear and Trembling – October 16, 1843	*Four Upbuilding Discourses* – December 1843
	Two Upbuilding Discourses – March 1844
	Three Upbuilding Discourses – June 1844
Philosophical Fragments – June 13, 1844	
The Concept of Anxiety – June 17, 1844	
Prefaces – June 17, 1844	
	Four Upbuilding Discourses – August 1844
Stages on Life's Way – April 1845	*Three Discourses on Imagined Occasions* – April 1845
Concluding Unscientific Postscript – February 1846	
	Two Ages: A Literary Review – March 1846
	Upbuilding Discourses in Various Spirits – March 1847

The Crisis and a Crisis in the Life of an Actress – July 1848

Either – Or (2nd edn.) – May 14, 1849

Two Ethical-Religious Essays – May 1849

The Sickness unto Death – July, 1849

Practice in Christianity – September 1850

Works of Love – September 1847

Christian Discourses – April 1848

The Lily in the Field and the Bird of the Air – May 14, 1849

Three Discourses at Communion – November 1849

An Upbuilding Discourse – December 1850

Two Discourses at Communion – August 1851

On My Work as an Author – August 1851

For Self-Examination – September 1851

Articles in *The Fatherland* – 1854–5

The Moment – 1855

"The Changelessness of God" – September 1855

Posthumous publications

The Point of View for My Work as an Author – [1848] 1859

Judge for Yourself! [1851–2], 1876

The Pseudonymous Authorship

Either – Or – A Fragment of Life, edited by Victor Eremita

Repetition – A Venture in Experimenting Psychology, by Constantin Constantius

Fear and Trembling – A Dialectical Lyric, by Johannes de Silentio

Philosophical Fragments – A Fragment of Philosophy, by Johannes Climacus

The Concept of Anxiety – A Simple Psychologically Orienting Deliberation on the Dogmatic Issue of Hereditary Sin, by Vigilius Haufniensis

Prefaces – Light Reading for People in Various Estates According to Time and Opportunity, by Nicolaus Notabene

Stages on Life's Way – Studies by Various Persons, Compiled, forwarded to the press, and published by Hilarius Bookbinder

Concluding Unscientific Postscript – A Mimical-Pathetical-Dialectical Compilation, an Existential Contribution, by Johannes Climacus

The Crisis and a Crisis in the Life of an Actress, by Inter et Inter

Two Ethical-Religious Essays, by H. H.

The Sickness unto Death – A Christian Psychological Exposition for Upbuilding and Awakening, by Anti-Climacus, edited by S. Kierkegaard

Practice in Christianity, by Anti-Climacus, edited by S. Kierkegaard

chapter 2

Either – Or and the First *Upbuilding Discourses*

ither – Or was a bestseller – it introduced a clever writer to the Danish literary scene.[1] This was probably in great part due to one of its sections, "The Seducer's Diary," which today is published on its own.[2] A volume of two religious discourses was ready at the same time as *Either – Or*, but Kierkegaard deliberately delayed its publication by a month. I will consider these early writings at some length because they set the stage, as it were – with them we first see literary strategies and conceptual tensions that inform the rest of his writings, as well as themes (and the glimmers of themes) that we will meet again and again, refined or refigured. Moreover, this set of writings nicely represents all the dimensions I spoke of earlier with respect to the overdetermination of his writings and thereby provides a good sample for examination.

I *Either – Or*

A Introduction

Either – Or: A Fragment of Life was originally published in two volumes under the same title, with a preface by the editor, Victor Eremita (the victorious hermit, or the cloistered victor), the first volume consisting of a miscellany of short pieces (essays, aphorisms, diary entries) and the second volume consisting of three "letters." The title of the work, *Either – Or*, is obviously designed to be provocative. The preface is, on the surface at least, a funny account of the serendipitous discovery of the papers that are gathered together – a story of a man fancying a desk in a shop window and how, after he took it home, his impatience led to finding a hidden drawer containing a pile of papers. Already the preface piques one's interest because of the anticipated voyeuristic pleasure we will have in exploring a hitherto hidden cache. But, in addition, the preface gives us important editorial guidance for reading the book.

The editor reveals his long interest in a "philosophical" issue: the relation between inner and outer. He questions "the accuracy of that familiar philosophical thesis that the outer is the inner and the inner is the outer" (EO1, 3), and he claims to find in these fortuitously discovered papers some "observations" that bear on his philosophical question, hoping to gain some insight from "the lives of two men," whom he calls A and B (4). A quick glance at the table of contents (with its assortment of genres) shows that this will be much more intriguing than any ordinary philosophical investigation. In addition to "The Seducer's Diary," the papers of A include essays on "The Musical-Erotic," "The Unhappiest One," "The First Love," and dramatic tragedy. Together they begin an unending story of love, passion, seduction, sorrow, and deception. The second volume, "Part Two, containing B's papers, letters to A," contains two long letters to A, and a very short final letter consisting of a brief introduction to a sermon (from a pastor friend) that B wants A to read.

Victor directs the reader to see the authors as follows: "A's papers contain a multiplicity of approaches to an esthetic view of life" (noting that "a coherent esthetic view of life can hardly be presented") and "B's papers contain an ethical view of life" (EO1, 13). The two sets of papers are, he says, two useful illustrations of cases in which inner and outer diverge – that is, one of the men "especially" shows that "the outer is not the inner" because "his exterior has been a complete contradiction of his interior," while the other man shows this incommensurability "to a certain extent" "inasmuch as he has hidden a more significant interior under a rather insignificant exterior" (4). The philosophical has become personal! Victor's assessment of the men is ambiguous because he does not indicate which figure, A or B, will correspond to each characterization. I propose that the work of reading this text is the work of continuing to ask the guiding question put forth by Victor and Victor's creator: how does the relation between inner and outer play a major role in life?

The common reading of *Either – Or* as a representation of a choice between the esthetic and the ethical ignores the editorial guidance in the preface. First, the preface makes clear that we are being presented with "a multiplicity of approaches to an esthetic" life view (rather than a set of necessary and sufficient conditions for *the* esthetic life view); this multiplicity could represent a set of different possibilities around which a life can center, or they could represent the infinitely varied center of every life. We can similarly assume that we are being presented with an approach (or approaches) to an ethical life view – rather than *the* ethical view of life. Moreover, although sometimes commentators speak as if the first volume represents the "either" and the second volume represents the "or," the fact that the whole title appears on the title pages of both volumes suggests that there might be an "either – or" within each volume, perhaps even several within each volume. Second, although it is often thought that the ethical wins out, the editor emphasizes and approves of the presentation's open-endedness: "these papers come to no conclusion" (EO1, 14). Indeed, he specifically distinguishes this work from those "in which specific characters represent contrasting views of life," and usually "end with one persuading the other" (14). Rather, "the point of view ought to speak for itself" – the goal is that "only the points of view confront each other" and A and B, the personalities, are "forgotten" (14). He affirms this, despite the fact that the last line of his preface expresses his "wish" that "the charming reader may succeed in scrupulously following B's well-intentioned advice" (15). Does this mean that the editor thinks it is not good advice, though "well-intentioned"? But then, why encourage someone to "scrupulously" follow it? Is it good advice? Then why not admit it is normative, rather than think it "fortunate" that the issue between them is left "open-ended"? In any case, the victory, if there is one, is hidden.

The editor also reports that he considered the idea of attributing the authorship of both A and B to one person, suggesting that, after all, both movements could have been experienced by a single person, and that both movements might be somehow related (e.g., sometimes when one has said A, one must also say B). Given the title he ends up with (*Either – Or*), it might seem that he has decided that this was not a good idea, yet he concludes, somewhat surprisingly, that he has been "unable to abandon the idea" (EO1, 13). In the context of his inability "to abandon the idea" of a single authorship, the title might be intended to reveal the way in which these two views of life are connected. Moreover, the subtitle of the whole work – *A Fragment of Life* – reinforces the notion of the two movements in a single life. The English version of the title has a slash between the "Either" and the "Or," suggesting them as mutually exclusive alternatives. But Kierkegaard used a dash in the original Danish, a form of punctuation he often used, and the dash is, for him, a "thought-stroke"[3] – a long pause; it need not indicate opposition between the two elements involved. Indeed, it can graphically tie the two life views together. Are they connected or are they mutually exclusive? Moreover, he had earlier noted that in determining the title, he allowed himself "some freedom, a deception" (13). What is the "deception" embodied in the title? The point is that the editor's preface appears to be at odds with itself in some ways, giving a mixed message both about the normativity of the ethical and about the tension between esthetic and ethical viewpoints. The questions remain: What is an esthetic "inner"; what is an esthetic "outer"; what is an ethical "inner" and what is an ethical "outer"? How many variations on the relation are possible?

It is impossible to do justice here to "A's Papers," but they open with some aphoristic fragments that the editor glosses as preliminary "glimpses" (EO1, 8) of the whole. Some are the dispirited moans of a soul that has "lost possibility" (41) and is too bored to move; they report a life achieving "nothing at all," resembling "the painting by that artist who was supposed to paint the Israelites' crossing of the Red Sea and to that end painted the entire wall red and explained that the Israelites had walked across and that the Egyptians were drowned" (28). Some express the indifference of any choice: "Marry or do not marry – you will regret it either way" (38). Others are more aggressive: "Let others complain that the times are evil. I complain that they are wretched, for they are without passion. . . . The thoughts of their hearts are too wretched to be sinful" (27). Still others are cynical: "When I became an adult, when I opened my eyes and saw actuality, then I started to laugh and have never stopped laughing since that time" (34). A wide range of mood and temperament is suggested and then displayed in part one, and we have our first explicit examples of what might count as "earnestness" and as "jest," two categories that will assume many forms throughout Kierkegaard's authorship.

The second volume, "Part Two," consists of what Victor terms three "letters to A" from a certain Judge William. Several features of the letters are worth noting at the outset. First, they do indeed have the form of letters to someone who is absent, but this is already a deliberate artifice, since we will learn later from William himself that he has been seeing A (the young man) frequently at his home and had even finished composing the second letter when A came to visit (EO2, 332). Second, the titles of the letters ("The Esthetic Validity of Marriage," "The Balance Between the Esthetic and the Ethical in the Development of the Personality," and, finally, "Ultimatum") were given to them by Victor, and he admits that other titles might be more "felicitous" (EO1, 10). In any case, because they are Victor's titles (not William's), they should guide us but not put blinders on us. Thirdly, the reader should be alerted to the fact that in William's first two letters one must distinguish William's voice from the frequent appearance of an (esthetic) interlocutor's voice, who makes proposals and objections that are usually, but not always, indicated by quotation marks.

B The first letter

1 The preservation of the esthetic

William's first "letter" to A announces its intention "to show that romantic love can be united with and exist in marriage – indeed, that marriage is its true transfiguration" (EO2, 31). The challenge William mounts is for the purpose of "upbuilding" (8) A, and has as its "particular task" to show that the esthetic is not left behind but is "preserved" and even "increased" in the ethical (symbolized by marriage) (142). William claims to offer a "richer and fuller esthetic ideal" than A has hitherto appreciated – namely, "the summit of the esthetic" (137). This is not just a critique of A's life view; it is also one of Kierkegaard's first published critiques of the age in which he lived.

William seems both repulsed by the esthete and drawn to him. On the one hand, William calls him "corrupted" (EO2, 6), "egotistical" (24), and "dangerous" (79, 80). But William's sympathy is drawn out by the "passionateness" (13) and "respect [for] earnestness" (15) he sees in A, and he admits that A's polemic contains "the truth" even if he and his opponents are not aware of it (29). The esthete is obviously tempting to William – "I actually at times with a certain reluctance feel that you dazzle me, that I let myself be carried away by your exuberance . . . into the same esthetic-intellectual intoxication in which you live" (16) – and he admits to some "unsureness" that leads him to be "at times too severe, at times too indulgent" (17). In the end William's reviews are always mixed, sometimes even within the same paragraph. The question whether William's response to the esthete is fair must acknowledge William's apparent self-awareness of A's pros and cons.[4]

William's critique has two prongs. On the one hand, he attempts to determine dimensions of the esthetic that A already accepts, and show A that on his own esthetic terms marriage fulfills the esthetic ideal better than erotic love on its own. But he also attempts to add to A's understanding an appreciation of an element that he sees as lacking in A's life view. He thus addresses the notions of immediacy and the historical.

William agrees with A about the value of immediacy or "beauty in the erotic" (EO2, 10). God loves "earthly love" (20), and just as first love is "the highest earthly good" (42–3), so too the "deeper eroticism" of marriage is "the most beautiful aspect of purely human existence" (30). He denies that "sensuousness is annihilated in Christianity" (49). He even questions A's hold on immediacy since A "think[s] too abstractly about everything," including love (128); esthetic abstraction amounts to "not coming into contact with actuality at all" (100).

But simple immediacy is not fully beautiful. William calls attention to a "second esthetic ideal, the historical" (EO2, 96). Failure to attend to this ideal precludes an appreciation of any love that is embodied, shared, and developing because an appreciation of beauty involves an exploration in depth; it involves reflection and this requires time. "Marriage," he concludes, "is precisely that immediacy which contains mediacy, that infinity which contains finitude, that eternity which contains temporality" (94). Marital love has more depth than love that has only immediacy because it contains "resignation" and "is able to relinquish itself" (presumably for the sake of the beloved): in marriage, "the true holding on is the power that was capable of relinquishing and now expresses itself in holding on, and only in this lies the true freedom in holding on" (97). A does not understand that "true art" is the art of "possession" (131), that time is needed for appropriation, development, and depth-appreciation. "Love should have a history" (98); it needs time for reflection on its immediacy, time to exercise the holding on, to acknowledge the striving and the expectation of victory, and to acknowledge the possibility of relinquishing.

William points out that what takes place in time, over time, cannot be easily represented, so it is a mistake to confuse the esthetic with what can be portrayed esthetically (EO2, 133). Or perhaps, this is better expressed by saying that the esthetic can be portrayed, "but not in poetic reproduction, but only by living it, by realizing it in the life of actuality" (137). The richest and fullest esthetic ideal is the esthetic in existence, which we recognize and create when we see ourselves as "creating and created" (137).

2 Harmony between the spheres
William proposes a "harmonious unison of different spheres: it is the same subject, only expressed esthetically, religiously, or ethically" (EO2, 60). He insists repeatedly on this harmony: "sensuous love has but one transfiguration, in which it is equally esthetic, religious and ethical – and that is love" (65); "if you cannot manage to see the esthetic, the ethical, and the religious as the three great allies, if you do not know how to preserve the unity of the different manifestations everything gains in these different spheres, then life is without meaning" (147).

The spatial imagery of concentric circles best expresses the harmony between the spheres. The religious is "concentric" with earthly love (EO2, 30); "love lets itself be taken up into a higher concentricity" (94). The reflected immediacy in which the esthetic is preserved in marriage amounts to "a higher, concentric immediacy" (29); this "higher concentricity" (27, 47, 55) correlates with a "higher unity" (30, 89). Concentricity is possible because the same thing can be treated differently. The notion of concentric circles illustrates William's claim that "the real constituting element, the substance [of marriage], is love [*Kjaerlighed*] – or, if you want to give it more specific emphasis, erotic love [*Elskov*]" (32). The repeated spatial image of concentric circles implies that esthetic abstraction is a certain "how" of treating things, whereas true artistry is a different "how" of treating those same things. Erotic love, esthetic love, is the more circumscribed relation. When duty speaks, it is not something new since duty echoes what the lovers themselves wish. Rather, inwardness is what keeps the fulfillment of duty from being unfree – the task is "maintaining the inwardness of duty in love" (152). William faults the esthete's "either – or," "either love or duty" (159). Duty commands one – that is all it can do. We have to *choose* to do what duty asks. In short, when we "translate duty from the outer to the inner," we are paradoxically "beyond duty" (148). The unity between duty and love is an example of the harmony between spheres and concentric circles. In sum, William has offered an "exploration" of "first love" and of marriage that uncovers the elements of the esthetic that need to be "preserved" in marriage, and, he says repeatedly, can be preserved (9, 117, 119, 124, 125, 141).

3 Inner and outer

The notion of "inwardness" thus shifts the question from "What is beauty?" and "What is love" to "How is one to show that one loves another?" The question is "What does the transfiguration of love look like?" William posits a genuine and nuanced dialectic between openness and hiddenness. On the one hand, he insists that duty must be translated "from the outer to the inner" (EO2, 148), and that in marriage "the internal is primary, something that cannot be displayed or pointed to" (152); he also aligns the esthete with the one who is always "outside" himself (140, 143, 146). This suggests a valorization of the inner, of interiority, but William effectively complicates things here, upsetting any fixed notions as to the value of the inner and outer, and any assumption that the ethical is univocally tied to inner while the esthetic is tied to outer. For example, he admits that A cultivates "secretiveness" (106, 118), but this does not mitigate the way in which the esthete remains "outside" of himself. Moreover, William's emphasis on the inner sits alongside his proposal that "openness" or "disclosure" (118) (which he equates with honesty and frankness) is the "life principle in marriage" (116) precisely because "openness . . . is the life-principle of love" (104).

How are we then to understand love in terms of the polarity between inner and outer, inside and outside, hiddenness and disclosure? The question of inner/outer is a pressing one precisely because we want to understand what kind of openness love involves. This is not a mere philosophical concern. He draws a very explicit contrast between "inside" and "outside," when he says to the esthete, "You are inside yourself only when there is opposition, but therefore you actually are never inside yourself but always outside yourself" (EO2, 143). Nevertheless, William's ideal of self-giving by going out of oneself shows a positive notion of "outside" – the positive notion of a person who "goes outside of himself"(109) is contrasted with the negative notion of a person who is "outside" himself (140, 143, 146).

The ideal of being "outside himself within himself" is paradoxical: "only within himself does the individual have the objective toward which he is to strive, and yet he has this objective outside himself as he strives toward it. That is why the ethical life has this duplexity, in which the individual has himself outside himself within himself" (EO2, 259).

Can one be open to another in such a way that one loses oneself and forgets oneself, and yet remains, in some sense, for oneself? If not, one has no self to give to others, no inwardness to disclose. Inwardness must be guarded against dissipation, and the transfiguration of the esthetic opens the inwardness without losing it. William's claim that "only the person who has lost everything has gained everything" (111) echoes the biblical notion that one gains one's life only by losing it.

C The second letter

William's second letter, "The Balance between the Esthetic and Ethical in the Development of the Personality," continues the concern with beauty as well as the theme of the preservation and transfiguration of the esthetic in the ethical. But we also find new accents.

1 The preservation of the esthetic

William adamantly denies that "the ethical is entirely different from the esthetic, and when it advances it completely annihilates the latter"; on the contrary, "everything comes back again, but transfigured [because] only when a person himself lives ethically does his life take on beauty, truth, meaning, security" (EO2, 271). He forcefully insists that the ethical "does not want to destroy the esthetic but to transfigure it" (253). Indeed, "all the esthetic returns" (178). To understand why it is not destroyed one must distinguish between absolute exclusion and relative exclusion: "in the ethical, the personality is brought into a focus in itself; consequently, the esthetic is absolutely excluded or it is excluded *as the absolute*, but relatively it is continually present" (177, my emphasis). He goes on to say that when the esthetic is excluded "as the absolute," it is "dethroned" (226). Saying that the esthetic is "made an auxiliary and precisely thereby is preserved" means that although "one does not live in it as before," it is "used in another way" (229). Although the imagery of concentric circles shifts to the imagery of dethronement, the meaning remains the same.

2 New accents: choice, paradox, imagination, and transparency

The letter opens with something new – a stark and repeated accent on the categories of "choice" and "freedom." These categories develop the earlier judgment that the esthetic has to be lived in existence (i.e., with contact, engagement, continuity) as well as reconfigure the understanding of the historical (previously emphasized as shared, developmental history) into an emphasis on "the moment" of choice and its responsibility.

Choice is the primary hallmark of the ethical: "On the whole, to choose is an intrinsic and stringent term for the ethical" (EO2, 166). Such choice is *practical* (it is about what to do in life) and *concrete*: the "self contains in itself a rich concretion, a multiplicity of qualities, of characteristics – in short, it is the total esthetic self that is chosen ethically" (222). William writes that "the person who chooses himself ethically chooses himself concretely as this specific individual . . . with these capacities, these inclinations, these drives, these passions, influenced by this specific social milieu, as this specific product of a specific environment. But as he becomes aware of all this, he takes upon himself responsibility for it all" (250–51). After all, "the ethical does not want to wipe out this concretion but sees in it its task, sees the material with which it is to build and that which it is to build" (253). In sum, "there is no abstract marriage" (305); the ethical person "is no hater of the concrete, but he has one expression in addition, deeper than every esthetic expression, inasmuch as he sees in love a revelation of the universally human" (256).

Although William does not use the term "paradox," the concept is integral to his description of choice. The "perilous" transition from esthetic to ethical (EO2, 232) is a paradoxical performance because "choice here makes two dialectical movements simultaneously – that which is chosen does not exist and comes into existence through the choice – and that which is chosen exists; otherwise it was not a choice" (215). In other words, "it is, for if it were not I could not choose it; it is not, for it first comes into existence through my choosing it, and otherwise my choice would be an illusion" (213–14). In choice a person paradoxically transforms himself – a person "remains himself, exactly the same that he was before, down to the most insignificant feature, and yet he becomes another, for the choice penetrates everything and changes it" (223). The point of saying that someone "becomes another" is lost if he ceases to be at the same time the same self, for then "he" would not be becoming another – there would be a different person rather than a transformed person.

The relevance of paradox brings in the relevance of imagination. The ethical task – to "become what he becomes" (EO2, 178, 225, 226) – paradoxically holds the inner and outer in tension: "The self the individual knows is *simultaneously the actual self and the ideal self*, which the individual has outside himself as the image in whose likeness he is to form himself, and which on the other hand he has within himself, since it is he himself" (259, my emphasis). It is only imagination that can enlarge the horizon of possibilities through presenting the ideal self as an "image" of what is not yet actualized: "What he wants to actualize is certainly himself, but it is his ideal self, which he cannot acquire anywhere but within himself. If he does not hold firmly to the truth that the individual has the ideal self within himself, all of his aspiring and striving becomes abstract" (259). The ability to make a free transition to another perspective assumes that we can sufficiently appreciate another context for it to attract us *before* we actually accept its categories or values. This paradoxical possibility toward which we strive must be concrete – imagination presents us with possibilities and concretizes them. Moreover, William correlates ethical choice with infinity: one's "finite personality is now made infinite in the choice, in which he infinitely chooses himself" (223). But only imagination can infinitize anything.

The ethical person sees "tasks" where the esthete sees only possibilities to be entertained or enjoyed (EO2, 251). Imagination is needed not only to see a possibility, or to concretize it, or to infinitize it, but also to construe it as a task. To see a "likeness" to which he *has to* "form himself" (259) is to see a possibility which is recognized or appreciated as a *demand*; such a "seeing-as" requires imagination. To see as a demand what could otherwise be seen (by you or others) as a neutral possibility is to explore it imaginatively (explore the various possibilities within the possibility) and thus to hold different descriptions in tension. To see a demand in a possibility is an imaginative extension.

There are other ways of using imagination: the esthete uses imagination to flit around in possibilities; the philosopher uses imagination to make things abstract, theoretically or conceptually excising them from actuality. But imagination can be used ethically to counteract abstraction (to see a possibility, to concretize it, to infinitize it, and to construe it as a task). Thus, one cannot fully appreciate William's position on the role of willing or choice in ethics without also acknowledging his appreciation of the ethical roles of imagination.

Although William claims that "with the ethical there is never a question of the external but of the internal" (EO2, 265), he re-envisions the relation between inner and outer yet again when he suggests that the "transparent" is the mark of the ethical (258). This notion of transparency, on which he relies heavily (179, 190, 248, 254), develops the first letter's emphasis on openness, as well as its preliminary suggestion that it "takes courage to be willing to appear as one really is" (105), "courage to be willing to see [one]self" (118). How can love show itself without belying itself? One answer is by being transparent, rather than trying to turn the inner outward. The contradiction that seems to make the inner, by definition, unable to be shown, is addressed by the notion of transparency. Transparency, or openness, is crucial, because "the person who can scarcely open himself cannot love, and the person who cannot love is the unhappiest of all" (160).

Finally, William points to a difference between the "how" and the "what": "In order for a person to be called a hero, one must consider not so much what he does as how he does it. . . . The question is always – how does he do it?" (EO2, 298). Two people can "do exactly the same" thing in two different ways (257) – the "ethical lies so deep in the soul, it is not always visible, and the person who lives ethically may do exactly the same as one who lives esthetically, and thus it may deceive for a long time, but eventually there comes a moment when it becomes manifest that the person who lives ethically has a boundary that the other does not know" (257). There are different ways of treating everything – time, evil, beauty; there are different ways of using everything – choice, passion, imagination.

D Assessment

The first two letters provoke us to think again about what love is, or more precisely, how to express love, whether some loves are incompatible with each other, and what role love plays in the choices we make (or what role choice plays in our loves). They also provoke us to think again about the notion of beauty in relation to love. One could say that the first letter makes a promissory note (a formal assertion that the ethical can retain and transfigure the esthetic) while the second letter is an attempt to make good on that note, by illustrating the particular ways in which choice expresses crucial dimensions of the esthetic. But this difference of emphasis should not obscure the important fact that both letters raise the question (in various ways) whether one can maintain an emphasis on a qualitative difference between categories alongside a meaningful sense of one of them being "preserved" and "transfigured" in the other.

1 Harmony yet qualitative difference

The first letter makes a case for the "esthetic prestige" (EO2, 6) or "esthetic meaning" (8) of marriage, and thereby posits the *compatibility* of the esthetic and the ethical. William almost immediately raises the stakes from the compatibility between esthetic and ethical to the *harmony* between three spheres: esthetic, ethical, and religious. Although he refers here to three spheres, William does not draw a distinction between the ethical and the religious. The idea of a qualitative difference between the esthetic and the ethical-religious is suggested by the graphic descriptions of their contrasting behavior. He presents us with the possibility that there can be a qualitative difference between certain categories at the same time as there can be "harmony" among their lived expressions. In other words, both letters present the possibility of understanding an "either – or" in different ways: first, an "either" that is tied to an "or" (the harmony in the "esthetic validity" of marriage); second, an "either" that is distinguished from an "or" (in virtue of a qualitative difference).

William considers it crucial that there be no confusion between esthetic categories and ethical categories. He is not, however, advocating their mutual exclusion; mutual exclusion is not the only alternative to conflating them. William repeatedly emphasizes that the two are in relation; in fact he has a long discussion of "life relationships" in which "the esthetic and the ethical meet" (EO2, 277) with examples of the difficulty of separating the two. William emphasizes the "dialectic" (215, 262) that retains the tension – rather than the absorption or submergence of one into another. In other words, this text presents the possibility of a disjunction that remains dialectical rather than mutually exclusive. It might seem strange that the message of *Either – Or* is about the harmony of spheres, but because this harmony allows for dialectical tension there is no confusion between the spheres. The claim that one must either live esthetically or live ethically, if taken to mean that these are mutually exclusive, is belied by the Judge's commitment to the unison or harmony among different dimensions of life.

2 Inner and outer

What first got Victor's attention was the way in which the papers of A and the letters of B might shed light on the thesis that "the outer is the inner and the inner is the outer" (EO1, 3). Since he questions the "accuracy" of the thesis, we are led to expect that he will try to show that such identity is neither possible nor desirable. It is clear from the beginning that Victor did not see the contrast between inner and outer as coinciding with that between B and A, but rather with that between the inner and outer in B and the inner and outer in A. Moreover, Victor does not see a decisive contrast between A and B with respect to the disparity between inner and outer. His judgment is that *both* illustrate a contrast between inner and outer, and the difference is only one of degree – in the case of one of these people, his exterior "completely" (4) contradicts his interior, whereas, in the other case, the exterior only partly contradicts the interior. The only evaluation he offers is, in the one case, by way of distinguishing between a "significant" interior and an "insignificant" exterior as a way of being incommensurate (4).

Having read the letters, we now find ourselves questioning how A and B both might have a significant interior with an insignificant exterior, differing only in degree. Does A have a significant interior (passion, immediacy) under an insignificant exterior (the frivolous, indifferent, cynical façade)? Or does B have a more significant interior (the inwardness of duty, the fidelity of love) under an insignificant exterior (the duty-bound married civil servant)? How is A's inner life in contradiction to his outer? How is William's in contradiction to his outer? Both value love and passion. Both resist abstraction. It is possible that even after reading all the papers and letters one still might not know which life view is the one Victor judges to be "completely" contradictory, and which is only contradictory to some extent. Moreover, by now we should question whether the inner is the only "significant" dimension, after all, since William has revealed ways in which the outer can be valuable – transparency, openness, going outside of one's self. Thus, we can find a variety of "either – or" in both volumes.

There are at least two styles found in the letters thus far. First the author (Kierkegaard) *orients* and guides the reader, alerting the reader to certain things. For example, when the Judge raises the question whether the esthete can rightly assess the character and values of the esthetic because he lives in it and only a higher stage can really see a lower one, this indirectly raises the question whether the Judge can rightly assess the ethical, for the same reason. The Judge offers what seems a weak and self-serving rationale when he says that he can judge because he is not stuck in necessity, but rather experiences freedom.

Second, the author (Kierkegaard) *disorients* the reader by presenting certain tensions. The letters cannot but be provoking and perplexing. One could say that both letters pose the question (in various ways) how "inner" can relate to "outer" – are there different kinds of "inner" and "outer," and can the valuations associated with each vary not only between "inner" and "outer," but also among various kinds of interiority and among various kinds of exteriority? In sum, the letters explore how different an "inner" can look, and how different an "outer" can look. They present us with different kinds of passion, different kinds of duty, different kinds of openness, different kinds of hiddenness, different kinds of immediacy, and different kinds of reflection. They repeatedly exchange valuations on these – at times passion is good, at times bad, at times hiddenness is bad, at times good, etc. In short, anything could be good or bad, depending on "how" it is done (EO2, 298). The qualitative difference lies in the way something is done, and all the dichotomies of inner/outer, inside/outside, internal/external, interior/exterior need to be reassessed in that light.

We cannot help asking certain questions. For example, why is the "transparency" endorsed by the Judge not simply an identity between inner and outer? How is the hiddenness endorsed by the Judge different from the hiddenness he criticizes in A? Is the idea of a "higher unity" (EO2, 30, 89) which the Judge endorses different from the "balance" between the esthetic and the ethical that he also endorses? In the end, however, it is clear that the letters particularize the universal perplexity of how to live in the question "Do I love rightly?"

E The ultimatum

The title given by Victor Eremita to the third letter, unlike the simply descriptive titles given by him to the first two letters, is a provocative one – "Ultimatum." This title gives the impression that here is something decisive. At any rate, Victor and Victor's author seem to want us to stand back and consider whether there is something decisive and in what it might consist.

The third letter is really only a brief introduction to its contents – namely, a "sermon" from a pastor friend of William, entitled "The Upbuilding that Lies in the Thought that in Relation to God We are Always in the Wrong." Judge William begins by suggesting that the substance of the earlier letters, his "attitude," "position," and "thought," remain "unchanged," but adds the somewhat odd note that he hopes "that in time the movements of thought will become easier and more natural for [him]" (EO2, 337). The claim for the continuity of his thought is striking, but William seems to hint that he is still not at home in this position, that he still strives to feel what he says at such length. More interestingly, William posits a similarity between the preceding letters and the sermon when he claims that "In this sermon he [the Pastor] has grasped what I have said and what I would like to have said to you," admitting that the Pastor "has expressed it better" than he was able to (338). This makes one wonder whether the title "Ultimatum" is misleading, since if the sermon is consonant with William's preceding letters, it cannot represent a new choice in any strong sense. Since it is, after all, Victor Eremita's title, we need to consider the sermon itself to determine whether it adds anything absolutely new to the picture or in any way forces a choice, or whether William is correct in his judgment that this sermon expresses William's own view.

The Pastor reminds us that other things do not have the freedom to be in the wrong before God: they follow God's laws necessarily (EO2, 346). But while it may seem flattering to construe such freedom as our "perfection," the thought that in relation to God we are always in the wrong confronts us more forcefully: because there are no degrees in relation to God (352), if we are in the wrong we are infinitely in the wrong. It is interesting, therefore, that the Pastor's sermon does not raise the issue of guilt or repentance, or sin or forgiveness, which one would expect to be raised in connection with being in the wrong. Instead, he casts the discussion of being in the wrong in a positive and hopeful light – it is an "upbuilding" thought.

The exploration of why the thought can be "upbuilding" rather than discouraging, why the confession that we are always in the wrong before God should be "joyfully" attended by thanksgiving (EO2, 341) has to do with its converse side – namely, "should not the thought that in relation to God we are always in the wrong be inspiring, for what else does it express but that God's love is always greater than our love?" (353). This thought is a happy one because it amounts to the thought that "you could never love as you were loved" (351) and the thought that "God's love is always greater than our love" (353). To be in the wrong before

God consists in being in an infinite debt of love.[5] It would be hard to understand why the Pastor thinks there is something "upbuilding" in the thought that in relation to God we are always in the wrong if it did not carry with it the message of God's great love and the promise of the "wisdom" of "God's governance" (351).

Only the supporting and empowering love of God could explain why the thought of always being in the wrong does not "vitiate the power of the will and the strength of the intention" (EO2, 353) but rather calms doubts and inspires to action (351, 353). Although being in the wrong is not something we should want to change, not wanting to change it does not mean we can be inactive; to be built up by the thought of being in the wrong demands something from us.

What does the sermon accomplish? Even if one emphasizes the sobering dauntingness of the sermon's message about being always in the wrong, the sermon remains hopeful. True, being built up is not something that can be achieved and finished (EO2, 348), but the thought that one is "always in the wrong" is "the longing with which [one] seeks God" and "the love in which [one] finds God" (353). Moreover, given how the Pastor makes the tie between being in the wrong and being loved by God, he could have drawn out the positive implication of there being no degrees in relation to God (352) – namely, that if we are loved, we are infinitely loved. The upbuilding reassurance found in the sermon is that God's love enables our love, and it is important that we personally appropriate it since "only the truth that builds up is truth for you" (354). The sermon highlights the anxiety we experience, but it affirms our ability to do what we need to do, because we are loved. It contributes the sobering and hopeful message that infinite debt reveals infinite love.

But to answer the question whether and in what way this is an "ultimatum," we need to ask why William thinks the sermon says what he wanted to say, only better. Is William right, or does the "ultimatum" put William in question? Does the sermon undermine William's position? Commentators disagree on this question, and this leaves the reader the opportunity to ponder more deeply what is at stake in the putative contrast between the Judge and the Pastor. The Pastor's final words, "Only the truth that builds up is truth for you" (EO2, 354) may well be the most important thing he says, and it could be considered the fount of all the works that follow.

F Conclusion

Either – Or serves as a paradigmatic example of some central strategies Kierkegaard uses. It serves first as an example of *indirection* in the writing – that is, of crafting a text that will suggest certain possibilities and raise certain questions and offer certain warnings, without being a straightforward representation of a conclusion. In a very general sense, one could say that the author (Kierkegaard) communicates indirectly in *Either – Or* because he communicates through a variety of authors he creates (Victor, A, the Judge, the Pastor). But the indirect communication is effected in more specific ways as well.

First, *Either – Or* reveals the importance of the category of *tension* to Kierkegaard's writings. In particular, the book suggests how form and content may be in tension. *Either – Or*, despite its title and form, does not communicate a single "either – or" between two options; rather, the two volumes communicate varieties of ways of understanding the tension between certain contrasts (between esthetic and ethical, between inner and outer, between concrete and abstract). In that sense, the book does not present a single "either – or." It does not advocate the mutual exclusion of the esthetic and ethical as lived experience. In another sense, however, the decisiveness of an "either – or" is shown to be important, so long as the decisiveness is located in the right place. "Either – or" means: do not confuse categories, and do not act "to a certain degree." The decisive difference is not located in the content of our actions. This book shows that the importance of a *qualitative difference*, as opposed to a quantitative difference, lies in the "*how*" rather than the "*what*"; it repeatedly leads us to appreciate the crucial distinction between what we do and the way we do it.

Either – Or is also a paradigmatic example of *concentricity*, or of the coincidence of central concerns – that is, it is a revealing example of how there is no either/or between theological, philosophical, literary, and personal concerns. The way in which one's personal, even romantic, interests can, in the space of one's literary artistry, coincide with one's religious or philosophical interests is exemplified in *Either – Or*. For example, we find a philosophical concern played out in terms of inner versus outer, abstract versus concrete: this represents a challenge to the dominant philosophy of the age, a "breakup" with German idealism and then further disillusionment with Schelling's lectures. We also find explorations of inner and outer in relation to love, both with respect to deception in love and to expressions of love in marriage. It would be difficult to read "The Seducer's Diary" and the Judge's discussions of erotic love and marital fidelity without thinking of Kierkegaard's personal engagement crisis. But the theme of a "broken engagement" stands as an emblem for all the losses, departures, and rejections in life. If everything were a dimension of his relation to God, the various strands would coincide. Explorations of being "in the wrong" could simultaneously refer to his personal experience with Regine Olsen and to coping with the perception of his father's guilt made salient by the father's death, as well as to the problems of suffering and guilt and repentance as tied to his relation to a God who both judges and forgives. Kierkegaard could be addressing both personal and theological concerns. If Kierkegaard did not see the relation to God as eccentric to the rest of his life, the themes of love, commitment, sorrow, grief, and doubt could all carry an infinite freight. That Kierkegaard wrote his way into and out of various events in his life does not preclude these writings from having a far greater import and relevance for readers.

Some of the most important insights in Kierkegaard's entire authorship are already in place in this, his first major work. Most important, we have seen the centrality of the notion of "lived tension," the compatibility of qualitative change and harmony between spheres, and the role of paradox and imagination. All these pieces will be picked up again and refigured, refashioned. Their placement in relation to different things will give them nuance and qualification, as well as the richness of added dimensions.

II *Two Upbuilding Discourses* (1843)

A month after *Either – Or* made its splash, Kierkegaard took a set of *Two Upbuilding Discourses* (the Danish *Taler* simply means "talks") to the printer. These were ready earlier, but he seems to have deliberately wanted to delay their publication (perhaps he wanted to avoid mitigating the impact of *Either – Or* in any way). All we know is that these discourses were quite different from anything else he had written, and that he signed his own name to them. I will examine these first two discourses in greater detail than I will the remainder because they are the beginning of a new genre that will comprise a significant portion of his authorship. As I noted earlier, it has been claimed that the category of "upbuilding" (*opbyggelige*, also translated as "edifying") is "the central theme of Kierkegaard's authorship." as well as that these discourses provide a "privileged viewpoint on the authorship as a whole."[6] The term "upbuilding" connects these discourses with *Either – Or* not only because the Pastor's sermon in the second volume insisted on the thought that "only the truth that *builds up* is truth for you," but also because Judge William himself had claimed that his letters were intended to be "upbuilding" (EO2, 354, 8). Let's look at the discourses in detail before assessing their import and their relation to *Either – Or*.

This first volume of discourses is dedicated to Kierkegaard's father (a practice he continued for the next seven volumes of discourses) and begins with a preface that serves, with minor variations, as the model for the prefaces of the next seven volumes of discourses. First, Kierkegaard distinguishes these discourses from "sermons," presumably because he does not have the clerical authority to give sermons. In this particular preface he also contrasts his title for them, namely, "upbuilding discourses," with a title that might seem equivalent, namely, "discourses for upbuilding." His explanation is that they are not discourses "for upbuilding" because he is not a "teacher."[7] This implies that the writing of these upbuilds him too – they educate him. Second, he addresses the discourses to his special reader – "my reader."

The first discourse, "The Expectancy of Faith" (EUD, 7–29) clearly exemplifies a religious genre: it opens with a prayer to our "heavenly Father," refers us to Paul's epistle to the Galatians, and ends with an appeal to our "Father in heaven." The deeply poignant reference to God as the one "who tests spirits in conflict, the same Father without whose will not one sparrow falls to the ground" (7) shows it to be the prayer of one who feels he has been tested, but who knows his trials come from (or at least are knowingly allowed by) God. The prayer suggests why the discourse is upbuilding – the mood is humble and sad, yet hopeful.

Given this prayerful framing and Scriptural reference, it may seem surprising that Kierkegaard puts this discussion into the context of New Year's Day, which is not a religious holiday but rather an occasion on which we offer to others our good wishes for the coming year – that is, our wishes for the good of others. He adds that it is a time when we recognize that, however much we love others, we cannot give them what we consider the highest good. But what is the highest good, and why is it not something we can wish for or give to others?

Implicitly guided by the passage from Paul's epistle, which includes the theological themes of justification by faith and how baptism in Christ eliminates all distinctions "between Jew and Greek, slave and free, male and female," the discourse centers on how faith is the highest good, one in which we can all share equally. The highest good is the "faith," "the eternal power in a human being," that expects "victory" (EUD, 19). The word "victory" is constantly repeated, but the character of the victory is indeterminate: Kierkegaard insists that there are two ways of failing to expect victory – namely, to expect nothing (to despair) and to expect something "particular" (23, 27). So the victory is described merely as "that all things must serve for good those who love God" (19) or "faith expects an eternity" (27). What is affirmed and expected in faith is a victory whose content cannot be described, a victory whose content is hidden from us – a hidden victory, so to speak, reminding us of one way to translate the name of the editor of *Either – Or*, Victor Eremita.

The good news is that "every human being has what is highest, noblest, and most sacred in humankind. It is original in him, and every human being has it if he wants to have it" (EUD, 14). Kierkegaard elaborates Paul's message about the inclusiveness of faith when he writes that the "very glory of faith" is this absolute equality – "every person" (13) is able to have this good. However, "no human being can give it to another" (14), nor is faith something that can be simply wished for:

"only by personally willing it could the other grasp it" (13); "it can be had only by constantly being acquired and can be acquired only by continually being generated" (14).

The contrast between wishing and wanting issues in a resounding assertion that every person can do it; you can do it; I can do it. This is meant to emphasize equality and personal appropriation, but it raises the question of how one gets faith. On the one hand, it seems good to contrast idle wishing for something with actively doing something about it; the idea that you can do it if you really want to implies that faith is a task. Although it cannot come from another human, it does seem to be up to me. This description of faith as something one can acquire, as well as the statement that everyone "has it if he wants to have it," that it is something "original" in everyone – all this is a religious message, a message of hope, but it is not yet the message that faith is a gift from God. If the discourse went no further, it would be at odds not only with the Pastor's message, but even with Judge William's own acknowledgement that what he has received is a "gift of grace from the hand of God" (EO2, 238).

It does go further, although it is easy to miss the place in which the notion of gift is introduced. This happens when Kierkegaard announces hopefully that "every person" can say "when people disdained me, I went to God; he became my teacher, and this is my salvation, my joy, my pride" (EUD, 12–13). He ends the discourse with an unambiguous statement of gift, for it is true of faith that "no person learns this from another, but each one individually learns it only from and through God" (28). We can each will to go to God, the teacher, who alone can gift us with faith. The most one can do for others is to build them up by presupposing faith in them and encouraging them to turn to God the teacher.

One way to read the strong emphasis on faith as dependent on my activity is to see it as reiterating Paul's emphasis on equality before God. Another way to read it is as a complement to the Jutland Pastor's message that we are always in the wrong before God, suggesting that there is a lack of tension in the Pastor's understanding that needs to be counterbalanced or corrected, or a one-sided passivity that needs to be put in question. But given the opening prayer and the acknowledgement of our dependence of God, the teacher, it seems implausible to read the discourse as cavalierly optimistic or naïvely confident.

This discourse is about faith in God, but it has another layer. Kierkegaard speaks of the perplexed person, the troubled person, who feels he is a prisoner mired in the "difficulty," even "the riddle," of wishing for the good of another (EUD, 8). But not just any other. The anxiety arises because it is a question of wishing the good for the person who is the "exception" to our general "goodwill" – namely, the one to whom the perplexed person is "more closely attached," "more concerned for his welfare" (8). The reference to "his" welfare is belied by the places in which "he" is identified as "the beloved" (9). The perplexity concerns "the one he loves most, and the more he loves, the harder it is" (9). What should he wish this New Year's Day for his beloved? The difficulty is that "he is unwilling to have the beloved slip out of his power, is unwilling to surrender him to the control of the future, and yet he must" (9); he must "let go" of the loved one (13). The perplexed person begins to think "there must be something wrong with his love" (14). One could say, then, that the discourse is about love, about loving others rightly, about the limits of what we can do for others (i.e., how we must let them go, and trust). In this respect, the relation to *Either – Or* is clear: namely, both concern themselves with "how to love rightly."

This discourse thus exemplifies the way in which Kierkegaard's concerns can be construed in terms of concentric circles – it shows how Kierkegaard's response to the personal in his life undergoes a literary "transubstantiation" and a theological/religious extrapolation. He expresses the particular in relation to something more general – the personal crisis is inflected literarily; the theological is both extrapolated from the personal crisis and applied to it. In this discourse he urges his listener(s) to trust God, to have faith in the future, to see the victory in eternity – the discourse describes a perplexity that we all face, and although the discourse is dedicated to his father (who died in 1838), the perplexity more likely refers to the more recent breakup with Regine Olsen (at the end of 1841).

To the question "How, then, should we face the future?" (EUD, 19), there is one answer: Have faith, expect victory in eternity. This is a question for his "devout listeners," and for his "listener," (he goes back and forth between the plural and singular, beginning and ending with "devout listeners"). It is also a question for himself, as is clear when he ponders: "But when I ask myself the question: Do you expect victory?" (27). That is, the one answer contains thoughts that coincide, or thoughts hidden within thoughts. One thought: You, devout listener, be faithful – do not lose faith in God, do not despair; faith is qualitatively different from other goods; have faith that you will have eternity. A coinciding thought: You, Regine, be faithful – do not lose faith in God, do not despair; faith is qualitatively different from other goods; have faith that you will have eternity. A coinciding thought: You, Regine, trust that I am faithful to you; have faith that we will have eternity together. One could even say that another coinciding thought concerns Kierkegaard himself: You, Søren Kierkegaard, be faithful – do not lose faith in God, do not despair; have faith that you will have God (and Regine) in eternity. The message is overdetermined – there is no need for an "either – or." If, for Kierkegaard, one only learns about love from God, then any reflection on his love for Regine is also a reflection on God's love.

The second discourse, "Every Good and Every Perfect Gift is from Above" (EUD, 31–48), elaborates Judge William's passing allusion to the "gift of grace from the hand of God," opening with a prayerful acknowledgement that "we are willing to receive everything" from God's "mighty hand" and God's "gentle hand" (31). Although Kierkegaard quotes in full the Scriptural reference (James 1:17–22), the discourse focuses mostly on the first sentence which it repeats six times: "Every good and every perfect gift is from above and comes down from the Father of lights, with whom there is no change or shadow of variation" (32).

The message – every good and perfect gift comes from the Father – soon transforms itself into the message that everything God gives is a good and perfect gift. That is, if it seems that what you, God, offer us is not a blessing, "increase our faith and our trust so that we might still hold fast to you" (EUD, 31). The message is intended to be both "soothing and comforting" as well as "curative and healing" (48). The discussion of gift distinguishes two kinds of temptation to be avoided: Do not think that you are tempted by God when you do not get your wish, and do not think that you can tempt God to fulfill your wishes. What God gives you is a good and a perfect gift – something good and good for you, rather than what you might wish for. The advice is simple: do not tempt God to undo what is done, because everything that God gives is a good and perfect gift, "even when what happens is strange in your eyes" (44). The courage to receive gifts is itself a gift (44), and the appropriate response is "always to give thanks" (45). These discourses were written soon after Kierkegaard separated from Regine, and it is not hard to think that when he writes of "the deep pain of having to confess again and again that you never loved as you were loved" (44), he is thinking of his relationship to her.

Aspects of the discourses interweave with those of *Either – Or*, and the interplay goes in both directions. Both these discourses raise the question of how to deal with the future when what we get from God is not what we wished for. One could say that in the discourses, there is no clear sense of what one wishes for, whereas in *Either – Or* one gets a sense that one wishes for the "harmony" between loves – esthetic, ethical, and religious. Judge William exulted "God has loved me first" and asked "What is a human being without love" (EO2, 216). The Pastor's sermon decisively accents how we can never love God as God loves us – in other words, we are loved infinitely by God (EO2, 351, 353). It could be that the equation between being "in the wrong" and being loved more than you could ever love, which we find in the Pastor's sermon, is given a more particular form in the discourses by the references to the "beloved" and the "pain" of admitting that you "never loved as you were loved" (EUD, 44). The "sermon" is at a distance from the writer of the discourses, whose personal experience of debt and excess love finds its own deepening and elevation when seen in the light of God's love. The infinite love of God toward us is another way of saying that everything we have is a good and perfect gift. Echoing Judge William's references to the notion of "repentance" (EO2, 216), this discourse suggests that true love of God is "love that is born of repentance" (EUD, 45). Kierkegaard explains: "in repentance it is God who loves you. In repentance, you receive everything from God, even the thanksgiving that you bring to him, so that even this is what the child's gift is to the eyes of the parents, a jest, a receiving of something that one has oneself given" (46).

It is interesting that he regards as a "jest" the fact that "God is the one who does everything in you and who then grants you the childlike joy of regarding your thanksgiving as a gift from you" (EUD, 46). This category will prove important in all of Kierkegaard's writings, and here we see that one meaning of "jest" has to do with the incongruity of our dealings with God. In other words, "jest" is going to bear a great deal more weight than the ordinary usage of the term would suggest – there is often an incredible poignancy about it. This is also going to be true of what Kierkegaard means by "irony."[8] "Jest" can be very serious, and we see here one way in which jest and earnestness are not incompatible.[9]

Either – Or and the *Two Upbuilding Discourses* bear out the thesis that Kierkegaard's transubstantiation of various personal life events does not preclude those writings from having a far greater import and relevance. Readers can discover in those writings things that awaken them and change their view of life because of a deep connection between the two dimensions running through Kierkegaard's authorship – that is, all the talk about love, sorrow, guilt, and forgiveness found its first meaning in his relation to God. If Kierkegaard wanted to express something of what love was, and if he thought that God was Love, then it would not be surprising that both strands would coincide, and be inseparable, in his writings.

notes

1 Although published earlier, neither *From the Papers of One Still Living* nor his university dissertation, *On the Concept of Irony*, brought him much attention.

2 It has long been found as such in Danish bookstores, and now both Princeton University Press and Penguin Classics offer an English edition.

3 The Danish is *Taenkestreg*.

4 William also allows that even if what he says does not fit A, it fits a "spokesman for this trend" (EO2, p. 53).

5 This parallels the duty to remain in love's debt, a notion of infinite obligation that will later get elaborated in *Works of Love*.

6 See chapter 1, notes 5 and 6.

7 Although he will later use the term "discourses for upbuilding" for the third part of his *Christian Discourses*.
8 E.g., "All things serve us for good, if we love God. *If* we love God. (The irony.)" (EUD, Supp., p. 476).
9 "Only that which is upbuilding truly unites jest and earnestness. Consequently, it is a jest . . . that God in heaven is the only great one whom one unceremoniously addresses with *Du* . . . but this jest is also the deepest earnestness" (EUD, Supp., p. 424).

further reading

Hannay, Alastair, and Gordon Marino, eds., *The Cambridge Companion to Kierkegaard* (Cambridge: Cambridge University Press, 1998).
IKC, EO1, vol. 3 (1995).
IKC, EO2, vol. 4 (1995).
IKC, EUD, vol. 5 (2003).
Jegstrup, Elsebet, ed., *The New Kierkegaard* (Studies in Continental Theology) (Bloomington, IN: Indiana University Press, 2004).
KSY, 2008.
Leon, Celine, and Sylvia Walsh, eds., *Feminist Interpretations of Søren Kierkegaard* (University Park, PA: Penn State University Press, 1997).
Pattison, George, *Kierkegaard: The Aesthetic and the Religious* (London: Macmillan, 1992).
Pattison, George, *Kierkegaard's Upbuilding Discourses: Philosophy, Literature, and Theology,* (London: Routledge, 2002).
Walsh, Sylvia, *Living Poetically: Kierkegaard's Existential Aesthetics* (University Park, PA: Penn State University Press, 1994).

chapter 3

Repetition, Fear and Trembling, and More *Discourses*

On October 16, 1843, three new works appeared – two pseudonymous works, *Repetition* and *Fear and Trembling*, and a volume of upbuilding discourses. *Fear and Trembling* is without doubt the more well-known, but they all gain from comparison and contrast. We begin with *Repetition*, which was completed first.

I Repetition

Repetition perfectly exemplifies the way Kierkegaard's works seem to succeed each other, each new work taking up again one or more of the thematic glimmers found in earlier texts and elaborating on them so that they retain something of the old, but something quite different as well. *Either – Or* had already broached the subject of "repetition," in terms of the esthete's contempt for repetition (EO2, 107, 125) and the possibility of "a completely different idea of time and of the meaning of repetition"(EO2, 141). In other words, the way *Repetition* (the book) exemplifies repetition thereby illuminates "repetition" (the category).

The title *Repetition* suggests that we have in hand a text that will address the significance of temporality. The pseudonymous author, Constantin Constantius, exemplifies repetition in his very name, not simply because of the literal repetition, but also because the name, Constant Constancy, invokes the temporal notion of continuity embedded in the repetition of faithfulness. The subtitle, *A Venture in Experimenting Psychology*, emphasizes a psychological interest, but it is important to note that the Danish word translated as "experiment" has nothing to do with scientific verification, but rather with imaginative construction.

Also reminiscent of *Either – Or* is the way this new book offers a presentation of a "young man" and his letters, an older or more experienced confidant or counselor (Constantin Constantius), and their contrasting views about love and relationships to women. That is, *Repetition* appears to repeat the literary scaffolding of *Either – Or*, but the appearance is misleading, because in this case everything seems to be turned on its head – the older man (Constantin Constantius) bears marks of an esthetic orientation, and the younger man is the one facing what he takes to be an ethical dilemma (at least insofar as he is concerned about guilt and innocence).

Constantius gets to orient the text by going first. In his long essay he gives us our first glimpse of the young man, but not until he has acknowledged his own concern with a philosophical question, a concern so extreme it "practically immobilized" him: he had been, he says, "occupied for some time, at least on occasion, with the question of repetition – whether or not it is possible, what importance it has, whether something gains or loses in being repeated" (R, 131). Continuing in the same breath (after a dash), he reports that at that time a thought "suddenly" occurred to him – namely, that he could take a trip back to Berlin to decide the question.

He explicitly puts the question of "repetition" in the context of the philosophical tradition, and then suggests the existential dimension of "repetition" as a movement that takes "courage" (R, 132) and that is "actuality and the earnestness of existence" (133). Only then does Constantius introduce the figure of a young man, with whom he had for some time played the role of "confidant" (134), but of whom he had become "very much aware" (133) a year ago when the young man's life took a dramatic turn. Always torn between being "an observer," whose "art is to expose what is hidden" or to ferret out secrets (135), and fully engaging with the young man (134), Constantius gives his account of the young man's dilemma. "Quite beside himself" (134), the young man reported that he had fallen in love – not reported exactly, since "as a grape at the peak of its perfection . . . love broke forth almost visibly in his form" (135). Yet "a few days later he was able to recollect his love" – i.e., "he was essentially through with the entire relationship" (136). This rather shocking turn of events, Constantius concludes, must involve some "misunderstanding" (136). During the next two weeks, the young man "began to grasp the misunderstanding himself; the adored young girl was already almost a vexation to him" – she was "the only one he would ever love" and yet "he did not still love her" (137). Constantius reports on the "remarkable change" that had taken place in the young man: "a poetic creativity had awakened in him on a scale I had never believed possible" (137–8).

The tale of Constantius's involvement with the young man's plight is a detailed one, but it is abruptly broken off when Constantius recalls us (and himself) back to his main theme – "But I must constantly repeat that I say all this in connection with repetition" which is "the new category that will be discovered." (R, 148). The story of his return trip to Berlin to see if he can repeat his earlier experiences there takes up the bulk of the essay. His disillusionment at the theatre ("There is no repetition at all") is compounded by his annoyance when he returns home to find only a "repetition of the wrong kind" (169). Although Constantius's Berlin "experiment" was not prompted by the young man's plight, their stories are intertwined in the telling, because Constantius's failed attempts to achieve repetition occur after he has advised the young man. He reports that his failure is humiliating since he "had now been brought to the same point" as the young man: "Indeed, it seemed as if I were that young man myself, as if my great talk, which I now would not repeat for any price, were only a dream from which I awoke to have life unremittingly and treacherously *retake* everything it had given without providing a *repetition*" (172). Note that the Danish word for repetition (*Gjentagelse*) is translatable as "take again," "take back," or "retake," as in a retake of a filmed scene.[1]

Although ostensibly an ordinary narrative, the temporal sequence is radically altered. Constantius's initial claim of concern with the topic of repetition (R, 131) is only accounted for at the very end of the essay, where he describes a strange and funny experience as the cause of his excitement about "the idea of repetition" (174). Moreover, there is often an ambiguity about when an event actually occurs – a confusing back and forth between recent past and distant past. After orienting (or is it disorienting?) our reading with the vagaries of this first essay, with its desultory ramblings, its staccato transitions, its refusal to take temporal sequence seriously, and its marked lightness of spirit, making fun of all kinds of repetition, Constantius marks a decisive break, which amounts to a new beginning – he begins this second part with a repetition of the title "Repetition."

This second part opens with a short introduction by Constantius, followed by seven letters from the young man to Constantius, then an even briefer commentary by Constantius, a final eighth letter from the young man, and a concluding commentary by Constantius. It is interesting that in his introduction to the young man's letters, Constantius seems to do an about-face. Qualifying his earlier approval of the Greeks, he suggests that the young man "is right not to seek clarification in philosophy, either Greek or modern" (R, 186). He then adds that the young man is right not to seek any explanations from himself (i.e. Constantius) either, for "I have abandoned my theory, I am adrift" (186). Constantius has somehow come to the conclusion that "repetition is and remains a transcendence" (186), a "religious movement" that he cannot himself make (187).

The first seven letters from the young man to Constantius indirectly raise the question of the religious, by extravagantly comparing his romantic plight with that of the biblical Job, highlighting Job's response to a test of his faith in God and the subsequent restoration by God of all that Job had lost. In a final eighth letter the young man announces that the girl has gotten married and that he has achieved repetition through regaining his self, through reuniting what had been split. Constantius closes the book with the judgment that the young man does not succeed in achieving the kind of repetition that is an exercise of freedom and a breakthrough to transcendence. He grants that the young man has achieved "the repetition [that] is the raising of his consciousness to the second power" (R, 229), a kind of reflective and relative achievement, but has nevertheless failed to get beyond the poetic.

A "The same sameness"

Given Kierkegaard's earlier study of German idealism and his previous engagement with some of the key items on their agenda in his unfinished work, *Johannes Climacus*, it is not hard to make the case that *Repetition* works, at least in part, as a challenge to German idealist philosophy: it is "incredible how much flurry has been made in Hegelian philosophy over mediation and how much foolish talk has enjoyed honor and glory under this rubric" (R, 148). Whereas Constantius thinks the Hegelian "mediation" is a synthesis that eliminates a dialectical tension, he thinks the "Greek view of the concept *kinesis* [movement]" highlights the paradoxical nature of a certain kind of transition – one in which "actuality, which has been, now comes into existence" (149). This is "the dialectic of repetition," namely, that "that which is repeated has been – otherwise it could not be repeated – but the very fact that it has been makes the repetition into something new" (149). The "new category" of repetition involves continuity and discontinuity; it does not annihilate what has been, but allows the old to be made new, re-newed, repeated as new. In sum, Constantius's opening remarks and his vehement return midway through the first essay to the philosophical dimensions of repetition suggest a decisive engagement with problems of temporality, freedom, and qualitative transition.

Constantius has done some philosophical groundwork by repeatedly narrowing down the category with which he was concerned. His question – "what would life be if there were no repetition?" (R, 132) reveals that he thinks that there is repetition. He then puts before us various illustrations of what might qualify as repetition – some are achievable and some are not, and some do not deserve to be called repetition. Routine habit, which he calls "the same sameness" (170), is achievable, but it is not genuine repetition. He has illustrated the impossible attempt to experience a "first" anything again. Re-reading a book with a renewed dimension of appreciation is a kind of repetition that is achievable, but it is not the kind of achievement with which he is concerned. It is clear that the paradoxical character of old-yet-new is a necessary but not a sufficient condition of the repetition with which Constantius is really concerned. His judgments assume two further conditions of the movement of repetition – namely, freedom and transcendence (a qualitative change, rather than a quantitative change within immanence). In the end, he offers a stipulative definition of "genuine repetition" (131), of "repetition proper" (148), as a movement that is not only paradoxical, but also free and qualitatively transcendent.

The question whether repetition is possible is therefore answerable only when it is qualified as to what kind of repetition – Constantius's stipulation is that repetition is achievable only where freedom is actualized in a qualitative transition to a transcendent order of consciousness. Repetition is not achievable where freedom is not actualized – so repetition is a task. Repetition is not achievable where a transcendence is not realized, and such transcendence, "if it is to take place at all . . . must take place by virtue of the absurd" (R, 185). This is what Constantius refers to as a "religious movement," a task of exercising freedom in a qualitative change, a transcendence of which he is not capable, but whose reality he does not deny (187).

Constantius's philosophical target is the kind of philosophy that emphasizes sameness, identity, and history as immanent teleology, and thus, he thinks, fails to be genuinely interested in the exercise of freedom – free choice, responsibility, guilt. The important question is whether freedom is genuinely possible or whether life simply happens to us, willy-nilly; the question is whether we are responsible, whether we can be guilty. For this reason, repetition is "the watchword in every ethical view" (R, 149). We are meant to move forward, to act rather than to contemplatively ponder or recollect; to be ethical is to *become* ethical and it involves a paradoxical change.[2]

The question whether genuine freedom is possible is also the question whether one can maintain immediacy in a lived, historically conditioned life. Constantius thereby asks whether in life there is only a choice between a simple immediacy and a simple reflection that loses something of the initial immediacy. Constantius construes philosophical "mediation" as a reflection that lacks the renewed immediacy. In the place of idealist philosophy's hallmarks of identity, immanence, and necessity, Constantius puts paradox, transcendence, and freedom.

The struggle to gain more than pure immediacy and more than pure reflection involves a reconstrual of the relation between particular and universal, and this amounts to raising a question about what it means to be an "exception" to the universal (R, 227). So Constantius, both in his own name and in the figure of the young man, examines different possibilities of what it means to justify oneself as an exception: e.g., Job

(207); the sinner (226–7); the true poet (228). The legitimate exception is "reconciled in the universal" (227); the legitimate exception "thinks the universal with intense passion" (227). But the battle is "as difficult as to kill a man and let him live" (226). Repetition is not merely the interest on which metaphysics founders (because repetition challenges identity, sameness, immanence). Repetition is the "watchword of every ethical view" (149) because it is about inner/outer, hidden/revealed – it is about deception.

B Imaginatively constructing: earnestness and jest

The reports by Constantius that frame this little book call the reader's attention to its obvious literary stylings and forestall any flat-footed reading which sees the text as merely a philosophical critique. First, Constantius makes an aside about imagination that seems true to human nature:

> There is probably no young person with any imagination who has not at some time been enthralled by the magic of the theater and wished to be swept along into that artificial actuality in order like a double to see and hear himself and to split himself up into every possible variation of himself, and nevertheless in such a way that every variation is still himself. (R, 154)

An author can create all these possibilities – "every possible variation of himself"; i.e., every possible variation of Constantine, every possible variation of Kierkegaard.

Moreover, the apparently profound proclamations about "actuality and earnestness of existence" are followed by a reference to an author with whom Constantius agrees and who is said to be "at times somewhat deceitful" (R, 133). This author is A, from *Either – Or*, and the deceitfulness is explained in a very positive way: it is not that the author "says one thing and means another" but rather that the author "pushes the thought to extremes, so that if it is not grasped with the same energy, it reveals itself the next instant as something else" (133). The reader should wonder whether this kind of deceitfulness is being practiced by Constantius himself. Later, he counsels the reader to "form his own judgment with respect to what is said here about repetition" as well as about "my saying it here and in this manner" (149). This "manner," he explains, means that he speaks in "various tongues," in the "language of sophists, of puns," and "babble[s] a confusion of criticism, mythology, *rebus*, and axioms, and argue[s] now in a human way and now in an extraordinary way" (149). This should alert the reader early on to the possibility that the description of the trip to Berlin is a parody of the attempt to re-experience a "first."

Constantius expressly says that the fact that there are few people dedicated to being good readers may lead some authors to write "in such a way that the heretics are unable to understand it" (R, 225), and he admits that the work will be difficult to understand because the "movement in the book . . . is inverse" (226). He refers back to the way he employed "jesting and flippancy" in relation to the young man (228). In part he achieves this by repeatedly poking fun at certain ways of understanding repetition, and in part by poking fun at the young man, although he denies that this excludes genuine "consideration" for him. We are right to remind ourselves here that Constantius's early emphasis on "earnestness" complements his later confessions of jesting, provoking us to reconsider the relations between earnestness and jest.

Only at the very end of the book, exemplifying an extreme inversion, does he go on to make readers aware of the trick he has played on them – namely, he has created the character of the young man whose letters are included in the book, and whose actions and attitudes are responded to and evaluated by Constantius. He decided at some point to bring into being a "poet" who faces an interesting dilemma (R, 228). All the movements in the book are "purely lyrical" (228) and everything Constantius says is "to be understood as obscurely pertaining to him [the young man] or as helping to understand him better" (228). This is why Constantius ends the book with the explicit reminder that "Although I frequently do the talking, you, my dear reader . . . will nevertheless be reading about him [the young man] on every page" (230–31) – note, "every" page.

In other words, Constantius deliberately provokes the character, experimenting with him to see how he will react. He warns us that he might overstate his view or express something he does not actually believe, merely to present options, to flesh out the picture of the young man; he admits to trying to "tease" (R, 230) the young man. Constantius's own callousness and cynicism might well be assumed poses that heuristically (or artistically) provide a strong contrast to the young man. In other words, Constantius is not trying to present himself to us (or to hide himself) – everything serves the presentation of a certain kind of young man, a certain picture of the possibilities available to such a poet.

C "What does it mean: a deceiver?"

Read in terms of a story of the young man's personal dilemma, the text illustrates many moods represented in the letters and many possible responses to the dilemma presented by both Constantius and the young man. The letters express melodramatic pathos and self-pity in their histrionics about a failed love relationship and the loss it involves: "My whole being screams in self-contradiction. How did it happen that I became guilty? Or am I not guilty? Why, then, am I called that in every language" (R, 200). They also express a much calmer existential anxiety on a more cosmic scale – a "nameless anxiety about the world and life and men and everything" (205).

The young man's self-understanding is that he truly loved the young woman, has fallen out of love, and thereby caused her suffering; he suffers from being the cause of her suffering and is torn between wanting to end her suffering and knowing that he cannot resume the relationship because the young woman cannot really be happy with him (nor he with her). His self-understanding is that he is being "faithful" to her (R, 192), even when he seems to be "unfaithful" (201). He is wracked by the fear that he is guilty (200, 202), but nonetheless repeatedly asserts that he is "still in the right" (201) since he is convinced that the relationship could never have worked. The ambivalence about his guilt and innocence is a constant thread in the text – guilt about committing "a wrong" (184) alongside assertions of innocence (185–6, 193, 200).

Various options of dealing with the young woman are presented by the two men, some involving deception and others merely being callous. The young man later describes his intoxication with the romantic fantasy of one of the options: "To make oneself out a scoundrel, a deceiver, simply and solely to prove how highly she is esteemed" (R, 190); "to be in the right this way, to be faithful, and yet to pass oneself off as a scoundrel" (192). Was Kierkegaard sending a message to Regine? If so, it is a very mixed message, or a very difficult message to understand, one which "the heretics" will not understand. The message that she was just a muse who became a burden, that she was herself guilty because she was selfish or manipulative – for whom was this message meant? Or is it supposed to be understood as the message of someone proposing a strategy of playing the scoundrel for her sake? "What does it mean: a deceiver?" (200) – does it mean that he never really loved her, or that he deceives her by claiming he is a deceiver? The latter is deception at a second order – he offers a deception while alerting the reader to the possibility of a strategy of deception. When Constantius questions "What kind of life would it be if along with my beloved I have lost honor and pride and lost them in such a way that no one knows how it happened, for which reason I can never retrieve them again?" (202), we might be seeing something of Kierkegaard's concern that his story must be told – people must learn what really happened. But this too is only one dimension of the book.

D "The Lord gave and the Lord took away"

Constantius and his literary creation, the young man, invoke a religious dimension in contrasting ways. Whereas Constantius generates an *a priori* religious category and elaborates on it somewhat abstractly in his commentaries, most of the young man's letters explicitly appeal to the concrete Scriptural image of Job.

Job represents, for the young man, "the voice of the suffering, the cry of the grief-stricken, the shriek of the terrified . . . a faithful witness to all the affliction and laceration there can be in a heart, an unfailing spokesman who dared to lament 'in bitterness of soul' and to strive with God" (R, 197). But, on the other hand, Job also spoke those "beautiful words" – "The Lord gave, and the Lord took away; blessed be the name of the Lord" (197). Job's dilemma raises the more general question: "How does the individual discover that it is an ordeal?" (209). And the young man's response to Job's response raises paradigmatically religious questions: questions of suffering and of guilt, before God and man, which imply theological questions about a lost innocence – about sin, repentance, God's justice, and grace.

There are hints of insights in the young man, particularly in the passing references to how repetition is "transcendent," rather than "esthetic, ethical or dogmatic" (R, 210), to how Job is not the highest ideal, "not a hero of faith" (210), and to how Job is "in the right" by "being proved to be in the wrong *before God*" (212). But these insights are not sustained or developed. They seem to be outweighed by two esthetic and ethical commitments he holds. One commitment is to an esthetic construal of Job (Job "resides in a *confinium* touching on poetry," 204) and to esthetic views of repetition: repetition is signified by Job receiving everything back double (212); repetition is achieved when he can say "I am myself again" (220). The other commitment is his ethical construal of Job – the shrill, petulant insistence by the young man that "the secret in Job, the vital force, the nerve, the idea, is that Job, despite everything, is in the right" (207). He is concerned with the recovery of a lost innocence, with "clean hands" (214), with how he feels and how he appears. As a result we have within the letters themselves two contrasting portrayals of Job, confusingly intermingled – there is no progression in the understanding of Job, only a variety of possibilities (as if Constantius is concerned to give "every possible variation" of Job). It will be the task of one of the upbuilding discourses that follow later in 1843 to develop the lessons one can learn from Job.

Constantius raises the possibility of a religious repetition – a religious movement of transcendence that he is unable to make himself, but whose reality he does not question (R, 186–7). Part of the reader's engagement with the text is to struggle with the character of the young man's achievement. How do Constantius's criteria of free and qualitative transition apply to the young man's form of reconciliation? How does Constantius's evident abstraction affect his own understanding of repetition?

In the book *Repetition* we see another take (a "retake") on the question confronted in *Either – Or* – how to live rightly, or how to love rightly. This work asks us to think about living the good life in relation to several alternatives – namely, living out of biological necessity, living out an unfolding immanent teleology, living out of routine, automatic habit (with its absolute stasis), and living from moment to moment in frivolous discontinuity (with its absolute movement). It asks us to think about what philosophical views preclude an understanding of significant freedom. It presents us with versions of repetition – the young man's version, Constantius's version, and the young man's version of Job's version. Each version embodies important insights, sharpening a sense of the differences between an immanent recovery and a transcendent renewal. The possibility of a religious repetition, which Constantius suggests would require that "the collision would have come from higher levels" (R, 229), is presented, but its unfolding awaits the next book, *Fear and Trembling*.

II *Fear and Trembling*

A Introduction

The title, *Fear and Trembling*, recalls St Paul's letter urging the Philippians to work out their salvation "in fear and trembling" (Philippians 2:12–13), and this passage in its own way alludes to the Old Testament notions of fear of God as devotion aligned with rejoicing: "Serve the Lord with fear, and rejoice before him; with trembling pay homage to him, lest he be angry and you perish from the way when his anger blazes suddenly" (Psalms 2:11–12). The subtitle, *A Dialectical Lyric*, conjures up either a contradiction in terms (a philosophical lyric) or perhaps, in another sense of dialectical, a tension-filled lyric. The name of the author, Johannes de Silentio, is obviously meant to be provocative – a book authored by silence, a message generated in silence or about silence. Moreover, the "motto" of the book is also provocative – "What Tarquinius Superbus said in the garden by means of the poppies, the son understood but the messenger did not" (Johann Georg Hamann). This is a motto about how communication can be made indirectly, so that the messenger does not understand the message he announces.

The author's "Preface," which should normally indicate the topic of the book, turns us in a philosophical direction. Despite Silentio's claim that he is "by no means a philosopher" (FT, 7), he explicitly invokes both Descartes and Greek philosophy, and makes indirect but unmistakable allusions to Hegelian philosophy: "In our age, everyone is unwilling to stop with faith but goes further" by trying to "transpose the whole content of faith into conceptual form" (7). Silentio longs for that ancient thought that recognized that faith is the "task" for a lifetime and is always attended by "anxiety and trembling" (7). Thus, the preface suggests that this book challenges any view that philosophy "goes further" than faith (5,7), and the "Epilogue," the other half of the book's framing, reinforces the idea that "no one goes further" than faith (122). Moreover, early on Silentio reveals his literary bent in saying that he writes in a "poetic and refined way" against a philosophical idea (7–8). We should expect then to find philosophical, religious, and literary dimensions in the work.

It is only when we leave the preface, with its proposal to present an alternative to the view that philosophy "goes further" than faith, that we are introduced to Abraham, the Old Testament figure commanded by God to sacrifice his son, Isaac. That neither the preface nor the epilogue makes any mention of Abraham suggests strongly that the book is much more than an engagement with the story of Abraham, or better, it is an engagement with the story of Abraham in a much broader context than as the illustration of a conflict between religion and morality.

Abraham is first mentioned in a lyrical section whose title is best translated as "attunement" or "tuning up" (creating the right key or mood for what follows).[3] We are introduced to Abraham indirectly, through imagining a man who could not understand the story of Abraham – and Silentio jokes that "if he had known Hebrew, he perhaps would have easily understood the story of Abraham" (FT, 9). He imagines four scenarios of Abraham's journey to Mount Moriah for the sacrifice; these are attempts to walk with Abraham, not to understand him, because they are not by a "thinker" who needs to "go beyond faith" (9). These four scenarios play out alternatives to the biblical story. In one of these, Abraham sacrifices himself rather than Isaac, but, rather surprisingly, in the other three scenarios, even though Abraham literally does as God commands, "faith" does not follow. Moreover, the implied contrast between a particular action and a particular manner of execution gains support from the refrains about a mother weaning her child that follow each scenario, since these present ways in which something loving is done that appears not to be loving.

The theme of getting Isaac back only comes into play in the following section, the "Eulogy on Abraham." In Silentio's view, Abraham's greatness lies in his love of God and his belief in God, expecting the impossible with a "hope whose form is madness" (FT, 17). Abraham's "ordeal" takes place in the context of Abraham's earlier faith and earlier trials: his faith in following God's command and emigrating from the land of his fathers, and his faith in the fulfillment of God's promise to give him an heir, holding on to that hope for 70 years (19). The claim that it is "great to give up one's desire, but it is greater to hold fast to it after having given it up" (18) refers to this long-held hope – thus, long before the trauma of Mount Moriah, Abraham experienced both resignation and a mad hope. Now that the promise of an heir is fulfilled, we find Abraham needing faith in the continued fulfillment of that same promise in the face of God's command to sacrifice Isaac (20). On the one hand, the eulogy raises the question whether Abraham is a murderer, but on the other hand, it seems to be only a rhetorical question, for Silentio has nothing but praise for Abraham's "supreme passion," his "divine madness" – indeed, "Abraham was the greatest of all" (16), even though Abraham "got no further than faith" (23).

The next part of the book, entitled "Problemata," will re-engage the philosophical dimension through the presentation of three "Problems," which will "draw out . . . the dialectical aspects implicit in the story of Abraham" (FT, 53). Before this "dialectical" analysis begins, however, we find yet another beginning, "A Preliminary Expectoration" (a "clearing of the throat" or, more gracefully, a "preamble from the heart"). This section is crucial because here Silentio does three things simultaneously that seem hard to reconcile: (a) he offers a positive evaluation of faith, (b) he claims not to understand faith, and (c) he offers a description of faith.

First, he is convinced that the "dialectic of faith is the finest and most extraordinary of all," that faith is not "inferior" to philosophy (FT, 33, 36); he even claims that "there is nothing I wish more" than to make the movement of faith (51). Second, he affirms repeatedly that he does not understand Abraham (33), that he is "shattered," "repelled," even "paralyzed," when he attempts to think his way into Abraham (33). From beginning to end, he insists that he "cannot understand Abraham" (99, 112). Alternatively, he says that he "perhaps can understand Abraham, but only in the way one understands the paradox" (119). He provokes the question of what it means to understand a paradox. His suggestion that "insofar as I can understand the paradox, I can also understand Abraham's total presence in that word" (118) proposes that one might understand *someone* without understanding what they say.[4]

The admiration and approval he can have for what he claims not to understand is peculiar, but it is even more surprising that Silentio, thirdly, claims to be able to "describe [*beskrive*]" (FT, 37) the faith he cannot understand. The description of faith is quite specific: Silentio clearly distinguishes "two" movements in the "double-movement" (119) made by Abraham: there is one movement in which "I renounce everything" and another movement in which "I do not renounce anything" but rather "receive everything" (48–9). The description of the double-movement of faith is developed primarily through the obvious contrast between Abraham and another figure, variously called "the hero," the "tragic hero" (34), and the maker of the "infinite movement" of "resignation" (35). This general contrast is between two radically different ways of experiencing life – namely, as the "knight of faith" (38, 46) or as the "knight of infinite resignation" (38). This "infinite movement of resignation" (47), which is the "last stage before faith" (46) is a "purely philosophical movement" in which I gain "my eternal consciousness" (48), and which "I venture to make when it is demanded and can discipline myself to make, because every time some finitude will take power over me, I starve myself into submission until I make the movement, for my eternal consciousness is my love for God, and for me that is the highest of all" (48). Clearly, "God" figures centrally in such a life, but for the "knight of resignation" God's love invites (only) a resignation of the finite world.

By contrast, in the "next" (FT, 115) movement, which follows the resignation of the finite, one receives back what one has resigned – "I receive everything" (49). This movement involves a "paradox," indeed, a "prodigious paradox" (33, 52, 53) – namely, the paradoxical reception of the finite again. The paradox is one of resignation alongside an impossible hope: "this having, after all, is also a giving up" (47). Silentio concedes: "I cannot make the final movement, the paradoxical movement" (51). Since the second movement is paradoxical, presumably it is qualitatively different from the first movement that he claims he can understand, yet Silentio goes on to "describe" the second movement in some detail. It is one in which one "does not lose the finite but gains it whole and intact" (37). He equates doing something "by virtue of the absurd" with doing something "by virtue of the fact that for God all things are possible" (46). The believer maintains a "hope" in what is impossible according to the conclusions of human understanding – the paradox is that the believer is "convinced of the impossibility, humanly speaking" (46), but thinks that "in the infinite sense it was possible" (47). It is a new understanding of what God's love and loving God mean – for the knight of faith, love is not simply renunciation. The qualitative distinction between the knight of faith and the knight of resignation lies in the relation to actuality: "temporality, finitude – that is what it is all about" (49). Unlike the knight of resignation, the knight of faith believes that God's love is commensurable with actuality – his aim is "to exist in such a way that my contrast to existence constantly expresses itself in the most beautiful and secure harmony with it" (50), so he is exceedingly conscientious at his job, takes walks in the woods, looks like a tax-collector, and fantasizes about what there might be for dinner. His relation to a God is commensurable with actuality insofar as faith involves the "courage to grasp the whole temporal realm now by virtue of the absurd" (49).[5] The qualitative (paradoxical) difference in what each knight does marks a major contrast.

At the very least, Silentio presents an insightful reading of the Abraham story by highlighting the way in which, for faith, there is a rejoicing as well as suffering resignation. Abraham's faith is not found in a negative distancing from actuality, from the finite world. Faith is not a matter of other-worldliness; it is not acosmic, but rather receives the world back again once one has been willing to give it up. The knight of faith ought to look like everybody else, his faith being undetectable from externals, and his faith being exercised in the most mundane worldly endeavors. Abraham, on the other hand, is presented as an "exception," and his ordeal is not only unique, but the most horrific imaginable – slaying his own son at God's command. Are we supposed to concentrate on the exceptional Abraham or on the ordinary person of faith?

Silentio answers this question by making a second contrast, *within* the category of the knight of faith. He suggests that faith can be found even in cases quite unlike Abraham: "it makes no difference to me whether it is Abraham or a slave in Abraham's house, whether it is a professor of philosophy or a poor servant girl – I pay attention only to the movements" (FT, 38). In other words, faith covers the extraordinary Abraham and the ordinary knight of faith. We all have "fear and trembling" insofar as we transcend the immanent and universal, the self-contained. This contrast is within a range of "exceptions," a range of "anxiety," not a qualitative difference.

In sum, Silentio's description of the "double-movement" of faith distinguishes the first movement of infinite resignation of the finite from another movement of receiving back the finite. Silentio sees himself as at best a "tragic hero" (FT, 34) who could make the infinite movement of resignation (35), and he asserts repeatedly that he can achieve (or has achieved) such resignation (48, 50); moreover, he can "describe" "the movements" of faith although he "cannot make them" (37). He can "describe," but he "cannot make the final movement, the paradoxical movement of faith" that he wishes to make (51); he cannot follow Abraham, because Abraham not only achieves infinite resignation, but "actually goes further and comes to faith" (37).

B The *problemata*

The three "Problems" now begin to expose "the dialectical aspects implied in the story of Abraham" (FT, 53). Each of the problems poses a question (addressing the issue of "the universal" first in terms of the universal as the ethical, then the universal as the divine, and finally the universal as the disclosed) and I suggest that there is a general formula for answering all the questions.

The answer to the first question "Is there a Teleological Suspension of the Ethical?" takes two forms. The first form is the conditional: *if, then*. *If* the ethical is "the universal," what "rests immanent in itself, has nothing outside itself that is its *telos* [end or goal]" (FT, 54), *then* the ethical is the highest and there can (by definition) be nothing that legitimately suspends the ethical. *If,* as modern philosophy holds, the highest is "social morality," *then* there can be no such thing as the "paradox that the single individual as the single individual is higher than the universal" (55).

A description of what *would* count as a teleological suspension of the ethical provides the second form of the answer; the answer is yes, Abraham's dilemma would count if it really differs from the case of the tragic hero or the knight of infinite resignation. Silentio's conclusion is that "the story of Abraham contains . . . a teleological suspension of the ethical" (FT, 56, 66). That is, "the difference between the tragic hero and Abraham is very obvious. The tragic hero is still within the ethical. He allows an expression of the ethical to have its *telos* in a higher expression of the ethical . . . Here there can be no question of a teleological suspension of the ethical itself" (59).

This first problem thus makes a second qualitative distinction – between two kinds of resignation, one for the sake of an end within the ethical and one for the sake of an end outside the ethical. This is an important addition to the earlier postulation of a qualitative contrast between the movement of resignation and the movement of receiving back.

By describing a movement which is qualitatively different from that which tragic heroes of ethical dilemmas perform, Silentio succeeds only in pointing out a clear instance of what would count as a teleological suspension of the ethical. This does not itself demonstrate that there is a "legitimate" teleological suspension. Along with Silentio, we ask "Is he justified?" (FT, 62). Silentio's earlier eulogy implied a positive answer, but here the only answer he repeatedly suggests is that any justification is paradoxical, "by virtue of the absurd" (56, 57, 59). But this is not an answer to the question of legitimacy. His only answer, in the end, is the conditional: *if* Abraham's story actually involves a break in immanence (the impossibility of resolution except by virtue of the absurd), *then* modern philosophy can only conclude that Abraham is not to be admired but rather condemned.

Although the problem began with a reference to ethics, it is motivated throughout by the need to "have a clearer understanding of what faith is" (FT, 55). Like *Repetition, Fear and Trembling* proposes a "new category," one needed "for the understanding of Abraham" (60). The "new category" is rendered necessary by the inconceivable situation in which there is a collision between duty as God's public will and duty as God's private will (60). The "new category" is either that of the "ordeal" (60) (as contrasted with "spiritual trial," 60) or that of a "private relationship to the divine" (60), namely, faith.

The second problem ("Is There an Absolute Duty to God?") resembles the first, and one could say that the second question is answered just as the first was: *if* modern philosophy is correct, *then* there could not be an "absolute" duty to God. The reference to "God," however, signals a shift towards a lengthy inquiry into the meaning of a relation to God. The opening pages of the problem provocatively suggest that modern philosophy's understanding that the ethical is "the divine" amounts to a tautology, with the result that there are no specific duties to God; every duty is a duty to God but not one in which I "enter into relation to God" (FT, 68). God, in this view, is God "in a totally abstract sense" (68) – God is duty, the universal, the ethical.

We learn more about what an "absolute duty" to God means when Silentio turns explicitly to the "remarkable teaching on the absolute duty to God" – namely Luke 14:26, "If any one comes to me and does not hate his own father and mother and wife and children and brothers and sisters, yes, and even his own life, he cannot be my disciple." (FT, 72). Silentio claims that "anyone who does not dare to mention such passages does not dare to mention Abraham, either" (75).

Silentio insists, as if with some authority, that the passage represents God's demand of "absolute love" and "must be understood literally" (FT, 73) – it should not be weakened or mitigated. Yet, just as authoritatively, he proclaims that this does not mean that God requires that a person's love for God be "demonstrated by his becoming indifferent to what he otherwise cherished" (73). In fact, "if [a husband] had any idea of what love is, he would wish to discover that she [his wife] was perfect in her love as a daughter and sister, and he would see therein that she would love him more than anyone in the kingdom" (73). So what then does Scripture mean by "hate" parents, siblings, or even one's life?

It is clear that Silentio cannot imagine a command by God to stop loving someone: "the absolute duty can lead one to do what ethics would forbid, but it can never lead the knight of faith to stop loving" (FT, 74). So, in this sense, he is not proposing a "literal" understanding of the passage. When all is said and done, it seems that "literal" hatred of others is precisely that willingness to resign all (while continuing to love and cherish what is loved) for the sake of an end beyond the ethical.

Moreover, this passage re-emphasizes the knight of faith's resignation made in virtue of an end beyond the ethical: the passage must be understood "in such a way that one perceives that the knight of faith can achieve no higher expression whatsoever of the universal (as the ethical) in which he can save himself" (FT, 74). That is, the paradox cannot be "mediated" by anything – no appeal can be made to either state or church to justify the sacrifice. It is worth recalling here that although the knight of faith does not achieve a "higher expression of the ethical," he does (according to Silentio) achieve a "different expression" of the ethical, a "paradoxical expression" of the ethical: "The ethical receives a completely different expression, a paradoxical expression, such as, for example, that love to God may bring the knight of faith to give his love to the neighbor – an expression opposite to that which, ethically, speaking, is duty" (70).

The question of the expression of love again brings in the relation between inner and outer, and here Hegelian philosophy is judged inadequate: "In Hegelian philosophy, *das Aüssere* is higher than *das Innere*" (FT, 69), or more exactly, each determines the other. By contrast, Silentio posits "faith" as "the paradox that interiority is higher than exteriority," the paradox that "there is an interiority that is incommensurable with exteriority, an interiority that is not identical, please note, with the first but is a new interiority" (69). The proposal of a "new interiority" that differs from exteriority as well as from "the first" interiority should make the reader wonder how this new interiority arises. If it is not mediated by reference to the universal, what moves the single individual from the first interiority to the new interiority?

So, is there an absolute duty to God? The answer is both "No, if modern philosophy is correct," and "Yes, this is what would count as an absolute duty to the absolute."

The third problem asks whether it was "ethically defensible for Abraham to conceal his understanding" (FT, 82) from Sarah, Eliezer, and Isaac, thereby inquiring about Abraham's case in particular rather than about the ethics of concealment in general. Still, the formula for the answer remains the same: "If there is no hiddenness rooted in the fact that the single individual as the single individual is higher than the universal, then Abraham's conduct cannot be defended" (82). On this understanding of ethics, the answer to the question must, by definition, be "No": if ethics demands disclosure, then what Abraham did was not "ethically defensible." Is it defensible in any other way? Not if Hegelian philosophy is correct, since "Hegelian philosophy assumes no justified hiddenness, no justified incommensurability" (82).

This implies again that if one denies all incommensurability, it is inconsistent to praise Abraham as the father of faith. As in the first problem, the suggestion here is that Hegel may have gotten ethics right, but he did not prove that ethics is the highest; he is right in thinking that "the immediate should be annulled," but wrong in thinking that faith is a "first immediacy" (FT, 82). Thus, he is unjustified in thinking that it needs to be annulled or gone beyond (99). Silentio in effect introduces another new category when he proposes that "faith is not the first immediacy but a later immediacy" (82) – and the inquiry into the character of this "later immediacy" coincides with the challenge to philosophical mediation. As with his earlier introduction of a "new interiority" (69), we are led to ask how this move is achieved; what takes the place of mediation, or precludes its need?

In this third problem, Silentio proposes a new strategy – namely, to "consider the whole question purely esthetically" (FT, 82), focusing on the category of "the interesting," a "border category, a *confinium* between esthetics and ethics" (83). All his poetic stories and their poetically modified versions serve to explore the idea of concealment and silence – they are all cases in which hiddenness is problematized. In all there will be at least four main cases – the Delphic couple, Agnes and the Merman, Sarah and Tobias, and Faust and Margaret. These "interesting" cases occur at the border between esthetics and ethics, and they suggestively involve categories like "the demonic," "repentance," and "sin." But, in the end, there is no analogy to Abraham.

C Two models?

The proposal of a "new category" (FT, 60) (be it "faith" or the "ordeal," or a "new interiority," or a "later immediacy") for the understanding of Abraham serves (as was the case in *Repetition*) as an alternative to modern philosophy's category of "mediation" (the resolution of all conflicts within immanence, quantitatively). The "Epilogue," however, complicates matters.

The work culminates with Silentio deploring the "urge to go further": "This urge to go further is an old story in the world" (FT, 123). This recalls the reader to Silentio's overwhelming concern in the preface to propose an alternative to the model that philosophy "goes further" – further than "doubt" (5) and further than faith (7).[6] But is the upshot going to be that faith "goes further" than philosophy?

When he described the movement of resignation as a "purely philosophical movement" because its immanent end can be shared publicly, he implied that although philosophy does not go further than faith, it is compatible with it and serves to provide a necessary preliminary movement. Silentio said he could make this movement, could understand it. The notion of faith as "one more movement" (FT, 47), made after a movement that can be made by philosophy, gives "going further" a quantitative dimension that is reinforced by the idiom of resignation as "antecedent" (47), as "the last stage before faith" (46), and of faith as "the final movement" (51). This invokes what one might call a *quantitative model* (or *additive model*) in which faith extends and supplements (goes further than) an earlier movement.[7] On this view, the first movement (of resignation) is the same whether or not one goes on to make the second movement (of faith). Since Silentio initially claimed to offer a challenge to philosophy's view that philosophy goes further than faith, it is not surprising that he proposes a model in which faith "goes further" than philosophy. Such a model in which Abraham "goes further" (37) engages the philosophical agenda and reverses it. It is the model that Silentio is motivated to offer because he is angry that "theology is willing to sell [faith] off at a low price" (48).

But selling faith off at a high price is still within the quantitative, economic model he mentions in the first line of the preface, where he complains about sales that lower the value of things.[8] Not surprisingly, there are in Silentio's discussion, therefore, the rudiments of another model of faith which one might call a *qualitative model*, in which faith does not go "further" than philosophy because they are on different tracks altogether, incommensurate with each other. Such a model of faith as genuinely incommensurable with philosophy cannot employ images of "going further" and "additional" movements. In this model faith is experienced in a qualitative shift. Silentio's language about the "paradoxical" element of faith suggests this, implying a radical discontinuity or qualitative difference.

This qualitative model is also supported by the important distinction that Silentio has already made in the first problem, between two radically different ways of making a movement of resignation – one is for the sake of an end immanent within the ethical universal, and the other for the sake of an end that is not immanent within the ethical universal. Abraham's act of resignation "transgressed the ethical altogether and had a higher *telos* outside it, in relation to which he suspended it" (FT, 59). Silentio makes this qualitative distinction explicitly but then seems to forget it when he later assesses how far he has come in his understanding. Is Abraham simply making an additional ("one more") movement? If one resigns in the paradoxical hope that what is resigned will be kept or regained, then is not Abraham's first movement qualitatively different? The resignation made in virtue of a "higher" expression of the ethical does not have such a hope – it is a qualitatively different way of resigning the finite. Thus, on this model, the relation between the two movements of faith is not one in which one can make the first regardless of whether one makes the second. The first movement is integrally related to the second, and affects it.

Silentio does not work this out, but prompts the reader to wonder whether there is a necessary or intrinsic connection between the kind of resignation that is done for the sake of an end beyond the ethical, and the hope and receiving back which mark faith. In fact, Silentio acknowledges at one point that although they can be conceptually distinguished, the two movements are inseparable – "this having, after all, is also a giving up" (FT, 47). The paradox lies in the simultaneity of the movements – if one makes the second, he does so "at every moment"; "After having made this [first] movement, he has at every moment made the next movement" (119). Note the tension between saying "after" and saying "at every moment." On this model faith is qualitatively different from philosophy. In other words, although Silentio repeatedly tells us that he can understand the first movement but not the second, on his own terms there is a kind of first movement he could not understand any more than the second.

Now we are reminded of the "motto," by which Silentio had brought to our attention the possibility that someone can fail to understand what he can nevertheless convey accurately. This might have been done to allay our fears that we readers might be misled by a description given by someone who does not understand what he is describing, but it raises the question "How much does Silentio understand?" That is, by raising the possibility of a qualitative contrast between the two movements that make up faith, as well as a qualitative contrast within the first movement, Silentio indirectly suggests two different models of faith. One is a model in which faith merely "goes further" than philosophy, makes an "additional" movement – it is a model of quantitative transition. In the other model the contrast between two ways of resigning the finite supports the incommensurability between philosophy and faith – this is a model of qualitative transition. There is irony in the very attempt to show that one movement does something "in addition" to the other, goes "further" than the other, alongside the attempt to show that their relation is paradoxical and hence incomprehensible. He distinguishes between two kinds of movement of resignation, but the quantitative model does not follow through on it. We are given two different pictures of faith, despite Silentio's lack of awareness. He is then like the messenger in the book's "motto" – he does not understand what he conveys, while conveying what is necessary for us to understand that he does not understand.

III More *Upbuilding Discourses* of 1843

Fear and Trembling was also concerned, like *Repetition*, with how to respond when one suffers a loss or when one feels tested by God, and while he was writing these books, Kierkegaard was also working on two more volumes of upbuilding discourses. These two volumes of discourses have been said to be even more biographical than the two books, but they are clearly in a different genre – they are, if we use the image of concentric circles, a larger circle. They represent a different form of struggle with the same challenge to faith represented by Job and Abraham, and they mine Scriptural passages for their words of consolation, comfort, hope, and encouragement. We can consider ourselves to be eavesdropping on the words of comfort and encouragement Kierkegaard hears from God. What he says in the first of these – that it is not intended to be used in a judgmental way, as warning or admonishment – is true of all the discourses. These discourses are extremely elegant, unlike didactic religious sermons – they have dramatic scenarios, rhetorical flourishes, and an abiding concern with the language in which they are expressed.

A *Three Upbuilding Discourses* (1843)

Three Upbuilding Discourses was published on the same day as the two books. The first two discourses are a pair of explorations of a single Scriptural theme – "Love Will Hide a Multitude of Sins" (I Peter 4:7–12). The first discourse begins like a concrete poem. The word "love" repeats in every sentence of the entire first (lengthy) paragraph – a refrain that is insistent and rhetorically effective because, in the English edition, the eye is carried down the page by the word "love" winding through the paragraph. What is it that is comforting, unchanging, undemanding, forgiving, never deceived? "It is love!" (EUD, 55).

The old proverb which declares that love is blind neglects something important about love – namely, love's vision. Love sees while it is blind: "It does not depend, then, merely upon what one sees, but what one sees depends upon how one sees; all observation is not just a receiving, a discovering, but also a bringing forth, and insofar as it is that, how the observer is constituted is indeed decisive" (EUD, 59). This theme is significant for the way it supports the social dimension of love. A loving vision minimizes "quarreling, malice, anger, litigation, discord, factionalism" (61) because it refuses to bring attention to it. Love hides the multitude of sin by refusing to go searching for it, or by giving the other person's words the benefit of the doubt. Love is upbuilding in that it recreates the goodness of the initial creation and is the way in which we are "God's co-worker in love" (62).

In saying that love goes beyond the external to the internal, that love sees what it hopes to see and finds what it seeks (EUD, 59–62), Kierkegaard does not explain here why this does not give license to hide one's head in the sand and ignore evil that should be dealt with; he will clarify this later in his writings.[9] But his example is telling – what Abraham did in praying for the residents of Sodom and Gomorrah was a way of hiding their sins (66). The discourse ends with a reference to the Scriptural passage in which the scribes and Pharisees "seized a woman in open sin" and brought her face to face with Jesus in the temple (67). Jesus's response (stooping down and writing in the sand, rather than condemning her) was a way of hiding her sin, a form of upbuilding.

The second discourse on the same Scriptural passage begins with quite a literary flourish – not (as did the first) assaulting the reader with a veritable avalanche of "love," but rather with an impressive description of apostolic speech. Peter's speech is "concerned, ardent, burning, inflamed, everywhere and always stirred by the forces of the new life, calling, shouting, beckoning, explosive in its outbursts, brief, disjointed, harrowing, itself violently shaken as much by fear and trembling as by longing and blessed expectancy, everywhere witnessing to the powerful unrest of the spirit and the profound impatience of the heart" (EUD, 69). Kierkegaard then does a careful exegesis of the passage, calling to our attention the contiguity of the "admonition" and the "comfort" (70) – for there is "comfort" in the suggestion "that love is able to live in the same heart in which there is a multitude of sins and that this love has the power to hide the multitude" (72). The discourse begins to wrap up with another story of a sinful woman, this time the one who came to the dinner Jesus was having in the pharisee's house, washed Jesus's feet with her tears, and anointed them (75). Jesus "made the love in her even more powerful to hide a multitude of sins, the love that was already there, because 'her many sins were forgiven her, because she loved much'" (77).

The third discourse, "Strengthening in the Inner Being," is set apart by beginning with a prayer, "Father in heaven! You hold all the good gifts in your gentle hand . . . you fulfill every prayer and give what we pray for or what is far better than what we pray for" (EUD, 79). The theme of "gift" is a constant motif in Kierkegaard's discourses, and here it receives an important elaboration: "Nobody can provide this strengthening for himself . . . *because the witness itself is a gift from God*, from whom comes every good and perfect gift" (98). He continues: "the inner being looks not at the gifts but at the giver . . . the giver is primary. . . . *God gives not only the gifts but himself with them* in a way beyond the capability of any human being" (99, my emphasis).

Kierkegaard picks up on his earlier reference to us as "God's co-worker" (EUD, 62) when he focuses on the "human being's high destiny – to be the ruler of creation" (84) and "God's co-worker" (86). He connects the strengthening of the inner being to an engaged appropriation of the world's actuality: "Not until the moment when there awakens in his soul a concern about what meaning the world has for him and he for the world, about what meaning everything within him by which he himself belongs to the world has for him and he therein for the world – only then does the inner being announce its presence in this *concern*" (86). The concern that is awakened in us craves "a knowledge that does not remain as knowledge for a single moment but is transformed into an action the moment it is possessed" (86). The end of the discourse develops the theme of "hope" from *Fear and Trembling*, and explicitly brings in Abraham: "the person who learns from God is strengthened in the inner being. Then even if he lost everything, he would still gain everything, and Abraham possessed nothing but a burial place in Canaan, and yet he was God's chosen one" (95). The hopeful cry, "the one God tests he loves" (98), encircles both him and Regine, for it is hard not to think of Regine when Kierkegaard writes that "the person who loved God and in this love learned to love people was strengthened in the inner being. If someone denied him his love, then that person helped him to find God's love" (97).

B *Four Upbuilding Discourses* (1843)

This set of discourses was published six weeks after the preceding set, but it is clear that the first of them, "The Lord Gave, and the Lord Took Away; Blessed be the Name of the Lord," is closely tied in Kierkegaard's mind with *Repetition* and *Fear and Trembling*. Ostensibly about Job, this discourse also calls Abraham to mind since it presents Job in the light of *Fear and Trembling's* thought about infinite resignation and joy in the finite. Kierkegaard focuses on the "beautiful words," the words that the young man in *Repetition* took refuge in: "The Lord gave, and the Lord took away; blessed be the name of the Lord!" (EUD, 114). Describing how Job's "heart was shattered" (114) by the news of the death of all his sons and daughters, and how Job "surrendered to sorrow, not in despair but with human emotions," Kierkegaard reminds us of Job's first words, the "judgment" through which "the dispute was settled" once and for all: "Naked I came from my mother's womb, and naked I shall return" (115). Before he ever spoke the words "The Lord gave," Job had already rested in the thought that all he had was not really his – it was all gift. Despite "the crushing weight of the loss," Job did not first say "The Lord took away" but rather "The Lord gave" – "Job's soul was not squeezed into silent subjection to the sorrow, but . . . his heart first expanded in thankfulness" (115). Job expressed his gratitude for all those things that had been taken, for they had all initially been good and perfect gifts from God that he had received with thankfulness. The magnificent discussion of the gift by which God gives Godself, found in the discourse on "Strengthening in the Inner Being," is here revived. What Job lost was "beautiful because the Lord had given it" (116) and it retained its beauty, turning Job from the gift to the giver.

Kierkegaard here re-presents Job after the work he had done on Abraham through Silentio. Is this Job just an elaboration of *Repetition's* Job – or is he a different Job? Here there is no mention at all of the restoration of Job's family and goods: Job "witnesses to joy" (EUD, 122) long before he receives back what he had lost! The second movement of taking joy in the finite received back is either assumed or seen as irrelevant. Here the emphasis is on how "the Lord did not take everything away" from Job, for he did not take away the "praise," the "peace," the "bold confidence," and "intimacy" with God (122). The emphasis in *Repetition* had been on Job's courage in challenging God, requiring an explanation from God – Job's refusal to give in. Here we are presented with a Job who held his ground somewhat differently – Job "held his ground after having overcome everything" is now taken to mean that "Job had overcome the world" (121).

The emphasis on Job's gratitude in this discourse sounds the note of thanksgiving for gifts that Kierkegaard develops in two more discourses on some of his favorite words: "every good gift and every perfect gift is from above" (EUD, 125). This discourse develops a dimension of the category of "gift" that will become more important in his later works – namely that "the condition" for receiving it is given along with the gift: "God is the only one who gives in such a way that he gives the condition along with the gift, the only one who in giving already has given" (134); "the condition is a gift of God and a perfection that makes it possible to receive the good and perfect gift" (137).[10]

The next discourse on the verse that "every good gift and every perfect gift comes from God" begins in a rather unexpected way – it focuses on the notion of "equality before God" (EUD, 141). This meditation on gift becomes an examination of how external inequality between people is nullified in the equality that lies in the recognition that every good gift comes from God. The one who gives needs to remember that no one can give unless he was first gifted by God: "no man can give what he himself has not been given" (156). The one who gives needs to remember that because he is handing on God's gift, he is "more insignificant than the gift" (147, 149, 151, 156–7); he is God's instrument of giving, not himself the author of the gift. The one who receives needs to remember that every good gift comes from God and thus he need not be crushed by a debt to the gift-giver. Kierkegaard takes great pains here to suggest how many forms there are of doing a loving thing in an unloving way, of being an unjust man even when one does a just deed (148). There are many ways of betraying "with a kiss" (147). One can self-servingly make someone feel indebted and humiliated; one can uncaringly "let him wait for it," make him "implore" you (148), either so that he will be more grateful to you or so that you can feel superior. Kierkegaard warns: "The longer you let the needy one plead, the deeper he is mired in his earthly need, until he may not be able to lift his soul up out of it even with the help of your gift" (148–9). The theme of the relation between inner and outer surfaces here in the advice that the giving should be "covert" and the giver should become as "invisible" as possible in the act of gift-giving (153), should vanish without waiting for thanks (154). The requirement is to give joyfully without calling attention to oneself – i.e., to hide oneself.

Equality follows from the "'divine law to love one's neighbor as oneself' in such a way that no person is so exalted in rank that he is not your neighbor in exactly the same sense as no person is so inferior in rank or so wretched that he is not your neighbor, and the equality is incontrovertibly demonstrated by your loving him as you love yourself!" (EUD,

142). Moreover, Kierkegaard insists that we cannot use the truth that the gift comes from God as an excuse for not expressing gratitude to the human giver: "if the person who receives the benefaction does not go out in his thankfulness to find his benefactor, he will never find God; it is in this search that he finds God" (152).

The fourth and final discourse in this volume is entitled "To Gain One's Soul in Patience." The soul is "the self-contradiction in the contradiction between the external and the internal, the temporal and the eternal" (EUD, 172), so "life must be gained and . . . it must be gained in patience" (160). Finally, invoking a biblical theme that he will refer to throughout the authorship, Kierkegaard says that the soul is "able to gain itself only by losing itself" (172).

The entirety of the 1843 discourses seem to have been Kierkegaard's way of dealing with his faith in God. He is exploring, looking for an explanation – taking examples of God's chosen ones as encouragement during sorrow or confusion.

notes

1 Edward Mooney sees *Gjentagelse* as a "'retake' as in a cinematic second or third 'take,'" in *Selves in Discord and Resolve: Kierkegaard's Moral-Religious Psychology from Either – Or to Sickness unto Death* (London and New York: Routledge, 1996), p. 28.

2 Of the sort that will later be elaborated in *Concluding Unscientific Postscript.*

3 The more common translation is "exordium," which simply means (another) "introduction" but this fails to capture any of the nuances of the Danish word *Stemning.*

4 In *The Concept of Anxiety*, Haufniensis writes that "To understand a speech is one thing, and to understand what it refers to, namely, the person, is something else" (CA, p. 142).

5 But of course this commensurability must also be understood in terms of the claim that "the paradox of faith is that there is an interiority than is incommensurable with exteriority" (FT, p. 69) – it is in this context that Silentio claims that "subjectivity is incommensurable with actuality" (FT, pp. 111–12).

6 Modern philosophy "is unwilling to stop with doubting everything but goes further" (FT, p. 5); "In our age, everyone is unwilling to stop with faith but goes further" (FT, p. 7).

7 For more detail on this, see my "Describing What You Cannot Understand – Another Look at *Fear and Trembling*," *Kierkegaardiana* 24 (2007).

8 I take it that this is something like what Stephen Mulhall argues, in *Inheritance and Originality: Wittgenstein, Heidegger, Kierkegaard* (Oxford: Oxford University Press, 2001), p. 382.

9 See *Works of Love.*

10 This anticipates the formulations to come in *Fragments.*

further reading

Caputo, John D., *Radical Hermeneutics: Repetition, Deconstruction, and the Hermeneutic Project* (Bloomington, IN: Indiana University Press, 1987).

Eriksen, Niels Nymann, *Kierkegaard's Category of Repetition* (Berlin: Walter de Gruyter, 2000).

IKC, FT/R, vol. 6 (1993).

Kierkegaard, Søren, *Fear and Trembling*, ed. and trans. C. Stephen Evans and Sylvia Walsh (Cambridge: Cambridge University Press, 2006).

KSY, 2002.

Lippitt, John, *Kierkegaard and Fear and Trembling* (London: Routledge Philosophy Guidebooks, 2003).

Matustik, Martin, and Merold Westphal, eds., *Kierkegaard in Post/Modernity* (Bloomington, IN: Indiana University Press, 1995).

Mooney, Edward, *Knights of Faith and Resignation: Reading of Kierkegaard's Fear and Trembling* (Albany, NY: SUNY Press, 1991).

Perkins, Robert L., ed., *Kierkegaard's Fear and Trembling: Critical Appraisals* (Tuscaloosa, AL: University of Alabama Press, 1981).

chapter 4

Philosophical Fragments, The Concept of Anxiety, and Discourses

K
ierkegaard has thus far written three books that have attempted to provide new categories for rethinking the possibilities for "the good life," each time within a particular horizon and through the use of a set of contrasts (e.g., esthetic/ethical-religious, two kinds of repetition, two movements of faith, and two kinds of resignation). The next take on this central concern, entitled *Philosophical Fragments*, offers a new opportunity to craft a provocative contrast between two positions – this time, the Socratic and the non-Socratic. This text introduces the Socratic position on knowledge of God (a position which encompasses both Greek idealism and nineteenth-century speculative idealist philosophy) and in five short chapters (plus an appendix and an "interlude") examines an alternative to it. This examination is important because it amounts to the question whether "self-knowledge is God-knowledge" (PF, 11) or whether there must be a revelation of God by Godself. That is, this text tries to illuminate the crucial generic difference between a religion of reason and a religion of revelation.

Fragments takes up certain themes found in Kierkegaard's earlier writings, and it will be interesting to see what he does to them through his new pseudonym, Johannes Climacus. It is especially tied to several earlier discourses. In "The Expectancy of Faith," his first published discourse, Kierkegaard had considered the character of a "good" gift, a gift that is both good and good for you, and suggested that the only unfailingly good gift is the gift of faith, which is something every person is able to have: "every human being has what is highest, noblest, and most sacred in humankind. It is original in him, and every human being has it if he wants to have it – it is precisely the gloriousness of faith that it can be had only on this condition" (EUD, 14). He concluded that "It is the only unfailing good, because it can be had only by constantly being acquired and can be acquired only by continually being generated"; the obverse of the fact that faith is something that each must "acquire" for herself is that "no human being can give it to another" (14). As if to counter the possible misunderstanding that human reason could generate faith, Kierkegaard reminded us that he was talking about the "gift" of faith by insisting that "no one can learn this from another, but each one individually learns it only from and through God" (28). He announced with hope that "every person" could "truthfully" say: "I went to God; he became my teacher, and this is my salvation, my joy, my pride" (12). In other words, God is the "giver of good gifts" by being Teacher. These themes are taken up and refined in *Fragments*, as if Kierkegaard is worried that what he had said to highlight equality – that faith was "original" in us – might lead to misunderstandings. Another early discourse ("The Lord Gave and the Lord Took Away") had claimed that God "gives the condition along with the gift," and that "the condition is a gift of God" (EUD, 134, 137). In other words, *Fragments* may be seen as picking up these glimmers of the giftedness of faith and attempting to clarify and/or qualify some of Kierkegaard's early claims about faith.

In general, *Fragments* develops a trajectory begun in *Repetition* and *Fear and Trembling* in which there is a polemic against theological immanence and philosophical mediation. *Fragments* also relates to *Fear and Trembling* in particular insofar as it develops its notions of "paradox" and of believing by "virtue of the absurd." Silentio's conclusion there – that "faith begins precisely where thought stops" (FT, 53) – is clarified and qualified in *Fragments*, where the activity and dynamic of thinking are much more to the forefront. This new book offers Kierkegaard his first real opportunity to examine the implications (for intellectual reflection) of his challenge to a philosophical understanding of faith. Here the notion of the "leap" which comes up in *Fragments'* companion piece, *The Concept of Anxiety*, will get a philosophical development in relation to rational thinking and argumentation. *Fragments* will develop the passing references in *Fear and Trembling* to "passion," but it will also introduce two new categories – namely, "offense" (which may have been anticipated by the notion of Job's trial and Abraham's "ordeal") and the "historical" in relation to faith.

I *Philosophical Fragments, Or, A Fragment of Philosophy*

A The framing

An appreciation of the text at any of its levels requires that we consider briefly the literary framing – in this case, the unusual title page, the preface, and the concluding "Moral." The title is *Philosophical Fragments,* or, *A Fragment of Philosophy*. Kierkegaard hereby enters a tradition of writers who produced "fragments" in some form – e.g., J. G. Hamann, H. S. Reimarus, K. W. F. Schlegel. The Danish words literally mean "philosophical crumbs/bits," a clear contrast to any philosophical totality or system. But, already, there is ambiguity: will we still find philosophy, however crumbly? or will we find that a fragment cannot be philosophical and be forced to ask "What is philosophy"?

The author that Kierkegaard creates for *Fragments*, Johannes Climacus, is also the subject of an unfinished work that preceded *Fragments*, a third-person narrative account (entitled *Johannes Climacus, or, De Omnibus Dubitandum Est*) of a 21-year-old student "ardently in love . . . with thinking," with "the comprehensible transition in which one thought connects with another" (JC, 118). His name (John the Climber) obviously reflects his belief that "coherent thinking," the ability "to climb step by step" from a single thought to a higher thought, was a *"scala paradisi* [ladder of paradise]" (JC, 118). Johannes Climacus is also the name of a fifth-century monk who wrote *The Ladder of Divine Ascent*, a recipe-like handbook for cultivating faith systematically, step by step. Given the account of faith recently given by Johannes de Silentio in *Fear and Trembling*, there obviously are many ironies in the use of this particular name.

The editor's name, S. Kierkegaard, is surprisingly prominent on the page, just below the name of Johannes Climacus. This is interesting because Kierkegaard wrote the entire book in his own name, and then, only the day before he sent the manuscript to the publisher, did he substitute the name of Climacus. This change of author on Kierkegaard's part seems to me the best evidence against the view that Kierkegaard conceived of and wrote his pseudonymous works by adopting *at the outset* the distinctive voice of a pseudonym. Although Kierkegaard changed only the authorship at the last minute, not anything in the text itself (except for some minor changes in the preface), it seems that adopting the pseudonymous author was an important move, probably intended to signal something about the oddness of the book's style.

The title page is unusual among Kierkegaard's works in that it poses three questions. These questions concern the relevance of the historical to faith and, presumably, are to be answered in the text: "Can a historical point of departure be given for an eternal consciousness; how can such a point of departure be of more than historical interest; can an eternal happiness be built upon historical knowledge?" Their presence on the title page suggests how central that concern is to the book.

The job of the preface seems to be the modest one of downplaying the import of the book, calling it a "pamphlet," and noting its inherent limitations; it also emphasizes that the author is a "loafer out of indolence" (PF, 5), one who in "carefree contentedness" "dance[s] lightly in the service of thought" (7). These are hints that this is not a philosophical treatise, and they make one wonder what sort of person this Climacus is. So, Climacus warns the reader against the temptation of looking for the author's "opinion," or of adopting it simply because it is the author's (7–8). The caution expressed in the preface has a counterpart in "The Moral" that Climacus appends as the last page of the book: namely, the claim that the book has intended only to highlight the differences between two positions (the Socratic position and the non-Socratic position), and does not try to suggest which type is "more true" (111).

Each of the first three chapters has an intriguing and descriptive title – one that highlights the distinctive form or genre of the chapter. The first chapter is entitled "Thought-Project," the second is subtitled "A Poetical Venture," and the third (entitled "The Absolute Paradox") is subtitled (paradoxically) "A Metaphysical Caprice." The third chapter on paradox has an important appendix, and this is followed by two chapters ("The Contemporary Follower" and "The Follower at Second-Hand") that address the relevance of the historical to faith by looking at various ways one can be related to a historical event. Breaking up these two chapters is the literary stratagem of an "Interlude," or intermission, intended to suggest a long passage of time between chapters 4 and 5.

B The contrast

"Thought-Project" introduces the seminal question: "Can the truth be learned ?"[1] This is a question about how we gain "the truth," but our only hint thus far about what "the truth" refers to is the notion of "eternal consciousness" or "eternal happiness" in the opening three questions. Climacus is here defining "learning" as an activity that involves the introduction of a radically new element – in Climacus's sense we do not "learn" when we are reminded of something we already knew but did not know we knew. The question is whether the truth can (must) be learned or whether humanity possesses it innately.

The Socratic position presents Socrates as the teacher for whom teaching is a reciprocal relationship, the teacher who recognizes that he learns from the student as well – i.e., the teacher (*laerer*) is in some ways the one who is taught, the learner (*laerende*). Climacus notes that the Socratic position illuminates the "highest" relation possible between human beings (PF, 10). This teacher is aware that he is only an occasion for the learner to recollect what he already knew but did not realize he knew. On this model many teachers could serve equally well as an occasion for a given recollection; thus, neither the teacher nor the moment of recollecting is decisive. Although one might argue that the moment of recollection is extremely important, Climacus regards it as indecisive because the knowledge is eternally present in the learner. Analyzing the

Socratic position, he indirectly points out a crucial philosophical distinction between two categories – the category of "occasion" and the category of "source." The Socratic insight distinguishes between the delivery of the baby and the source of the new life. The "thought-project" precisely generates the non-Socratic alternative by negating or inverting in turn each characteristic of the Socratic view, in relation to four formal or abstract categories: The Truth, The Teacher, The Learner, The Moment.

Climacus proposes to generate the non-Socratic alternative simply by adopting the rule of inversion, or philosophical negation: "This is the way we have to state the difficulty if we do not want to explain it Socratically" (PF, 13). Climacus applies the rule as follows. If the moment of learning the truth is to be decisive, it must be that the truth is not already potentially present – we must not even be seeking the truth, for that would imply that we had it in some sense. If the moment of learning the truth is to be decisive, the teacher must be someone who has something we need, something we cannot gain however deeply we look inside ourselves to find it. If we do not want to fall back into the Socratic model, we must introduce a new category – namely, "untruth" or "sin" – in order to describe our pre-learning position. The condition for learning the truth is not already in us – otherwise everything is Socratic. We notice a little theologizing here. We could not have been created in this sad state, without the truth or the condition for understanding it, because that would entail that our creation was a faulty one, that we were made imperfect (15), and that seems incompatible with an omnipotent and benevolent Creator. The only conclusion that saves the appearances is that we have deliberately forfeited both the truth and its "condition" – i.e., we have sinned by turning away from, rejecting, the truth. The learner can be "reminded that he is untruth and is that through his own fault" (15). However, this acknowledgement of guilt brings him no closer to the truth in one sense, because he still has to be given the truth. And not only the truth, but the "condition for understanding it," because "if the learner were himself the condition for understanding the truth, then he merely needs to recollect, because the condition for understanding the truth is like being able to ask about it – the condition and the question contain the conditioned and the answer" (14).[2]

Socrates is right – if I already have the question, then in some sense I already have the answer. Therefore, any genuine alternative to the Socratic position must assume that we do not already have the question, the desire, the wonder, and that no other human can transform us in this way; the only teacher who could give us what human beings lack is God. Being given "the condition" is being enabled to ask the question again. We can see already that this discussion re-addresses the questions (embedded in the first upbuilding discourse) of what is "original" in us and what we can "acquire." This "thought-project" raises for the reader the very important issue of volitionalism, or the role of the will and freedom in faith, and begins a process of clarifying and qualifying the early claims that Kierkegaard took for granted.

The chapter has put forth a set of alternatives – either innate truth or revealed truth, either inside or outside, either Socrates is right or he is not. Climacus assumes that these are the only candidates – that all attempts to speak of "the god" and immortality fall under one rubric or the other. But he puts forth the contrast in a very peculiar way, as is revealed by some oddities at the end of the first chapter. First, Climacus himself questions whether the hypothesis he has logically generated is even "thinkable" (PF, 20). After all, as he has already pointed out, if we are "turned around" by the gift of the condition, we become "a person of a different quality" (18); it is like "the change from 'not to be' to 'to be,'" and "the person who already *is* cannot be born, and yet he is born" (19). How can a person who *is* not (who is in the state of "not to be") *become aware* "in the moment" that he is "born"? Like the paradox of coming into existence that was discussed in *Repetition*, the idea of a non-Socratic "rebirth" is paradoxical: it seems to be something one's understanding cannot consciously undergo; a case of conceiving something that one can only conceive on condition that it has already happened to one. Nevertheless, Climacus goes on as if there is no problem – "This, as you see, is my project!" (21). In other words, my project involves a paradoxical moment that cannot be thought.

Now another objection is introduced (by the imagined interlocutor who Climacus imagines interrupts him) – specifically, that Climacus disingenuously claims to be the inventor of something that was not invented by him (since every Dane would see this apparently made-up story of sin and redemption as, at bottom, the Christianity he or she is familiar with). Climacus turns that objection that this non-Socratic alternative is nothing new on its head and suggests that it could not have been invented by *any* human being. And what would *that* mean?[3] The reader must grapple with this question, and perhaps draw some uncomfortable implications. It would mean that Christianity is absolutely different from philosophy. And what would *that* mean? The "thought-project" is a pedagogical tool by which Climacus appears to have attempted, through a logical deduction, to invent a hypothesis that cannot have been invented. That literary cleverness tries to provoke the reader into realizing something he could not have been told directly. Had Climacus said simply at the outset that philosophy was not Christianity, or that Hegelianized Christianity was not Christianity, the reader would have said, "Of course, I know that, I'm a Christian." The reader needs to see for himself how a rationalized religion and a revealed religion differ.

Chapter 2 furthers that goal by re-visioning the abstract "thought-project" in terms of a "poetical venture," a poem: this time the alternative is developed through poetic categories, like kings, maidens, love, and lilies. Like chapter 1, it begins again with Socrates, reminding us that "between one human being and another, this is the highest: the pupil is the occasion for the teacher to understand himself; the teacher is the occasion for the pupil to understand himself" (PF, 24). But this mutuality cannot be the case on a non-Socratic model, so we need to reconsider the non-Socratic Teacher. Climacus, as "poet," begins to "unroll the tapestry of discourse" so that we may see love unconcealed: the inadequate but necessary analogy is that of a king who wants to express his love for a maiden (26), and is faced with the sad fact of inequality and hence an incommensurability of understanding. The Teacher who is not motivated by any mutual gain can only be motivated by "love" (24) – the Teacher is now the Lover.

The Loving Teacher wants to share himself with another, to bring her to the truth, but since equality is a *sine qua non* for beings to share love, the inequality must be overcome: the Loving Teacher becomes the Incarnate Teacher. The poet's "solution" to the dilemma (the descent of the king to the level of the maiden) is meant "to awaken the mind to an understanding of the divine" (PF, 26) – God is Teacher, Lover, and Savior through an Incarnation. It is, by the way, not hard to see the sensitivity to the feelings of the maiden, the concerns about deception and overwhelming the maiden, as echoing the concerns about personal relationship found in *Repetition*. In any case, questions about God's immanence or transcendence take on a new form in the poet's solution, as does the theological question of God's hiddenness. Climacus here expresses Kierkegaard's ever-present concern with issues of inner and outer: "Look, there he stands – the god. Where? There. Can you not see him?" (32). Later chapters will continue to address this historical-hiddenness.

At the end of chapter 2 we find another ironic twist in the form of the charge of plagiarism that Climacus imagines being raised against him. The poem is as strange an attempt as the thought-project was, because Climacus himself offers an apparent argument against the possibility of any human author of this poem – namely, that although there have been many ways of imagining gods, the one thing that no human could have conceived was that "the blessed god could need him" (PF, 36) (and only the need of love to give itself would account for the god's becoming a human being). In other words, Climacus is not offering a metaphysical argument for the unimaginability of the hypothesis, but rather suggesting that the idea of the god descending to our level out of love would be thought too good to be true and could not be entertained by human beings. The possibility must be revealed to us, suggested from outside.

Climacus has provided first an abstract and then a poetic account of the non-Socratic alternative, and chapter 3 spirals back again with a return to Socrates. Entitled "The Absolute Paradox," and subtitled "A Metaphysical Caprice," this chapter begins with another description of the Socratic paradox. Instead of the earlier formulation of the Socratic paradox from Plato's dialogue, *The Meno*, here we find two other descriptions of the Socratic paradox. First, we see Socrates' uncertainty about whether he was "a more curious monster than Typhon or a friendlier and simpler being, by nature sharing something divine" (PF, 37). Second, we see the more general paradox that "the ultimate potentiation of every passion is always to will its own downfall," in its specific intellectual form such that it is the "ultimate passion of the understanding [*Forstand*]" to will its own downfall (37). "Paradox," Climacus says, "is the passion of thought" and "the ultimate paradox of thought" is "to want to discover something that thought itself cannot think" (37). The paradoxical passion of thought is always to seek to know more, so that thought constantly and inevitably approaches its limits, and when it makes sense of what it had seen as the unknown, it goes on and seeks yet another unknown. Climacus offers an analogy with the paradox of self-love, wherein self-love wants its satisfaction and finds it in love of what it desires, yet thereby constrains itself: the lover is "changed by this paradox of love" (39), and the result of self-love is that the self no longer has primacy, but love of the other takes precedence. The paradox of the understanding is that it too unseats itself by attempting to satisfy itself.

All these paradoxes are ingredients in a Socratic understanding of life. Socrates was aware of "the unknown" – "let us call this unknown *the god*" (PF, 39); he knew the unknown as the "frontier" which is "expressly the passion's torment, even though it is also its incentive" (44), but, according to Climacus, Socrates did not see the possibility of the "absolutely different" (46). Climacus's contribution is to highlight how "the understanding cannot even think the absolutely different; it cannot absolutely negate itself but uses itself for that purpose and consequently thinks the difference in itself" (45). The paradox is that the understanding cannot by itself know "the absolutely different": "if the god is absolutely different from a human being, then a human being is absolutely different from the god – but how is the understanding to grasp this?" (46).

On the non-Socratic model, then, the Teacher (Lover, Incarnate Savior) becomes the Absolute Paradox. The difference Climacus speaks of is not an epistemological issue as such – it is a difference constituted by "sin" (PF, 47). If the god, as Loving Teacher, wants to teach this difference the god must teach to an equal, so "the paradox becomes even more terrible": the paradox has the "duplexity by which it manifests itself as the absolute – negatively, by bringing into prominence the absolute

difference of sin and, positively, by wanting to annul this absolute difference in the absolute equality" (47). The Absolute Paradox is the Teacher
who wants to reveal an absolute difference between us, and yet can only
do this by becoming a human being (like us). The message is duplex –
the Paradox is the person of the Teacher who says at one and the same
time "You are different from me" (because of sin) and "I am like you" (a
vulnerable human being). Socrates knew human paradox, the paradoxical condition of the human being, but he did not know the "Absolute
Paradox" – the paradox intensified when the paradoxical human being
faces the paradoxical God.

Climacus here broaches some philosophical questions about the
character of what are called "proofs" for the existence of God and introduces the epistemological concept of "leap." He points to the limits of
demonstrations of existence – both the assumption of unproven initial
premises and the subjective "contribution" (PF, 43) of drawing the final
conclusion. The latter is a "letting-go" that he calls a "leap": "anyone
who wants to demonstrate the existence of God (in any other sense than
elucidating the God-concept and without the *reservatio finalis* [ultimate
reservation] that . . . the existence itself emerges from the demonstration
by a leap) proves something else instead" (43).

What is particularly interesting here is that the notion "leap" (which
might suggest a kind of will-power notion of faith) is then qualified by
the concept of "passion" found in the opening reference to the "passion
of thought." The understanding cannot understand the paradoxical message, yet, on the other hand, its dynamic is to passionately seek its own
downfall, which is precisely what the Absolute Paradox is. Climacus
calls this a "mutual understanding" between the understanding and the
paradox, but one achieved "only in the moment of passion" (PF, 47). The
appendix to this chapter on the Absolute Paradox serves to explore more
of the details of this "mutual understanding" and this relation to God
in an infinite, paradoxical passion. Moreover, the "passion" (47) alluded
to at the end of this chapter is then, in the appendix, called a "happy"
passion (49). Insofar as a passion is a suffering or an undergoing of something, the purely volitional aspect of a "leap" is qualified. Later, this
notion of faith as a happy passion is elaborated more fully, by contrast
to both "a knowledge" and an "act of will" (62). Drawing on Aristotle's
understanding of passion, Climacus expounds a notion of passion that
is not mere feeling or mere event – it is an affective response that is cog-
nitively oriented and stable. The "moment of passion" is a construal of
what is neither intellectually coerced nor willfully arbitrary.

The appendix, "Offense at the Paradox," brings several major issues
to the fore. The first issue concerns the nature of the "offense." The
possibility of a "mutual understanding" of their difference, by the understanding and the paradox, is the possibility of a happy encounter. But the

opposite possibility is highlighted too – the possibility of an unhappy encounter – because the affront to the understanding is not so much an intellectual one as a moral one. The consciousness of sin and what we learn about ourselves offends our self-esteem. Secondly, Climacus suggests that "offense" is a category that vacillates between active and passive, or transcends the dichotomy between active and passive: do we take offense or are we offended? The duplexity in the experience mirrors the duplexity in all the descriptions of surrendering the understanding.

Thirdly, Climacus tries to make very clear that the Absolute Paradox is not the paradox met simply by the natural dynamic of the understanding, the infinite passion of thought seeking its downfall – rather, the understanding meets an absolute difference that affronts it. There is a break, a revelation we face from outside. Subtitled "An Acoustic Illusion," this appendix is a peculiar addition to the text insofar as it addresses the very serious question of the relation of the understanding to the paradox of the God-Man-Teacher in a rather jesting way.[4] It reassesses the nature of the "passion" and the "mutual understanding" which ended the earlier chapter, but does so by irreverently personifying both the paradox and the understanding as engaged in a rather comical exchange. It uses the notions of "acoustical illusion" and echo in such a way that the reader feels tossed back and forth rather confusingly, having a hard time deciding who is really saying what. We find a playful encounter, yet a tremendous amount of seriousness informs the appendix because the notion of offense is tied to the consciousness of sin that the Paradox brings with it.

Chapter 3 and its appendix are thus particularly important in fleshing out the non-Socratic alternative because they raise the question whether Climacus (or Kierkegaard) is here describing an irrationalist position. On the one hand, there is the language of "the absurd," but on the other hand, the effect on the understanding is qualified by Climacus's parallel with self-love – namely, that even when "self-love has foundered . . . it is not annihilated but is taken captive . . . it can come to life again, and this becomes erotic love's spiritual trial. So also with the paradox's relation to the understanding" (PF, 48). The understanding is never "annihilated." The contrast between the "probable" and the "absurd" brings to the forefront of our imaginations the category of the "Wholly Other" or the absolutely different that informs a radical notion of transcendence. But it also raises the question of the historical character of the incarnation of the god and its epistemological implications.

Climacus emphasizes the historical origin of the Christian faith – not only the indispensability of the existential "moment" in which a potential believer faces the (announcement of the) Paradox, but also the indispensability of the ontological "moment" in which God comes into time. The question whether the historical is "decisive" or "indifferent" raises several different senses of the historical. The claims that "knowing all the historical facts with the trustworthiness of an eyewitness . . . by no means makes the eyewitness a follower" (PF, 59) and that "faith cannot be distilled from even the finest detail" (103) suggest that historical information is insufficient to generate faith. But the claim that "we can let ignorance . . . destroy one fact after the other, let it historically demolish the historical – if only the moment still remains as the point of departure for the eternal, the paradox is still present" (59) is a stronger and more problematical claim. If we allow history to "demolish the historical" what does it mean to say that "the moment still remains" – what moment? What should we make of the suggestion that a religious faith has as its object certain historical events about which nothing at all need be known historically?

Climacus's claim that in this non-Socratic understanding of faith, it is "more than enough" for a potential believer that there be the brief report that some people in history have "believed that in such and such a year the god appeared in the humble form of a servant, lived and taught among us, and then died" (PF, 104) has been criticized for implying that there need not have been a Jesus Christ, but only the story of a Jesus Christ. But this criticism neglects Climacus's own strong insistence on the distinction between the "condition" and the "occasion." The "occasion" of the report of the story of Christ is not enough to allow faith, because "the condition" must also have been given. The question of the role and relevance of the historical, however, remains.[5]

As a book about sin and its consequences, this seems a serious book, yet two years after *Fragments* was published, Climacus commented on a review of *Fragments* that (according to Climacus) ignored all the "irony," "satire," and "parody" in the text and thereby gave "the most mistaken impression one can have of it" (CUP, 275n). But if the satire, irony, and parody, were not borne out in the text of *Fragments* itself, it would not matter what Climacus later said (and this is true of all the works that Climacus comments on). Similarly, Climacus's later self-attribution of "humorist" (CUP, 451) would mean little if we had not already seen it borne out in the text. All in all we have a lighthearted joker who is in deadly earnest. This is without doubt a classic example of the way in which "jest" is used by Kierkegaard in the service of earnestness, long before he thematizes their dialectical reciprocity.[6]

"The Moral" with which the book ends claims to take no stand as to which position is more true, but only to present the qualitative difference between the Socratic and non-Socratic understandings of faith. Some people take "The Moral" at its word and see the book as impartial. Others read it as disingenuous (or ironic), arguing that the non-Socratic position has in fact been implicitly presented as superior. Still others read the presentation of the contrasting positions as provoking the reader to come up with another position entirely that benefits from the insights of both without inheriting their problems.

In the end, *Fragments* is also valuable as a text because it suggests something that can help make sense of why Kierkegaard wrote the books he did. Some have suggested that Kierkegaard is in the strange and contradictory position of trying to directly communicate what he says is not directly communicable. But the impossibility of faith by "second-hand" that Climacus insists on leaves open the possibility that a Socratic relation among human beings is possible, once the condition is given historically. Kierkegaard and Climacus can both be seen as providing an "occasion" for their readers.

II *The Concept of Anxiety*

All of Kierkegaard's works thus far have presented us, the readers, with possibilities – different dimensions of human life, different ways of responding to the world, each other, and ourselves. Here, in *The Concept of Anxiety*,[7] Kierkegaard works at a different level, a meta-level, where he brings us face to face with the implications of possibility: our recognition of possibilities in life reveals our freedom to us, and with this comes an awareness of the fundamental mood or disposition of anxiety. That is, this text will present us with a possibility – namely, that freedom's possibilities reveal anxiety, that to be human is to be free, and to be free is to be anxious. It is difficult now to realize how unusual such a book was in its time. We take for granted now works entitled *The Meaning of Anxiety* and *Escape from Freedom*,[8] as well as French "existentialist" explorations of the dilemma of freedom and Heideggerian discussions of "Angst" – but such studies are in large part due to Kierkegaard's pioneering effort.

Anxiety is an appropriate topic for psychological exploration, and it is no surprise that the book is put forth in its subtitle as "A Simple Psychologically Orienting Deliberation," but the remainder of the subtitle puts the deliberation in relation to a quite different discipline – the deliberation is "on the Dogmatic Issue of Hereditary Sin." This might lead a potential reader to suspect that the book is irrelevant to someone who no longer has a concern with the religious category of inherited (or "original") sin, or even "sin" as such, but the book is about much more than the traditional story of the Garden of Eden or Paradise Lost. Or perhaps it is better to say that this is a book that goes deeper than that story, because this inquiry into the issue of inherited sin engages the fundamental question of human freedom and responsibility. Certain accounts of sin will put in jeopardy any robust notion of individual human freedom, and for this reason this discussion is an important one both for those who care about a particular religious account of sin as well as those who are, for other reasons, interested in the question of human freedom. The re-visioning of a traditional Christian doctrine that is found in this book issues from an anthropology in which freedom and its consequences are put front and center. Moreover, the famous category of "the leap" is developed.

The actual trajectory of the book begins with a concern with the consequences of sin that leads to a look at the origin of sin, that then involves a study of how the self who sins is constituted. That is, the book addresses the question whether sin can be inherited – but this involves the questions "what is sin" and "how can innocence be lost," which locates us in the middle of a discussion of the structure of the self, analyzing what can be psychologically gleaned about the self prior to the act of sin. The logic of the investigation, however, can just as easily be read in the opposite direction: namely, a concern with the various ways in which a human being both expresses freedom and imprisons freedom, which issues in a particular understanding of what sin is. After all, only if we first understand what the self is can we then understand the origin and consequences of sin for the self. Moreover, one does not need to agree with the author about the theological nature of sin to begin with, since he repeatedly construes the question in terms of the evil of "selfishness"[9] – so we can begin with shared assumptions, if there are any, about our experience of freedom and our intuitions about selfishness. His point is that the common saying that sin is selfishness is useless "if a person does not first make clear to himself the meaning of 'self'." (CA, 78).

A Introductory ambivalence

The short title – *The Concept of Anxiety* – already embodies a kind of vacillation that will resurface constantly throughout the text. The good news is that the book is devoted to an experience that we come face to face with repeatedly during every day of our lives. The bad news is that it is such a systematic scholarly presentation! The scholarly apparatus implied in the table of contents is daunting for any reader drawn to the book because of a personal concern with anxiety and looking for some help. Still, the author is not a professor of psychology, but someone with a funny name (Vigilius Haufniensis – the Vigilant Observer of the Harbor, the Watchman of Copenhagen) and no credentials in sight.[10] Moreover, the dedication to his professor is warm and humane, and the preface betokens a popular book, written "as spontaneously as a bird sings its song" (CA, 7). We move on hopefully.

The author's introduction, however, picks up and carries on the academic philosophical tone of the formidable table of contents, targeting the philosophical thinking of the day, explicitly labeled "Hegelian philosophy"[11] (CA, 13), for confusing ethics and logic, or life and logic. This challenge to philosophy reappears[12] but the author makes clear in the introduction that his main concern is the "harmful" (14) effect of superimposing Hegelian thought on ethics and dogmatics (theology). His primary goal is a practical one, not a theoretical one. On the one hand, Haufniensis is worried by the philosophically influenced dogmatic claim that "faith" is "the immediate," since it misleadingly convinces everybody (echoes of *Fear and Trembling*) "of the necessity of not stopping with faith" (10). According to Haufniensis, "faith loses by being regarded as the immediate, since it has been deprived of what lawfully belongs to it, namely, its historical presupposition" (10). On the other hand, he is worried about overcoming sin in "courageous resistance" (15) – in other words, with the "earnestness" and "appropriation" that the contemporary age has forgotten. Both worries will in fact be addressed indirectly by the book's "task": namely, "the psychological treatment of the concept of 'anxiety,' but in such a way that it constantly keeps *in mente* [in mind] and before its eye the dogma of hereditary sin" (14).

There is a constant tension in the book between the poetic and the academic, figured in the repeated back and forth by Haufniensis – "It is not my intention to write a learned work" (CA, 54), but I have a "schema" I want to justify (137). Here if anywhere in Kierkegaard's writings, the form of the book battles against the content. It is an elaborate psychological study, yet he is not after quantity in collecting empirical data. He suggests that a good psychologist will actually have a "poetic originality" that can "create both the totality and the invariable from what in the individual is always partially and variably present" (55) – that is, he is concerned with imaginatively constructed examples.

B The need for such a deliberation – the dilemma of qualitative sin

According to Haufniensis, sin is a theological category, a concept in dogmatics. We need an ethics that recognizes the actuality of sin, but sin is not a category of ethics. Haufniensis suggests that we do what we can – namely, that we inquire into the *possibility* of sin or the conditions in which sin takes place. Psychology can help with this inquiry. Psychology can discover and explore the state of anxiety that occurs in every human life "before the ethical manifests itself" (CA, 15): "this abiding something out of which sin constantly arises . . . this predisposing presupposition, sin's real possibility, is a subject of interest for psychology" (21). The task of the introduction is complete, he says, when the requisite distinctions between the domain and competency of ethics, dogmatics, and psychology have been delineated. With perhaps feigned modesty, Haufniensis warns the reader that the introduction may be correct, while the following "deliberation itself concerning the concept of anxiety may be entirely incorrect" (24). In other words, the reader must judge for herself whether Haufniensis is a good psychologist.

Haufniensis begins by putting under the microscope the Christian tradition's claim that "by Adam's first sin, *sin came into the world*," and he suggests that this "common" statement is usually misunderstood (CA, 32–3). He seeks to clear this up, not so as to reject the concept of inherited sin, but rather to see that it is "rightly understood" (98). In the process, he offers a concise but comprehensive rejection of traditional accounts of inherited sin as something passed on through reproductive generation or biological transmission. Haufniensis here makes a radical challenge to Christian theology – with one fell swoop he dismisses many classic and ecclesiastically authorized renderings of the doctrine of the fall of Adam and its consequences – and he does it so unassumingly that one might miss the resulting devastation. He also challenges any account of sin "as a disease, an abnormality, a poison, or a disharmony" (15), and he challenges "predestination" (62). To anticipate, Haufniensis offers a radically new theory: that we are guilty only of our own sin; the guilt of sin cannot be handed down through generations. Every person loses innocence the same way that Adam did (35): "innocence is always lost only by the qualitative leap of the individual" (37), and Adam and we are "completely alike" (112) in terms of the qualitative leap. And yet, the notion of something inherited has a place.

Haufniensis's project is very specific. He is out to "discover the truth that may be found" in the expression about Adam's sin – it has a "limited truth" (CA, 57). The "Genesis story," he admits, "presents the only dialectically consistent view" and "its whole content is really concentrated in one statement: *Sin came into the world by a sin*" (32). But the problem is that a "poor" myth was "substituted" in order to try to "explain" something that cannot be explained (32). That "poor" myth that attempts to explain inherited sin by giving the human race a "fantastic beginning" (25) not only does not explain what it intends to, but is also in danger of making Adam so different from the rest of the human race that it jeopardizes the doctrine of atonement (33n).

How did sin come into the world? How does sin now arise? The story of inherited sin makes it seem as if the answer to each question would be essentially different. But in both cases, "sin cannot be explained by anything antecedent to it" (CA, 112), otherwise there would be an infinite regress, going back further and further to locate its cause (34); the "fantastic"[13] theological stories of the human's state prior to "the fall" amount to saying that "sinfulness precedes sin" (32). The "sudden" quality of sin is an "offense" to the understanding; it is a "difficulty for the understanding" (32).

Haufniensis's theological innovation is informed by philosophical analysis – his intellectual debts are many and he is in conversation with many thinkers of his day.[14] One interesting comparison can be made with the account given by Kant's *Religion Within the Limits of Reason Alone*, particularly the way it goes beyond Kant's account. Haufniensis is in agreement with Kant that the original reversal of our maxims, or the fall into sin, is a mystery – it cannot be accounted for theoretically. He also agrees with Kant that no explanation for sin will be satisfying in which sin is seen either as a "necessity" or as an "accident" (98), because neither of these options accounts for the human responsibility ingredient in the notion of sin. For both men, if we are to be accountable for sin, we must each individually sin; guilt for sin cannot be inherited. For Kant, guilt for sin is something that we are never without, yet we can assign no time to the performance of the sin. But this leaves us with nothing explained. Haufniensis will go further than Kant in several ways.

Haufniensis makes explicit a distinction that is only implicit in Kant's book – the distinction between a qualitative transition and a quantitative transition.[15] He agrees with Kant that there is a mysterious moment of transition, a transition that cannot be theoretically accounted for yet must be assumed for the sake of ethics – and for him it is the "qualitative leap."[16] Haufniensis argues that the failure to distinguish qualitative from quantitative is most pronounced and dangerous in Hegelian philosophy: "Hegel's misfortune is exactly that he wants to maintain the new quality and yet does not want to do it, since he wants to do it in logic" (CA, 30n). Better said, Hegel wants to do it in life, but does it only in logic. For Haufniensis, everything depends on the plausibility of a distinction between qualitative and quantitative transitions – one will be confused "so long as one does not hold fast to the distinction . . . between the quantitative accumulation and the qualitative leap" (54). This distinction has already played a role in Kierkegaard's earlier writings, and it will play an important role in almost all of his writings. From early to late the polemic against the quantitative "more" persists: "never in the world has there been or ever will be a 'more' such that by a simple transition it transforms the quantitative into the qualitative" (72); "each repetition is not a simple consequence but a new leap" (113). Thus far, however, Haufniensis has still not gone beyond the philosophical or theological accounts in which we end up only with mystery. The beginning of any explanation will occur in psychology's domain and an account of human anthropology.

C Anxiety

First, Haufniensis goes further than Kant who suggested that freedom was the hallmark of humanity, because Haufniensis suggests that to be free is to be anxious, and he offers a psychology or phenomenology of anxiety. He explores the condition that makes for the possibility of sin, sin's "presupposition" (CA, 48) – namely, the mood or disposition of anxiety. Programmatically he announces: "Anxiety means two things: the anxiety in which the individual posits sin by the qualitative leap, and the anxiety that entered in and enters in with sin, and that also, accordingly, enters quantitatively into the world every time an individual posits sin" (54). The book's task is to explain these two things.

Haufniensis assumes a specific anthropology in which the human being is "a synthesis of the psychical and the physical" (or soul and body) but a synthesis that is "united" in a third thing, namely, "spirit" (CA, 43). What is this third thing? To put it most simply, spirit is freedom. To say that "spirit" establishes (71) or constitutes and sustains (81) the synthesis of body and soul is to say that we are posited "as spirit" (98) when we actualize our freedom in any way (91).[17] Before that there is innocence, or spirit "dreaming" (41); where the "synthesis" is "not actual" yet (49), spirit is not yet posited "as spirit" (98). Freedom is something that has to be achieved, since "in innocence freedom was not posited as freedom" (123).

Dreaming spirit (spirit before it is posited as spirit) is anxious even in its innocence because it is tempted by possibility: "in anxiety there is the selfish infinity of possibility, which does not tempt like a choice but ensnaringly disquiets with its sweet anxiousness" (CA, 61). Unawakened freedom is tempted by possibility – not the choice between good and evil (49, 52) but "the anxious possibility of *being able*" (44). Haufniensis here makes the distinction between fear and anxiety (42) which other thinkers will draw on later – namely, we experience fear in the face of "something definite" (42), whereas we experience anxiety about possibility. Possibility is not yet a thing – it is no thing – it is nothing. Anxiety about possibility is anxiety about nothing – "Anxiety and nothing always correspond to each other" (96).

The "task" of the book is to "immerse oneself psychologically in the state that precedes sin and, psychologically speaking, predisposes more or less to sin" (CA, 76). This immersion occurs through metaphoric description and imaginatively constructed examples. The most well-known passage is worth repeating here:

Anxiety may be compared with dizziness. He whose eye happens to look down into the yawning abyss becomes dizzy. But what is the reason for this? It is just as much in his own eye as in the abyss, for suppose he had not looked down. Hence anxiety is the dizziness of freedom, which emerges when the spirit wants to posit the synthesis and freedom looks down into its own possibility, laying hold of finiteness to support itself. Freedom succumbs in this dizziness. Further than this, psychology cannot and will not go. In that very moment everything is changed, and freedom, when it again rises, sees that it is guilty. Between these two moments lies the leap, which no science has explained and which no science can explain. (61)

When Haufniensis describes anxiety in technical terms as a *"sympathetic antipathy and antipathetic sympathy"* (CA, 42), he is really doing no more than reminding us of the psychology of love/hate or attraction/fear responses that we have all experienced. He asks: "How does spirit relate itself to itself and to its conditionality? It relates itself as anxiety. Do away with itself, the spirit cannot; lay hold of itself, it cannot, as long as it has itself outside of itself. Nor can man sink down into the vegetative, for he is qualified as spirit; flee away from anxiety, he cannot, for he loves it; really love it, he cannot, for he flees from it" (44).

Haufniensis expects his readers to draw on their own experiences of anxiety in order to understand how these experiences reveal an abyss. Rather than be dizzied by the abyss, by the infinite, one tends to grasp onto finite limited goods, rejecting the trauma of the infinite. Sin is looking at the infinite possibilities and choosing to grasp the finite. Sin is a lack of courage in the face of the infinite. We are not purely passive observers of the abyss – we climb up and look down, and we are responsible if our freedom succumbs, if we sink in anxiety (43).

In sum, spirit is freedom and expresses itself in anxiety. Haufniensis varies the formulations but they amount to the same thing: "anxiety is freedom's possibility" (CA, 155); anxiety is "freedom's disclosure to itself in possibility" (111). Psychology is the science that comes closest to describing "freedom's showing-itself-for-itself in the anxiety of possibility" (76–7). The self is posited only in the exercise of its freedom – man simply is the "freedom to know of himself that he is freedom," which he discovers by turning inward (108). The self recognizes itself as free, having actualized its freedom in that recognition. Anxiety is "the final psychological expression for the final psychological approximation to the qualitative leap" (91); it is "the psychological state that precedes sin" which "approaches sin as closely as possible" but "without explaining sin, which breaks forth only in the qualitative leap" (92). We are conditioned by anxiety, but we are not determined to sin by it.

D Sinfulness – the quantity of sin

Second, Haufniensis goes further than Kant in exploring the consequences of sin, in explicating a plausible sense of what is right in the doctrine of inherited sin. What remains of the notion of inherited sin (and this is all Haufniensis thinks is really at stake) is that there is a way in which our location in history makes a difference in how we face the possibility of sin. He makes a simple distinction – between actual *sin*

fragments, concept of anxiety, discourses

and the "quantitative approximation" of "*sinfulness*" (CA, 57). Sin is an all-or-nothing qualitative act done in freedom and bringing with it guilt; the "quantitative approximation" of "sinfulness" is the additional anxiety brought by sin into the world and the effects of sin on the world (the "objective anxiety") which we inherit. We inherit an "historical knowledge of sinfulness" (75) that can overwhelm us – the knowledge of the sins of others as well as the knowledge of our own previous sin – and we are different from Adam in the occasion we have to reflect on all this. Anxiety is "entangled freedom" (49). It is freedom entangled in the "historical nexus" or the "historical environment" (73) – we are born into a historical context and we are affected by the "example" of others (74–5). Although these do not determine us to sin, they weigh us down. In this way, our context is not one of innocence, although we are not born guilty. The act of sin arises in anxiety and brings with it more concrete anxiety: the "consequence of hereditary sin" is that "anxiety will be more reflective in a subsequent individual than in Adam, because the quantitative accumulation left behind by the race now makes itself felt in that individual" (52). The burden of this anxiety grows: there is a quantitative accumulation, so that the context into which we are each born reeks more of sin and anxiety than the previous generation's context. In this sense we inherit the consequences of sin but we are not guilty of a sin committed by someone else. He makes his intention clear: "every notion that suggests that the prohibition tempted him, or that the seducer deceived him . . . perverts ethics, introduces a quantitative determination" (43); "sinfulness moves in quantitative categories, whereas sin constantly enters by the qualitative leap of the individual" (47).

Haufniensis is walking the tightrope of denying that sin is necessary or accidental, while allowing that it is inevitable. Only our temporality provides the possibility of such a distinction – at no single time is it logically necessary that we sin, but our fallibility is tied to our temporality in that as temporal, extended beings in time, we will come up short at some time. The history of sin is the condition of sinfulness that surrounds us – the effects of sin in the world have their effect on us. But this quantitative historical residue is the only way in which we are different from Adam, and "this 'more' is never of such a kind that one becomes essentially different from Adam" (64, also 98). The claim that it is the "consequence of the relationship of generation" (64, 72) means that "this anxiety is obscurely present as a more or a less in the quantitative history of the race" (53).

E The absence of sin-consciousness – spiritlessness

Having examined the origin of sin as a qualitative free act whose presupposition was anxiety, Haufniensis turns in chapter 3 to examine the absence of consciousness of sin, or "spiritlessness": "spiritlessness is the stagnation of spirit" (CA, 95) and is worse than paganism. He compares it to a "vegetative sludge" (94–5) whose downward momentum is away from spirit. It is noteworthy that the features he focuses on have to do with the contrast between content and the way in which the content is held. He implicitly invokes a contrast between the "what" and the "how" when he writes: "To a certain degree, spiritlessness may therefore possess the whole content of spirit, but mark well, not as spirit but as the haunting of ghosts, as gibberish, as a slogan, etc." (94). Suggesting the emptiness of much of modern life, he writes: "Man qualified as spiritless has become a talking machine, and there is nothing to prevent him from repeating by rote a philosophical rigmarole, a confession of faith, or a political recitative" (95).

It is interesting that it is precisely here that he alludes to Hamann again (to whom he appeals both at the beginning and at the end of the book). He asks: "Is it not remarkable that the only ironist and the greatest humorist joined forces in saying what seems the simplest of all, namely, that a person must distinguish between what he understands and what he does not understand?" (CA, 95). This allusion to Socrates and Hamann respectively, which is made explicit in the book's opening epigraph, proposes a relation between spirit and understanding, and between spiritlessness and not understanding.

F Sin-consciousness and the potential for subjectivity

The following chapter shifts the focus from the lack of sin-consciousness (spiritlessness) to the presence of sin-consciousness. Although it may not be clear at first, this will indirectly reveal a more positive normative account of the human being, because the presence of sin-consciousness is the condition for the achievement of genuine subjectivity.

The person who has sinned has two options. He can, acknowledging his sin, experience "anxiety about evil" (CA, 113) – that is, anxiety about committing new sin. This anxiety of the "bondage of sin" (119) can undermine a person. Alternatively, the one who is conscious that he has sinned may, whether out of stubborn pride or rebelliousness, be anxious "about the good" (118). That is, he may want to shun anything that might lead to the good of a "restoration of freedom, redemption, [or] salvation" (119). Such a person is analogous to those New Testament figures who were possessed by demons and reacted with hostility against the presence of Christ – such a person is "demonic" (118). This category, which Silentio had touched on fleetingly,[18] is here developed more. The demonic closes himself off within himself, he constricts himself lest he be touched or affected by the good. In this sense, the demonic refuses a good gift. Such "inclosing reserve" (123) is the hallmark of this psychological attitude – it is comparable to a vengeful silence or with-drawal into a cocoon of resentment. Whereas the person who is in the bondage of sin, anxious about the evil of further sin, reaches out for the help of the good, the demonic refuses contact with the good. This "negative self-relation" (129) is like cutting off one's nose to spite one's face. The demonic refuses to be forgiven, and so he refuses to repent. The demonic uses his freedom to prevent further use of his freedom – "free-dom is posited as unfreedom" (123), freedom is made a prisoner. The demonic refuses to "disclose" himself; he rejects "transparency" (127n), most notably by refusing to communicate (128–9). It is interesting that Haufniensis here allies the ideas of isolation and lack of communication with the demonic – in other words, these are never the norm for the single individual; they are to be avoided.[19] However, he suggests that there are "traces" of the demonic in every person (122) – the temptation to refuse what the full-scale demonic person refuses.

Haufniensis ties freedom to truth. Truth is related to historical acts of freedom: "what I am speaking about is very plain and simple, namely, that truth is for the particular individual only as he himself produces it in action. If the truth is for the individual in any other way, or if he pre-vents the truth from being for him in that way, we have a phenomenon of the demonic" (CA, 138). Haufniensis has now made a transition to the normative ideal of "earnestness" (146), since "inwardness, certitude, is earnestness" (151). Examples of lack of certitude include "arbitrariness, unbelief, mockery of religion . . . superstition, servility, and sanctimo-niousness" (139). But, surprisingly, he also thinks that "an adherent of the most rigid orthodoxy may be demonic" (139). To such a dogmatist, he responds with disgust: "He knows it all. He genuflects before the holy. Truth is for him the aggregate of ceremonies. He talks of meeting before the throne of God and knows how many times one should bow" (139–40). On this particular understanding of "certitude," both super-stition and dogmatism lack the certitude of inwardness.

Haufniensis's "schema" explores the category of demonic anxiety about the good, but in the process it introduces a new category: "sub-jectivity" – the demonic lacks earnestness, certitude, and inwardness, and "certitude and inwardness are indeed subjectivity" (CA, 141). The implied correlation of certitude and inwardness with the expansiveness of the non-demonic is a little surprising, but Haufniensis is stipulating the meaning of these terms, and his examples illustrate his intention. Moreover, he importantly qualifies what he means by subjectivity – he wants to talk about subjectivity, "but not in an entirely abstract sense" (141). For Haufniensis, "abstract subjectivity is just as uncertain and lacks inwardness to the same degree as abstract objectivity. . . . [A]bstract subjectivity lacks content" (141). With this polemic against the abstract, Haufniensis recalls the understanding of the religious as commensurable with the world found in Kierkegaard's earlier works. Haufniensis had noted earlier that "to explain how my religious existence comes into relation with and expresses itself in my outward existence, that is the task" (105). Just as he thinks "every human life is religiously designed," so too he thinks that "a religious existence pervades and interweaves the outward existence" (105).

G Anxiety as teacher

The psychological deliberation thus far has been quite detailed – we saw intimations of the depth of our vulnerability as well as ways in which we can try to evade our freedom. The mood has been somber for four chapters, and yet it has been repeatedly claimed by Haufniensis that the experience of anxiety shows the potential for perfection that animals do not have: "The greatness of anxiety is a prophecy of the greatness of the perfection" (CA, 64). Moreover, "the moment when he is greatest [is] not the moment when the sight of his piety is like the festivity of a special holiday, but when by himself he sinks before himself in the depth of sin-consciousness" (110). A positive evaluation of anxiety had also been suggested in chapter 2, when Haufniensis alluded to "another role" that is played by anxiety – namely, that anxiety can be "rightly used" (53). Although he did not find it easy to redeem that promissory note, he finally did so, and chapter 5 takes up again and develops "the right way" to be anxious (155); it fleshes out the positive evaluation of anxiety as an "adventure" we must all go through.

Anxiety has educational value: the right way to be "educated by anxiety" is to be "educated by possibility" (CA, 156). First, we have to realize that "in possibility all things are equally possible" – "the terrible as well as the joyful"; this is part of being educated according to our "infinitude" (156). The graduate of the school of possibility must be "honest toward possibility" (157), but this is not just a theoretical acknowledgement that all things are "equally possible." It is also the acknowledgement that possibility is "the weightiest of all categories" (156) – actuality is "far lighter than possibility" (156) because possibility places demands on us. Moreover, it is a very practical acceptance of the hard facts of life – the graduate "knows better than a child knows his ABC's that he can demand absolutely nothing of life and that the terrible, perdition, and annihilation live next door to every man" (156). The individual who is educated by possibility needs to hear only one story (of someone falling low), and "in that very moment, he is absolutely identified with the unfortunate man; he knows no finite evasion by which he may escape" – he know that "in actuality, no one ever sank so deep that he could not sink deeper" (158). The danger, Haufniensis warns, is "suicide" (159). This sentiment had already been expressed earlier in the book, though to a different end – "No matter how deep an individual has sunk, he can sink still deeper, and this 'can' is the object of anxiety" (113).

Haufniensis makes the hopeful proposal that "only he who passes through the anxiety of the possible is educated to have no anxiety, not because he can escape the terrible things of life but because these always become weak by comparison with those of possibility" (CA, 157). The task of ethics – to "renounce anxiety without anxiety" (117) – sounds, on one construal, too easy, and on another, too hard. Perhaps it is best construed as working through anxiety, as extricating ourselves from "anxiety's moment of death" (117) (its paralysis, its hopelessness) without annihilating anxiety. In sum, the "individual through anxiety is educated unto faith" (159).

It turns out that Haufniensis has indirectly addressed one of his worries, namely, the way in which dogmatics has been misled into thinking that faith is "the immediate" (CA, 10). Faith is not immediate – it must be worked towards through anxiety. In this sense Haufniensis engages with one of Kierkegaard's perennial concerns, which Haufniensis expresses as follows: "Here the question about repetition reappears: to what extent can an individuality, after having begun religious reflection, succeed in returning to himself again, whole in every respect?" (106). In other words, what is possible to us after the loss of innocence? Is there a second immediacy? What should we make of anxiety and the experience of guilt? These particular questions exemplify the way in which Kierkegaard's texts work out concentric circles of concern. His life-experience and his faith-experience are of a piece.

III *Upbuilding Discourses* (1844)

The publications of 1844 were interestingly braided together. After drafting the first four chapters of *The Concept of Anxiety* at the end of 1843 and the beginning of 1844, Kierkegaard was unable to complete the book, and turned his attention to *Fragments*. In the short interim period (January to February 1844) he composed two upbuilding discourses, which he published on March 5, 1844. These had the rather mild-mannered titles, "To Preserve One's Soul in Patience" and "Patience in Expectancy," but both form an interesting complement to the themes in *The Concept of Anxiety*. The first discourse opens with a remarkable emphasis on "danger," "terrors," the "abyss," and "anxiety" (EUD, 181, 185) – the way not to lose one's soul is to preserve it in patience. Patience is the response to anxiety, and the discourse makes clear that the danger and anxiety are not necessarily tied to traumatic earth-shattering events, but to everyday little things. The danger that one can be "desouled in spiritlessness" (198) or experience "soul-rot" (207) echoes *The Concept of Anxiety*; the warning that "the outcome of the temptation is frequently the most dangerous temptation – whether we were victorious and were tempted to arrogance and thus fell after having been victorious, or we lost so that we were tempted to want to lose everything" (202) resonates with the discussion of the demonic in *The Concept of Anxiety*.

Before he turned back to *The Concept of Anxiety*, however, Kierkegaard wrote both *Fragments* and another set of three discourses during March 1844. The first discourse is particularly interesting in showing how a theme is treated differently in the two genres. The discourse's intention to "startle the soul out of its security" (EUD, 239) is balanced by its attempt to break "the spell of brooding seriousness so that there is joy again in heaven and on earth" (249). Whereas in *The Concept of Anxiety*, the emphasis on anxiety as dizziness is presented as the response to the infinite abyss that is meant to be struggled through, here Kierkegaard has sympathy for the person who was made dizzy when "the infinite manifested itself to him" and, being overwhelmed by it, made God's will into "a terrible law" (247) – because that person "had no youth" (250). This quite personal dimension, echoing his own sense of the loss of his childhood because of too rigorous a religious upbringing,[20] is appropriate to the discourse rather than to the pseudonymous work. This volume of discourses was published on June 8, 1844.

Philosophical Fragments and *The Concept of Anxiety* were published at about the same time (June 13 and June 17, respectively). Soon after, Kierkegaard began another set of discourses. Although it was not published until the end of August that year, it echoes the spectrum covered in *The Concept of Anxiety*, from anxiety to victory. "The Thorn in the Flesh" has as its stated goal "to terrify" (EUD, 331); "woe to the person who wants to build up without knowing the terror" (344). "Against Cowardliness" resonates with the category of the demonic as cowardly resistance to the good (359), speaks of "sin" repeatedly (349, 350, 353, 369) and about "inclosing reserve" (341), but in addition to its insight into the subtle psychology we use to evade demand, it is filled with words of great sympathy, compassion, and encouragement in the face of the difficulty of making and keeping resolutions to do the good.

IV *Stages on Life's Way* and *Three Discourses on Imagined Occasions*

After publishing these 1844 discourses, Kierkegaard went on to work on two books, one a pseudonymous work called *Stages on Life's Way* and the other a volume of discourses, both of which were published in April 1845.

Stages on Life's Way is, no doubt, a fascinating book and may even be a favorite of many Kierkegaard scholars, not least because it is the site of the famous banquet ("In Vino Veritas") modeled on Plato's "Symposium," as well as the site of a fictional "diary" fished up from the bottom of a lake, entitled "Guilty? Not Guilty?" It would be natural for a new reader to think that one good place to start reading Kierkegaard would be with the book entitled *Stages on Life's Way*. But I am not going to do an analysis of this book – in part, because of space limitations, and in part, because I think the notion of "stages" is not a helpful way to think about Kierkegaard's project. The title *Stages on Life's Way* may seem a convenient shorthand for the categories of the esthetic, the ethical, and the religious that we have seen in the previous works. The book, after all, is divided into three main parts, and it is often assumed both that the three parts represent the "stages" (*Stadier*) of the title, and that each of the three parts corresponds to an ascending order of the esthetic, the ethical, and the religious. But I suggest that, appearances to the contrary notwithstanding, this is not the book to which a reader should go looking for a summary of Kierkegaard's thinking about these categories.[21]

In fact, even in the book, *Stages*, Frater Taciturnus (who presents the fictional diary in the third part) does not refer to the esthetic, the ethical, and the religious as "stages" (the word in the title, *Stadier*); rather, he calls them "three existence-spheres [*Sphaerer*]" (SLW, 476). Taciturnus' picture of the religious involves "the harmony of the spheres of life" (462) and the locus of simultaneity:

> There are three existence-spheres: the aesthetic, the ethical, the religious.
> . . . The aesthetic sphere is the sphere of immediacy, the ethical the sphere of requirement (and this requirement is so infinite that the individual always goes bankrupt), the religious the sphere of fulfillment, but, please note not the fulfillment such as when one fills an alms box or a sack with gold, for repentance has specifically created a boundless space, and as a consequence the religious contradiction: simultaneously to be out on 70,000 fathoms of water and yet be joyful. (476–7)

We might then expect the third part to be the site of exploration of the three spheres, rather than the whole book. More importantly, he also refers to a "sphere of freedom" (366), so the word "sphere" applies more broadly and, also, has connotations of a dimension or category rather than a stage. The major drawback of the word "stage" was recognized early on by Kierkegaard, who referred to "the stages – child, youth, adult, oldster" as examples of a "vegetative-animal process";[22] his example shows that the word "stage" makes one think of a temporal, successive, and non-deliberate process one passes through and leaves behind. The word "sphere," on the contrary, invokes a richness of potential integration.

Taciturnus alludes to the integration of these "spheres" when he says that a person "must be esthetically developed in his imagination, must be able to grasp the ethical with primitive passion in order to take offense properly so that the original possibility of the religious can break through at this turning point" (428).[23]

In other pseudonymous texts, Kierkegaard also refers to "spheres" of existence. In *Either – Or*, the Judge proposes a "harmonious unison of different spheres. It is the same subject [love], only expressed esthetically, religiously, or ethically" (EO2, 60). He also says, "if you cannot manage to see the esthetic, the ethical, and the religious as the three great allies, if you do not know how to preserve the unity of the different manifestations everything gains in these different spheres, then life is without meaning" (147). In *Concluding Unscientific Postscript*, Climacus nuances the distinction between three "existence spheres," adding irony and humor as border categories (CUP, 501). In sum, whatever its limitations, the word "sphere" is less misleading than the word "stage."

While finishing up *Stages*, Kierkegaard was also working on a set of three discourses that are on the "imagined" occasions of a confession, a wedding, and at a graveside. The primary aim of the discourses is to let us "witness," as the author is doing, "how a person seeks to learn something from the thought of death" (or love or sin) (TDIO, 102). It makes no difference that there is no actual confession, wedding, or death as the occasion for these discourses, because they are not about anything "external," but rather "earnestness lies in the inner being and the thinking and the appropriation and the ennobling that are the earnestness" (73, 74). There is no "teacher" or "learner" in a technical sense, because "the meaning lies in the appropriation" and "the appropriation is the *reader's* . . . triumphant *giving of himself*" (5). All the discourses depend on a crucial and repeated distinction between mere knowledge and "appropriated" knowledge (21, 22, 25, 36, 37, 38): "the knower is changed when he is to appropriate his knowledge" and "he essentially appropriates the essential only by doing it" (37, 38). For example, the difference between "earnestness" and "jest" (73) is located in the difference between appropriated knowledge and unappropriated knowledge: there is jest when one thinks about death in general, but not about one's own death (as if death can be tricked into overlooking you). There is a huge difference between really having an opinion and merely reciting one –

> this other side is just as important, because not only is that person mad who talks senselessly, but the person is fully as mad who states a correct opinion if it has absolutely no significance for him. . . . Alas, yet it is so easy, so very easy, to acquire a true opinion, and yet it is so difficult, so very difficult, to have an opinion and to have it in truth. (99–100)

It will not be long before Kierkegaard gets the chance to develop this theme at length.[24]

notes

1 This amounts to the question "Must/can the truth be taught/learned?"
2 See my "Kierkegaardian Faith: 'The Condition' and the Response," *International Journal for Philosophy of Religion* 28 (1990).
3 As Stephen Evans puts it, any alternative "that could be invented by a human being essentially presupposes the Socratic view that the potential to discover the Truth lies within human nature" (*Passionate Reason: Making Sense of Kierkegaard's "Philosophical Fragments,"* Bloomington, IN: Indiana University Press, 1992, p. 17).
4 See Sylvia Walsh, "Echoes of Absurdity: The Offended Consciousness and the Absolute Paradox in Kierkegaard's *Philosophical Fragments,*" IKC, vol. 7, pp. 33–46.
5 See C. Stephen Evans, "The Relevance of Historical Evidence for Christian Faith: A Critique of a Kierkegaardian View," in *Kierkegaard: On Faith and the Self,* chapter 9, pp. 151–68, (Waco, TX: Baylor University Press, 2006).
6 As he will do in *Concluding Unscientific Postscript.*
7 Known to some by its earlier translation, *The Concept of Dread.*
8 Rollo May, *The Meaning of Anxiety* (New York: W. W. Norton, 1950, rev. 1977); Erich Fromm, *Escape from Freedom* (New York: Henry Holt and Company, 1941).
9 Nineteen times in chapter 2 he refers to selfishness, especially, pp. 77–8.
10 Interestingly, Kierkegaard scratched out his own name as author, and substituted the pseudonym.
11 He actually refers to "thesis, antithesis, synthesis" and "mediation" (CA, p. 11).
12 Chapter 2, the polemic against the union of thought and being (CA, 78n); chapter 3 (CA, pp. 81–90).
13 He uses this word or variations on it 11 times in the space of 10 pages (CA, pp. 25–36).
14 His reading in Kant, Schelling, Hegel, Schleiermacher, is documented.
15 Kant does refer to a *metabasis eis allo genos* – see Ronald M. Green, *Kierkegaard and Kant: The Hidden Debt* (Albany, NY: SUNY Press, 1992).
16 The word "leap" (*spring*) occurs at least 57 times in the first four chapters (about 70 pages); until now the "leap" had been mentioned but not analysed.
17 It is interesting that the only definition Haufniensis gives of sin has to do with our temporality: "He sins who lives only in the moment as abstracted from the eternal" (CA, p. 93).
18 FT, p. 97.
19 See Ronald L. Hall, "Language and Freedom: Kierkegaard's Analysis of the Demonic," IKC, vol. 8, pp. 153–66.
20 He recollected a childhood "in the grip of an enormous depression" because he was "rigorously and earnestly brought up in Christianity, insanely brought

up, humanly speaking . . . a child attired, how insane, as a depressed old man" (PV, p. 79).

21 The book is presented as "Studies by Various Persons," none of whom is named at the outset, and the whole compilation and publication is credited to Hilarius Bookbinder.

22 JP, 1:67, p. 25.

23 Moreover, when he does refer to "stages" it does not apply to the standard tripartite division, but rather, "the stages are structured as follows: an esthetic-ethical life-view under illusion, with the dawning possibility of the religious; an ethical life-view that judges him; he relapses into himself" (SLW, p. 435).

24 See *Concluding Unscientific Postscript*.

further reading

Beabout, Gregory, *Freedom and Its Misuses: Kierkegaard on Anxiety and Despair* (Milwaukee, WI: Marquette University Press, 1996).

Daise, Benjamin, *Kierkegaard's Socratic Art* (Macon, GA: Mercer University Press, 1999).

Evans, C. Stephen, *Kierkegaard's "Fragments" and "Postscript": The Religious Philosophy of Johannes Climacus* (Atlantic Highlands, NJ: Humanities Press, 1983).

Evans, C. Stephen, *Passionate Reason: Making Sense of Kierkegaard's Philosophical Fragments* (Bloomington, IN: Indiana University Press, 1992).

Grøn, Arne, *The Concept of Anxiety in Søren Kierkegaard*, (Macon, GA: Mercer University Press, 2008).

IKC, CA, vol. 8 (1985).

IKC, PF/JC, vol. 7 (1994).

IKC, SLW, vol. 11 (2000).

IKC, TDIO, vol. 10 (2006).

KSY, 2001.

KSY, 2004.

Mercer, David E., *Kierkegaard's Living Room: The Relation Between Faith and History in Philosophical Fragments* (Montreal: McGill-Queen's University Press, 2001).

Nielsen, H. A., *Where the Passion Is: A Reading of Kierkegaard's Philosophical Fragments* (Tallahassee: Florida State University Press, 1987).

Roberts, Robert, *Faith, Reason, and History: Rethinking Kierkegaard's Philosophical Fragments* (Macon, GA: Mercer University Press, 1986).

fragments, concept of anxiety, discourses

chapter 5

Concluding Unscientific Postscript and *Two Ages*

I *Concluding Unscientific Postscript to Philosophical Fragments*

About two years after the publication of *Philosophical Fragments*, a second book authored by Johannes Climacus appeared (February 27, 1846).[1] The full title reflected both its great length and his delight in being provocative – *Concluding Unscientific Postscript to Philosophical Fragments. A Mimical-Pathetical-Dialectical Compilation. An Existential Contribution.* Since it is a "postscript" to the earlier book, it presumably will function in the way a "P.S." appended to the letter one has just written adds something one feels was left out and still needed to be said. We will see that this postscript not only develops important elements in *Fragments*, but also adds a new and crucial supplement.

Despite its length this book has become more popular than one could have predicted from the few copies that were sold in Kierkegaard's lifetime. Probably the main reason for the book's popularity is that it explicitly announces its concern with "what it means to live as a human being" (CUP, 256) and what it means that "the knower is an existing person" (196). This gives the book an incredibly broad appeal, one that allows it to be relevant in a pluralistic age. Climacus attempts a retrieval of classical philosophy's concern with questions of the good life: "Greek philosophy," he says, knew what it meant to exist (122), whereas people in our day "have entirely forgotten what it means *to exist* and what *inwardness* is" (242). Although Climacus's ultimate concern is with what it means to "become a Christian" (617), there is much of value in the book for those whose main concern is not Christianity as such, but rather the exploration of ethical and religious "subjectivity" and the polemic against intellectual abstraction. His evaluation of the ethical and the religious expands the audience of *Postscript*. For him, "the ethical is and remains the highest task assigned to every human being" (151). Moreover, the understanding of God in the bulk of *Postscript* is a historically unrestricted notion tied to ethical subjectivity: for example, Climacus writes that "freedom, that is the wonderful lamp. When a person rubs it with ethical passion, God comes into existence for him" (138). So, when he writes that "It is really the God-relationship that makes a human being a human being" (244), it must be remembered that "God is not something external, but is the infinite itself" (162). Thus, even those who find no use for the notion of a paradoxical God-Man may resonate with Climacus's resolute refusal to think of God as an object (even the greatest object) and with his emphasis on "the infinite."

Postscript is the site of the development of many familiar "Kierkegaardian" themes, and it is also the place where Kierkegaard puts his methodology front and center. One good example of this is found in what is probably Kierkegaard's most anthologized selection (the chapter provocatively entitled "Truth is Subjectivity"), namely, the passage about the passionate pagan. He writes: "If someone who lives in the midst of Christianity enters, with knowledge of the true idea of God, the house of God, the house of the true God, and prays, but prays in untruth, and if someone lives in an idolatrous land but prays with all the passion of infinity, although his eyes are resting upon the image of an idol – where, then, is there more truth?" (CUP, 201). In this passage, Climacus illustrates a contrast between a subjective approach to truth and an objective approach to truth, between a "how" and a "what," and his conclusion is that "the one prays in truth to God although he is worshiping an idol; the other prays in untruth to the true God and is therefore in truth worshiping an idol" (201). The implication that the passionate pagan is praying "in truth," as opposed to the indifferent Christian who is actually worshiping an idol gains Climacus as many enemies as it does fans, and for opposite reasons. On the one hand, it puts in question any simple affirmation of the superiority of Christianity. On the other hand, what some see as tolerance and a worthy appreciation of passion in life as opposed to rote-worship, others see as endorsing relativism and arbitrary irrationalism.

This famous passage illustrates the general way the book is crafted by its author to expose the instability of many commonly held assumptions. Climacus saw the age in which he lived as one that thought it knew it all – they were all Christians (because they had been baptized in the state church) and therefore they had "the truth," a truth of which non-Christians were deprived. Their smug security needed to be threatened because it obscured for them the fact that they "have forgotten what it means *to exist*, and what *inwardness* is" (CUP, 249). And Climacus reveals his own awareness of the need for careful crafting of this challenge – "this must not on any account be done didactically" (249). For Climacus, "what it means to exist humanly" must be understood before anyone can understand "what it means to exist religiously"

(249) – and it is counterproductive to preach such things to people. Aware that the problem is not a lack of knowledge, he writes *Postscript* with passion and satire that witness to his conviction that the best way to communicate is through a "mixture of jest and earnestness that makes it impossible for a third person to know definitely which is which – unless the third person knows it by himself" (69). As Climacus notes midway through the book – "with regard to something in which the individual person has only himself to deal with, the most one person can do for another is to unsettle him" (387).

One of his own images illustrates the way in which he purports to unsettle the age: he presents a picture of someone and asks a pointed question. For example, he asks: "When a man has filled his mouth so full of food that for this reason he cannot eat and it must end with his dying of hunger" (CUP, 275n), what is the way to help him? Is it by "stuffing his mouth even more or, instead, in taking a little away so that he can eat?" This is a provocative image and the goal is to get the reader to see that what seems to be a ridiculously obvious answer has troubling implications. That is, the answer is to take something out of his mouth, and the extrapolation is that when people are so full of "knowledge" that they cannot digest or appropriate any of it, when they are so sure they know what it is to be Christian that it becomes a passionless matter of course, "the art of being able to *communicate* becomes the art of being able *to take away* or to trick something away from someone" (275n). A communicator takes away someone's knowledge when he "takes a portion of the copious knowledge that the very knowledgeable man knows and communicates it to him in a form that makes it strange to him" (275n). Here Climacus guides the reader by letting her in on one of his strategies – namely, to make the familiar "strange." The reader is asked to come up with the solution to the stuffed mouth that is starving, and then see that it must be applied to herself. Such indirection is a means of unsettling the reader because it puts before the reader a challenge to something she thinks is obvious – in this case, what "truth" is and how one gets it.

A An overview

The epigram, the preface, and the introduction, are full of advice by the author, Climacus, about how to read the book. The brief preface is an obituary for an earlier book – it is an expression of gratitude for the "unnoticed" (CUP, 5) passing of *Fragments*. It is a humorous and ironic preface by an author who expresses his gratitude for being ignored and his fear of admirers. Although Climacus will only explicitly call himself a "humorist" hundreds of pages later (483), this preface, and everything that comes after it, will have prepared us for the announcement.

The question that motivates the book is posed in the introduction in two ways, both of which raise some questions. The first is as follows: "I, Johannes Climacus, born and bred in this city and now thirty years old, an ordinary human being like most folk, assume that a highest good, called an eternal happiness, awaits me just as it awaits a housemaid and a professor. I have heard that Christianity is one's prerequisite for this good. I now ask how I may enter into relation to this doctrine" (CUP, 15–16). On the last page of the introduction, he asks, "How can I, Johannes Climacus, share in the happiness that Christianity promises?" (17). Indeed, the very formulations of the question make us wonder. For example, should one be interested in one's relation "to a doctrine" (as in the first formulation) or one's relation to God? Might a desire to share in the happiness Christianity offers (as in the second formulation) reveal a self-serving prudential interest? But what is even more striking is the context in which Climacus places these questions. The first formulation of the question is immediately prefaced by the claim that he is asking the question while using himself "in an imaginatively constructing way [*experimenterende*]" (15) and it is soon followed by the admission that "I am merely presenting the question" (16).

Climacus has remarkably created an inquirer who by his own behavior raises for us the question of how to inquire. Is Climacus himself "infinitely, personally, impassionedly interested" when he poses his question, when he insists: "So I prefer to remain where I am, with my infinite interest, with the issue, with the possibility" because it is "certainly impossible" that a person who has lost his "infinite concern" for it "can become eternally happy" (CUP, 16)? Has Climacus reached the point where he asks the question in the medium in which it can be answered – in "infinite interest"? Or, is this preference to "remain" where he is the mark, not of passionate seeking, but rather, of someone who knows the truth about gaining truth, but simply prefers to stay where he is, turning away from the work it involves? Is the "possibility" he remains with a disinterested possibility? Or is he precisely where one must be in order to genuinely seek the Christian religious?

Climacus puts himself at one remove from any question whether he is interested or disinterested because any evidence of his interest is still within the confines of an imaginative construction. Indeed, the book ends with Climacus's reminder that it is an imaginary construction and with a different formulation of the motivating question. He writes that "in the isolation of the imaginary construction, the whole book is about myself, simply and solely about myself," and he formulates the question a third and final time: "I, Johannes Climacus, now thirty years old, born in Copenhagen, a plain, ordinary human being like most people, have heard it said that there is a highest good in store that is called an eternal happiness, and that Christianity conditions this upon a person's relation to it. I now ask: How do I become a Christian?" (CUP, 617). This question, he says, "is indeed the content of the book" (618), but it is still unclear what we are to make of the way Climacus asks this question. Is the shift to "How do I become a Christian?" decisive? But this question remains within the confines of an imaginary construction.

Part one consists of a very brief look at what Climacus calls "The Objective Issue of the Truth of Christianity." The discussion is not about the objective truth of Christianity, however, because "Christianity cannot be observed objectively" (CUP, 57), but is rather a polemic against an objective approach to the truth of Christianity. Whereas *Fragments* had pitted Socrates against a non-Socratic (thinly disguised Christian) alternative, here Climacus endorses "the Socratic secret" that inwardness is more valuable than objectivity (38). Here he pits Socrates against "the Hegelian notion that the outer is the inner and the inner is the outer" (54) – this is because "spirit is inwardness; inwardness is subjectivity" (33) which "cannot be observed objectively at all" (54). In other words, the question of the relation(s) between inner and outer, which has been imbedded in all the works thus far, takes the form of the relation(s) between subjectivity and objectivity.

Climacus explicitly puts the Hegelian category of "mediation" on his agenda because he thinks that it precludes the need for subjective decision, since it is part of a continuous movement without a decisive break (without a break for decision) (CUP, 33). Christianity, by contrast, is a matter of "decision," and "all essential decision is rooted in subjectivity" (33). This is the beginning of Climacus's continued engagement with the problem of Hegelian "mediation," and one of the most interesting things that happens in *Postscript* is the way in which we are repeatedly faced with criticisms of mediation made in the name of categories that resemble mediation. Much of the work of the book is the work of distinguishing Climacus's alternatives to mediation (namely, dialectic and joining-together) from the form of mediation he criticizes (synthesis, both-and). Already we see that Climacus's disagreement with Hegel about "mediation" does not imply the rejection of another category that sounds very Hegelian, the category of "dialectic." For Climacus, only an appreciation of the "dialectical" can prevent "zealotism" or fanaticism (35n):

> even the most certain of all, a revelation, *eo ipso* [precisely thereby] becomes dialectical when I am to appropriate it; even the most fixed of all, an infinite negative resolution, which is the individuality's infinite form of God's being within him, promptly becomes dialectical. As soon as I take away the dialectical, I am superstitious and defraud God of the moment's strenuous acquisition of what was once acquired. (35n)

Climacus insists that "every boundary that wants to exclude the dialectical is *eo ipso* superstition" (44), and that "dialectic" is indispensable (35, 44, 45n), because "God is negatively present in the subjectivity" (53). In sum, although he will later contrast Hegel's dialectic with a Greek "existence-dialectic" (309), he has an appreciation of at least one meaning of "dialectic" for Hegel – namely, as Hegel writes in his *Logic*, dialectic is an "*immanent* transcending, in which the one-sidedness and restrictedness of the determinations of the understanding displays itself as what it is, i.e., as their negation."[2] Climacus assumes the importance of this kind of back and forth, the relevance of negativity, and the avoidance of one-sidedness. Dialectic is relevant to Christianity because there is "no direct and immediate transition to Christianity" (49) – but ironically, this is also precisely the reason that "mediation" is irrelevant to it.

When Climacus turns to part two, "The Subjective Issue, The Subjective Individual's relation to the Truth of Christianity, or becoming a Christian," he begins the lengthy "existential contribution" (alluded to in the subtitle) that is the heart of the book. One of the central categories in part two will be that of "appropriation," and it is worth noting right now that the similarity of the words makes it easy for a reader to confuse the "appropriation" process essential to subjectivity with the "approximation" process that was highlighted as part of objectivity.[3] The subjective issue is essentially the "Socratic wisdom" (CUP, 204), and for this reason it becomes necessary to distinguish between Socrates and Plato, and to make clear that Socrates had not been done justice to in *Fragments* (206n).

Insofar as part two was presented in the introduction as the "renewed attempt" or the "new approach" to the issue of *Fragments*, it seems perfectly in order that this lengthy part, the bulk of the book, serves as a postscript to *Fragments* precisely by supplementing the sketchy treatment of Socratic subjectivity in *Fragments*. The bulk of the *Fragments* explored the non-Socratic account of faith whereas the Socratic version of subjectivity was presented in very short compass – a few pages sketched out the formal position on the immanence of truth and presented a very minimalist picture of inwardness and subjective paradox. This postscript will take a step back to examine more fully the Socratic account before it takes two steps forward to look again at the distinctively Christian account. But it is probably more accurate to say that Climacus takes two steps back – and lingers. Climacus undertakes a total revision of the Socratic position, which he now proposes to show in its richness and depth (in contrast to Platonic and Hegelian speculative philosophy). This lengthy presentation of the possibilities of Socratic inwardness is perhaps also attributable to the fact that Kierkegaard saw this as a conclusion to his authorship – i.e., in his purported last word, he needed to give generous credit to an achievement (human subjectivity) that he now conceded was "so strenuous for a human being that there is always a sufficient task in it" (CUP, 557).

The bulk of over 550 pages in part two, all on "the subjective issue," means we need to find a way to make it manageable. There are several fine commentaries on *Postscript* that consider it in detail,[4] and there are undoubtedly lots of ways to divide up part two for purposes of analysis. My own sense is that for our introductory purposes part two, "The Subjective Issue," can fruitfully be divided as follows. The first division explores in five chapters the generic nature of subjectivity – what it means to exist in general. The second division begins with chapter 4 of section 2, taking up the distinctively Christian issue of whether an eternal happiness can be built on historical knowledge. This explores the character of religious existence, developing the earlier Climacan contrast in *Fragments* between Socratic (or immanent) religiousness and non-Socratic (doubly paradoxical) religiousness; here they are called "religiousness A" and "religiousness B," and here the formal structure of non-Socratic religiousness is fleshed out through a much more developed account of "pathos" in relation to "dialectic." In sum, the part of the book that specifically addresses the distinctively Christian religiousness is the shortest part of all, which is explained by Climacus's suggestion that he had already treated it in *Fragments* (CUP, 561).

B Indirect communication and appropriation

Section 1, "Something About Lessing," is composed of two chapters that appear slight compared to the magnitude of section two, and they appear indirect since they refer to the eighteenth-century German philosopher, G. E. Lessing. But they serve two crucial functions for the remainder of the book. First, they provide a cautionary parenthesis around everything to follow, and second, they articulate four theses that will be played and replayed throughout the text. Section 2 will prove to be a progressive backtracking and retrieving and redeveloping of these four theses.

The first chapter is a deeply ironic account of the difficulty, the "knotty difficulty" (CUP, 65), of learning from someone how not to appeal to her or him. Here Climacus expresses a "debt of gratitude" to Lessing, while describing Lessing as an author who deliberately tried to preclude anyone from having a debt to him. Climacus details a conflict between a desire and its mode of fulfillment: the desire is to appeal to Lessing, whose thought seems in many ways congenial with his own, resonating with it in a variety of ways, while at the same time learning from Lessing that he should not appeal to Lessing. Lessing stands in for Climacus; Climacus uses him to examine the difficult character of his own authorship. How do you *teach* someone not to appeal to you? How do you *teach* someone to be autonomous, to "go his own way" (277)?

How do you *teach* another to be free (74, 277)? How do *you* teach *another* the indispensability of being alone with the truth? How do *you* teach *another* that the God-relationship is only between a single person and God; how do *you* teach *another* that God "can never become a third party" (66)? This brief expression of gratitude thus amounts to a strong caution to the reader against appealing to Climacus, taking him as an authority. The caution becomes a set of parentheses into which everything to follow in the entire book is placed.

The next chapter advances four "possible and actual theses by Lessing." The two theses that are possibly attributable to Lessing are (a) "The subjective existing thinker is aware of the dialectic of communication" and (b) "In his existence-relation to the truth, the existing subjective thinker is just as negative as positive, has just as much of the comic as he essentially has of pathos, and is continually in a process of becoming, that is, striving." These are followed by two theses actually historically attributable to Lessing: namely, (c) Lessing said that "contingent historical truths can never become a demonstration of eternal truths of reason, also that the transition whereby one will build an eternal truth on historical reports is a leap," and (d) Lessing said: "If God held all truth enclosed in his right hand, and in his left hand the one and only ever-striving drive for truth, even with the corollary of erring forever and ever, and if he were to say to me: Choose! – I would humbly fall down to him at his left hand and say: Father, give! Pure truth is indeed only for you alone!" (72–125)

Climacus's peculiar "debt that is no debt" mostly concerns Lessing's appreciation of an issue that is central to Kierkegaard's entire authorship – namely, the "dialectic of communication" of subjectivity or inwardness. Climacus insists that "objective thinking" has a legitimate domain: namely, that where the content of the communication can be completed and encapsulated, "direct communication" is "within its rights" (CUP, 76n). But where one is trying to communicate "subjectivity" or "inwardness," the main point is the appropriation and in that case the communicator is trying not only to express her thought in words, but at the same time to communicate her own relation to what she says.

Climacus tries to unsettle the reader's comfortable assumption that communication is unproblematical, to disabuse the reader of the simplistic assumption that all communication is the same. As if we just need to say it! One of Climacus's main strategies in the text is the simple but profound one of asking questions. In this case he asks the reader quite straightforwardly: Suppose someone wanted to communicate that "truth is inwardness," that "objectively there is no truth, but the appropriation is the truth" (CUP, 77), how could they achieve this? Or suppose they wanted to communicate that "the way is the truth, that is, that the truth is only in the becoming, in the process of appropriation" or that "all receiving is a producing" (78). Where the message is not "the result" (73, 78) but rather the importance of the appropriation or the process or the becoming, the message cannot be communicated directly. To present it as a "result" is to cancel it out (75, 77). In other words, how can the words, which are necessarily in the form of a completed "result," communicate the importance of the striving? How can one communicate that truth exists only insofar as it is appropriated – since the presentation of the truth in words will mislead the reader into taking it as a result. How can something in the form of the "universal" represent the need for aloneness with the truth? Are not words about passion, even words of passion, always an abstraction? So how could a book communicate that the book's message has to be appropriated passionately? In other words, the reader has to be made to experience a difficulty where before he had none.

"Double-reflection" (CUP, 73, 75) is a reflexive reflection – the communicator reflects something and is reflected back into herself. Words are an inevitably necessary "first reflection" – an expression or externalization of a thought in public language – but the concerns of becoming a human being, an existing subject, require a "second reflection," namely, the "second reflection . . . [that] renders the existing communicator's own relation to the idea" (76). The "first reflection" will directly communicate something (since it is in the form of a language we understand), but not what is most crucial to the communicator. Bringing us quickly back to earth from this philosophical talk of "double-reflection," Climacus suggests that indirect communication is the communication of what is "essentially a secret" (79). Where the "essential content" of a message is a "secret," the secret may seem to be directly communicated, but is only understood by one who is in a certain state. You can literally tell someone a secret they do not understand because they are not in the right condition for appreciating it. They can "know the secret" without truly knowing the secret.

In sum, the necessity of indirect communication is presented in this section as a function of two difficulties. First, the agent is always in a process of becoming (73–74n, 277) – so, how can one communicate what one does not have completely or is not yet fully? Second, the essence of truth lies in the appropriation of truth – so, how can one communicate what one is inwardly?

Communication as a reflection of inwardness is another site for exploring the tension between inner and outer. Climacus's emblem for this problem of communication is a striking one – imagine trying "to paint a picture of Mars in the armor that makes him invisible" (CUP, 79n). He later repeats – word for word – this paradoxical image of the difficulty, highlighting how "the point is the invisibility" (174). The difficulty of directly communicating passion or becoming is parallel to that of painting Mars in the armor that made Mars invisible – we fail if we paint the armor but we also fail if we refuse to paint at all. The task is a difficult one, again involving the art of indirection. The most one is capable of is "artistically, maieutically helping another person negatively to the same view" (80). The criterion of learning is the striving that follows – the learning lies in the earnestness of going on – but the mechanism of that maieutic is the "reciprocity between jest and earnestness" (71).

The second thesis possibly attributable to Lessing is explored in terms of the "process of becoming" (CUP, 80), which expresses itself as a "prodigious contradiction" (82) – the "synthesis" of negativity and positivity, of comic and pathos. The importance of the "dialectic" of existence – the way in which each of us is a contradiction that has to be lived, rather than resolved – is affirmed. The third and fourth theses focus on a detailed discussion of the "leap"[5] and the importance of "continued striving."

Although section 1 was an indirect foray via Lessing, the four theses expounded set the stage and anticipate all the succeeding discussions of subjectivity in section 2. Moreover, section 1 can also be seen as a development of the statement of Christianity in embryo in the introduction: the leap, the rejection of approximation, and the importance of passion. Already we can see the beginning of a pattern that I suggest will continue in the book. There is a repeated circling back, again and again – a progression in which something is presented first concisely in very short compass and then later retrieved and taken up again for a wider or deeper coverage, and that coverage is then retrieved and taken up again for even deeper coverage. Backtracking and ever-widening circles of coverage pull into a tight unity what at first seems to be a grandiose verbal indulgence. But the effort it takes to grasp the unity is worth it – to paraphrase T. S. Eliot, in the end we come to the beginning and know the place for the first time.

C Subjectivity and truth

Section 2 ("The Subjective Issue, or How Subjectivity Must be Constituted in Order that the Issue Can be Manifest to it") begins with three chapters: chapter 1, "Becoming Subjective"; chapter 2, "Subjective Truth, Inwardness; Truth is Subjectivity"; chapter 3, "Actual Subjectivity, Ethical Subjectivity; the Subjective Thinker." All three chapters will recur continually but indirectly to the four theses found in the section on Lessing, expanding on the dialectic of communication and the dialectic of existence. Their titles suggest a likelihood of overlapping concerns, but we know that Climacus admired the gymnastic dialectical ability of Lessing to produce and alter and produce "the same and yet not the same" (CUP, 68), so we should look for something "not the same" in these chapters. As a rough approximation, I suggest that chapter 1 focuses on subjectivity as the ethical; chapter 2 focuses on subjectivity as truth; chapter 3 focuses on subjectivity as the concrete paradox of existence.

Chapter 1 is a prolonged tribute to the "infinite validity of the ethical" (CUP, 143). It begins by claiming that an understanding of subjectivity is only found in the activity of *becoming* subjective – subjectivity is a "task" (130), "the highest task" that we have (133, 158, 159, 163–4), and a task for a lifetime (163, 179). Moreover, that task is identical with becoming ethical: "The ethical is and remains the highest task assigned to every human being" (151). Climacus affirms that "the development of subjectivity consists precisely in this, that he, acting, works through himself in his thinking about his own existence, consequently that he actually thinks what is thought by actualizing it" (169). He illustrates this by giving four examples of what he had earlier called a "doubly-reflected subjective thinking" (79) – four questions that must be appropriated subjectively: namely, what it means to die, what it means to be immortal, what it means to thank God, and what it means to marry (171–80). These are questions that cannot be asked objectively – or rather, when they are asked objectively, they lose their deepest meaning. To try to pose these essentially subjective questions in an objective manner, he says (alluding again to his earlier example) is to try to "paint Mars in the armor that makes him invisible" (174). Just as one cannot become a lover objectively (132), so Christianity can only be understood subjectively – objectively it does not exist (130).

One implication of the subjectivity of the ethical is the emphasis on the "single individual": "each individual actually and essentially comprehends the ethical only in himself" (CUP, 155). Climacus (later acknowledging the danger of "acosmism" or withdrawal from the world (341), claims here that the emphasis on individuality fosters community: the "ethical is the eternal drawing of breath and in the midst of solitude the reconciling fellowship with every human being" (152). Ethics is "infinitely concrete" (155) and supports "reconciling fellowship" because "every subject becomes *for himself* exactly the opposite of some such thing in general" (167), and because it militates against the loss of individual responsibility that seems to follow from a Hegelian view of world history.

Despite its similar sounding title, chapter 2 does more than repeat chapter 1 – the approach to subjectivity now assumes a new focus on "truth." This chapter is a perfect example of the way in which Climacus is indirectly trying to loosen the grip that certain pictures of truth and knowledge have on us. The picture of truth as "correctness" as well as the assumption that truth comes only in the form of "objective" knowledge hold us in thrall, and, as every therapist knows, it is counter-productive to simply challenge the patient directly. Climacus is a master at using simple examples to make profound points. For example, he wants to make the point that "the objective truth as such does not at all decide that the one stating it is sensible" (CUP, 194). But simply saying that will insure that it is taken for granted or summarily dismissed – the alternative is to present a picture and then ask the reader to decide what is wrong with this picture. He puts forth a story of a patient who has escaped from a "madhouse" and wants to forestall the possibility that he would be recognized and taken back when he reached the city. His goal was to convince everyone of his sanity and he assumed that he could do this best "by the objective truth" of what he said (195). On arriving at the capital city, he visits a friend of his: "he wants to convince him that he is not lunatic and therefore paces up and down the floor and continually says, 'Boom! The earth is round!'" That is, Climacus lays out this story of "the man who hopes to prove that he is not lunatic by stating a truth universally accepted and universally regarded as objective" (195) and implicitly asks "What is wrong with this picture?" The obvious answer he expects is that "the patient was not yet cured," but the important thing is to get the reader to see why. Once we locate where the problem is not – it is not a problem with the objective truth of the lunatic's statement – we come to see new possibilities.

But having distinguished the "what" and the "how," and having gotten the reader to judge that the "what" is not sufficient, Climacus leaves us struggling with different possibilities of their relation. One possibility is that the "how" is sufficient – but even as he proposes that "the *how* of the truth is precisely the truth" (CUP, 323), he alerts us that unlimited passion is not sufficient (194n). Another possibility is that the "how" and "what" are complementary, but even this proposal is presented in such a form that the reader must stop and ponder: "Just as important as the truth, and of the two the even more important one, is the mode in which the truth is accepted" (247). And what is the difference, if any, between the claim that "Truth is Subjectivity" (which is found in the chapter title) and the claim that "Subjectivity is truth" (a claim he makes repeatedly in the chapter (203, 207, 213)[6] – is it to get the reader to wonder whether what is at stake, after all, is the second version, that not all truth is subjectivity, but that he refers only to a certain class of truths. He calls the reader's attention to his claim about "essential knowing" (197), that "only ethical and ethical-religious knowing is essential knowing" (198), by repeating in a footnote "that what is being discussed here is essential truth, or the truth that is related essentially to existence, and that it is specifically in order to clarify it as inwardness or as subjectivity that the contrast is pointed out" (199n). So the emphasis on the participatory nature of subjectivity, as opposed to the observational status of objectivity, is not put forth as covering all truth. He will go on to make this point more sharply: truth is not something you can have, like an apple; "the truth is supposed to be the truth in which to exist" (310). The importance of indirect communication, already detailed in the section on Lessing, is brought to bear specifically on his project. Climacus realized "the form of communication" (249) that would be necessary – namely, that "if I wanted to communicate anything about this, the main point must be that my presentation would be made in an *indirect* form" (242), not "didactically" (249).

The new accent brought in by chapter 2 is that although subjectivity is truth, there is also a perspective from which subjectivity is untruth. He writes: "It cannot be expressed more inwardly that subjectivity is truth than when subjectivity is at first untruth, and yet subjectivity is truth" (CUP, 213). This bizarre formulation provokes the reader to figure out what could possibly be at stake. One way to reconcile these perspectives is as follows: when subjectivity is opposed to objectivity, then Socratic subjectivity is truth (206–7), but when subjectivity is opposed to a revelation or breakthrough from outside (or when sin is acknowledged) then Socratic subjectivity remains untruth. It is only when subjectivity as untruth, convinced of its sinfulness, goes more deeply into subjectivity, by being thrust back by the repellent force of the Absolute Paradox, that we can say once again that subjectivity is truth (213).

Somewhat surprisingly, Climacus ends both these chapters with a peculiar autobiographical report. He concludes both discussions of the ethical task of subjective inquiry with the sentiment, "This almost sounds like earnestness" (CUP, 183, 234). Chapter 1 tells a story about how, about four years before, as an "outsider in literature," sitting with a cigar in Frederiksberg Gardens, Climacus decided to become an author (185). The account is marked by flippancy both in the suggestion that the decision was born of "indolence" (186, 187) and in the suggestion that it aimed at "entertainment" (187). The content of the decision at that point was simply that, not being able to make things easier, he would do what he could do – namely, "make something more difficult" (186), indeed, "make difficulties everywhere," a project he compares with providing someone with an "emetic" (187). This dispassionate and light-hearted account of the beginning of his writing contrasts sharply with the apparent earnestness of the preceding descriptions of passionate thinking about death, immortality, gratitude to God, and marriage. At the end of chapter 2 the authorial motivation is rendered more specific; however, in this second account, the jesting tone of the earlier account is replaced by the counterpoint of an apparently earnest motivation. Although he still attributes his decision to the result of "whim" (234) and boredom, he describes the further specification of his vocation in terms of what he calls "the most heartrending scene I have ever witnessed" (238) – a scene in a cemetery, in which an old man laments the death of his son in a serious conversation with his grandson. In response to overhearing this amazing conversation, Climacus "gained a more definite understanding of [his] own whimsical idea that [he] must try to make something difficult" (241): he now knows what he will make more difficult because the conversation he overheard revealed to him the "dubious relation between modern Christian speculative thought and Christianity" (241). He resolves to "find out where the misunderstanding between speculative thought and Christianity lies" (241) in such a way that it will make becoming a Christian difficult.

In apparently sincere distress over the fact that "because of much knowledge people have entirely forgotten what it means to *exist* and what *inwardness* is" (CUP, 242), he decides that in order to make becoming a Christian more difficult, he needs first to make existing and inwardness more difficult. But we should note that he is not making it more difficult to become a Christian, but rather he is making it difficult for someone to keep on thinking it is a simple matter of being baptized; moreover, he later qualifies this, saying that he is not making it more difficult than it really is (213, 381). These two accounts of his authorship illustrate the "dialectical reciprocity of jest and earnestness" (71) he had mentioned in relation to Lessing.

Chapter 3 brings us back full circle; it takes up everything that has preceded it and culminates in a picture of "The Subjective Thinker." This chapter places subjectivity in the new-yet-old perspective of the existing concrete human being as a "prodigious contradiction" (CUP, 350), a phrase Climacus had earlier used in explicating Lessing's second thesis (82). The notion of "paradox" emerged implicitly in Climacus's earlier claim that "truly to exist, that is, to permeate one's existence with consciousness, simultaneously to be eternal, *far beyond it*, as it were, and nevertheless *present in it* and nevertheless in a process of becoming – that is truly difficult" (308, my emphasis). His image of "what existing is like" was concrete: imagine "a man who wants to go somewhere as quickly as possible (and therefore was already in something of a passion) astride a horse that can hardly walk" (311). Eternity and temporality in tension: imagine being the driver of a carriage hitched to "Pegasus and an old nag," together (311). We are, in existence, paradoxical contradictions. Moreover, it is because existence is paradoxical that when existence is penetrated with reflection, it generates passion – "existence, if one becomes conscious of it, involves passion" (351).

The question that runs through the chapter – "Indeed, what is an individual existing human being?" (CUP, 355) – cannot be answered abstractly, because we do not live in the "fantastic medium: pure being" (304). We are supposed to exist, not to abstract from existence (315).[7] The polemic against abstraction is not a polemic against thinking (314). That is, "existence is not thoughtless, but in existence thought is in an alien medium" (332). The goal is "concrete thinking" (332), since "the one who is thinking is existing" (309). The subjective thinker has the "task of understanding the abstract concretely" (352). Although "existence separates the ideal identity of thinking and being" (330), they are both required. The "task" of every individual is "to become a whole human being" (346). It is a "defect" to make "one-sidedness into the whole" (349); both "one-sidedness" and an "abstract many-sidedness" are defective – the aim is to gain concreteness in our many-sidedness. We must exist in a variety of dimensions simultaneously, coordinately – "in existence, the important thing is that all elements are present simultaneously" (346).

The implication of becoming whole, given that we are a paradoxical contradiction, involves the need "to understand extreme *opposites together* and, existing, to understand oneself in them" (354, my emphasis). In abstraction things can be understood successively or combined in thought, but to understand himself the existing individual has to hold opposites in combination in concrete existence – that is, not mediating or resolving them into a synthesis, but maintaining them as distinctive elements with a tension between them. The subjective thinker must become an "existing work of art" (303); "the subjective thinker's form, the form of his communication, is his style. His form must be just as manifold as are the opposites that he *holds together*" (357, my emphasis). The dialectic of indirect communication parallels the dialectic of existence. In sum, "To exist is an art. The subjective thinker is esthetic enough for his life to have esthetic content, ethical enough to regulate it, dialectical enough in thinking to master it" (351).

In examining the "task," "form," and "style" of "the subjective thinker" (CUP, 349), it is interesting that Climacus begins, not with the usual trio of thinking, feeling, acting, but with another trio, when he writes: "With respect to existence, thinking is not at all superior to imagination and feeling but is coordinate" (346–7). The general character of the ethical task is not to elevate either thinking or feeling or imagination at the expense of one of them – no, "the task is equality, contemporaneity, and the medium in which they are united is *existing*" (348). In sum, "For a subjective thinker, imagination, feeling, and dialectics in impassioned existence-inwardness are required. . . . [I]t is impossible to think about existence without becoming passionate, inasmuch as existing is a prodigious contradiction" (350). This suggests a role for the imagination in the ethical. To exist in subjectivity is to "see," to "be," to "think" opposites *together* – this paradoxical task cannot even be addressed (much less achieved) without a particular appeal to the activity of imagination in holding opposites in tension. Climacus had, in fact, noted this earlier with respect to the momentary realization of the unity of finite and infinite which generates "passion": "In passion, the existing subject is infinitized in the eternity of imagination and yet is also most definitely himself" (197). Imagination is required for the exploration of our concreteness. What is concrete is what is non-finalized, in process: insofar as one is existing, then, one is inexhaustible, and this open-endedness requires the impulse of imagination to go beyond what is at any time actually given, to the "not yet."

Climacus also highlights imagination indirectly by providing another perspective on possibility, detailing how possibility can play a role in ethical development. Earlier he had contrasted the ways in which "possibility is superior to actuality and actuality is superior to possibility" (CUP, 318) – this is a good example of the strategy of putting forth a provocative apparent contradiction in the hope that the reader will be forced to stop and engage with it. In this case, the contradiction is resolvable by noting the difference in the arenas in which each claim applies – that is, esthetically and intellectually possibility may be superior to actuality but ethically actuality is superior to possibility. Now, however, he gives us another perspective on possibility in relation to ethics, a way in which possibility can pose a challenge. Possibility is the mode in which the ethical presents a demand on us: "What is great with regard to the universal must therefore not be presented as an object for admiration, but as a *requirement*. In the form of possibility, the presentation becomes a requirement" (358). Ethics consists in actualizing the possibility common to both the prototype and the observer (359). The importance of seeing a possibility as a demand (i.e., imaginatively seeing-as) is also emphasized when he writes that "in asking ethically with regard to my own actuality, I am asking about its possibility, except that this possibility is not esthetically and intellectually disinterested but is a thought-actuality that is related to my own personal actuality – namely, that I am able to carry it out" (322–3). In other words, "ethically understood, if anything is able to stir up a person, it is possibility – when it ideally requires itself of a human being" (360). Climacus reveals a use of possibility as ethically upbuilding: instead of admiring another's ethical actuality, we see that actuality as a possibility for us, and one that has a claim on us.[8] Thus, despite his occasional disparagement of imagination as the "fairy-land of the imagination" (357), Climacus's view of ethical subjectivity involves a commitment to the positive and even indispensable role of imagination.

These first five chapters have all focused on generic human subjectivity. Climacus presents the next chapter (chapter 4, section 2) as if it will do something different. Its title ("The Issue in *Fragments*: How Can an Eternal Happiness Be Built on Historical Knowledge?") suggests that we are now going to relate back directly to *Fragments* and the issue of Christianity. And the first of its two divisions, division 1, does directly provide "Orientation in the Plan of *Fragments*" by means of three brief sections which challenge Hegelianism's interpretation of Christianity.

Postscript raises the question whether there is a difference between finding out "what Christianity is" and finding out if it is objectively true (CUP, 371), and it focuses on the former task. It also raises the question whether there is a difference between finding out "what Christianity is" and "becoming a Christian" (371). It answers in the affirmative because, on the one hand, since people do become Christians, there must be a period before one becomes a Christian in which one has "found out what Christianity is" (372), and, on the other hand, "to become a Christian then becomes the most terrible of all decisions in a person's life, since it is a matter of winning faith through despair and offense" (372). Climacus denies that one can "know what it is to be a Christian without being one" (372), and he contrasts "knowing what Christianity is" with "being a Christian" (384). In other words, Climacus purports to "know what Christianity is" (372) and to be able to provide an introduction to becoming a Christian without himself "being a Christian," "becoming a Christian," or even "know[ing] what it is to be a Christian" (372).

D The return to pathos again

Division 2 turns away from the "orientation" to *Fragments* and toward "the issue itself" – that is, the "pathos-filled and dialectical" "existence-issue" of relation to an eternal happiness (CUP, 385, 386). But if we were expecting to continue the treatment of Christianity explicitly, we are surprised to find a very long treatment of "pathos" (387–555) that seems to return us to the generic subjectivity that was treated before chapter 4. We are back again to the "existential pathos" (387) of "what it means to exist" (396). This discussion of pathos is the culmination of all the earlier attempts in *Postscript* to highlight "inwardness" and passion. While the earlier discussion of ethical subjectivity addressed the form of the subjective thinker or ethical subject, here we find incredible detail about the various deepening expressions of existential pathos.

Existential pathos is the "transformation" (CUP, 389) of one's life "in relation to an eternal happiness as the absolute good" (387) – "the pathos of the ethical is to act" (390). Subjectivity means immersing ourselves deeper and deeper into existence. The various expressions of pathos ("resignation," then "suffering," and finally "guilt") reveal deeper and deeper immersions into existence – deeper expressions of the task of avoiding abstraction and becoming a concrete subject.

The "initial" expression of existential pathos, "resignation," is an orientation of absolute "respect" appropriate to an absolute end; it is the willingness to reorient ourselves by resigning everything to its relative status in relation to the absolute end. Resignation involves a joining-together – "the task is to practice one's relation to one's absolute *telos* so that one continually has it within while continuing in the relative objectives of existence" (CUP, 408). The tension in this contradiction generates passion: one lives "in" relative ends but the absolute end is not exhausted in them (405); one is "not to leave the world" (406), but to "preserve the absolute choice in the finite" (411).

But this proposal prompts us to ask how this kind of joining-together can be distinguished from the "both-and of mediation" (CUP, 400) that Climacus "abhors" (406) – "a devil of a fellow who can *both-and* and has time for everything" (401). Climacus suggests that mediation performs a kind of leveling or reduction: "this both-and means that the absolute *telos* is on the same level with everything else" (401). Mediation wants to "include this *telos* among the others" (402), but the absolute end can never be "included" among our other ends (391, 393).

We are already in place when we take up our existential task, so the execution of our resignation in concrete renunciation involves suffering. Suffering is the "essential" expression of existential pathos – it is not an accidental accompaniment. This willingness to change our relation to relative ends, in our concrete situation of immediacy, amounts to a "dying to immediacy" (CUP, 526). Moreover, this understanding of suffering does not imply that we should want "misfortune," or that we should impose torment or penance on ourselves, because such muscular effort on our part would be antithetical to the acknowledgement of our complete dependence on God.[9]

But suffering is not the deepest we go into existence – we go deeper, into a "consciousness of guilt" which is the "decisive" expression for existential pathos (CUP, 527). Even as we try to begin the task of becoming subjective, we realize that we have already been relating to relative ends inappropriately – "a bad beginning" has already been made (526). This "bad beginning" is not just our condition of finitude or temporality – it is something for which we are responsible, but whose origin we cannot locate in time. It is the evidence of our "self-assertion" (528) – our tendency to want to deny that we are completely dependent on God. The notion of "joining together" weaves in and out of this section on guilt: the "totality of guilt comes into existence for the individual by joining his guilt, be it just one, be it utterly trivial, together with the relation to an eternal happiness" (529). In fact, "the joining together yields the qualitative category" (529): "all immersion in existence consists in *joining together*" (529–30); we need to comprehend "the requirement of existence: *to join together*" (531). The "existence-art" is to "join together" (535–6). But again our task is to see how this joining-together might be distinguished from the "both-and" of mediation.

In the discussion of existential "pathos" Climacus had already hinted that such pathos was "religious," and went so far as to contrast its "religiousness of hidden inwardness" with the "paradoxical religiousness, Christian religiousness" (534). Before moving on to a discussion of the paradoxical religiousness, he adds a very brief transitional section. As a kind of shorthand, he gives the name "Religiousness A" to the religiousness of hidden inwardness, and the name "Religiousness B" to Christianity (556). These pages are few but noteworthy, and may well be the centerpiece of the whole book because they are the site of the crucial claim he had neglected to make in *Fragments* about the richness and indispensability of Religiousness A to becoming a Christian.

Although Climacus's apparent goal is to contrast Religiousness A and Religiousness B quite starkly, he, in the process, offers a revealing assessment of Religiousness A's value in relation to Christianity (B). Climacus insists that "Religiousness A must first be present in the individual before there can be any consideration of becoming aware of the dialectical B" (CUP, 556), and that "if Religiousness A does not enter in as the *terminus a quo* [point from which] for the paradoxical religiousness, then Religiousness A is higher than B" (558). He reminds us that religiousness A is "by no means undialectical" (556). Religiousness A is characterized by infinite interest in "an eternal happiness (immortality and eternal life)" (559), so it is clear why it is pathos-filled. But it is also dialectical: that is, Religiousness A is an "inward deepening, which is dialectical"; there are in A "dialectical concentrations of inward deepening" (556) because it concerns an individual's "appropriation" of an eternal happiness (556) and there can be no certainty about this (397, 424, 455). Even in resignation, there is a "fear of error" that opens room for a "dialectical decision" (386). Religiousness A is already a "dialectic of inward deepening" precisely because it is not a "direct" relation to the absolute (560n). In sum, the qualification of individual appropriation of and infinite interest in what cannot be guaranteed is already dialectical. And this is undoubtedly why Climacus judges that "Religiousness A . . . is so strenuous for a human being that there is always a sufficient task in it" (557).

E The dialectical again

It is only after he has made these unusually strong claims for the value of the ethical-religious that Climacus goes on to the section on "The Dialectical," which is where he summarizes what we learned in *Fragments* about Christianity. The substantial priority Climacus gives to subjectivity and Religiousness A seems due to his own sense that it was important to insist on these as a necessary preliminary to the possibility of Religiousness B (Christianity).

Climacus's claim that "Religiousness A is not the *specifically* Christian religiousness" (CUP, 555, my emphasis) suggests that Religiousness A and Religiousness B are not parallel ways of being religious; they are not counterparts to each other. The "specifically Christian religiousness" (555) specifies or qualifies the eternal happiness (556). Religiousness B (the "paradoxical-religious") is the "final qualification of the religious" (554n); it is a specification of Religiousness A because "the specific for Christianity is the dialectical in second place" (559).

But none of this should obscure the qualitative difference between the religion of inward deepening and the religion of the Absolute Paradox. This is why Climacus goes on to explore the "dialectical in second place" (CUP, 559). Affirming the "qualitative dialectic of the absolute paradox" of Christianity (561),[10] this section on "The Dialectical" is "essentially what *Fragments* has dealt with," so he can be brief (561). In those brief pages, however, he fine-tunes the connection between the "dialectical" and the notion of the "crucifixion of the understanding" (564) and importantly qualifies the *Fragments'* notion of "the absurd." Believing against the understanding is a question of being deprived of the possibility of a retreat or "withdrawal" back into merely the eternal (572) – that is, the Absolute Paradox "annihilates a possibility" (581n). What is at stake is that Christianity requires that we lose "the last foothold of immanence" (569). To believe against the understanding means "to exist, situated at the edge of existence" (569).

Climacus's entire discussion of what it means to exist in Religiousness B highlights an appreciation of human beings as temporal being in the world. There is a double qualification of time, of the temporal, of history – in time there is a relation to the eternal in time. Our existence in time and our particularity is accentuated by being related to the eternal in time in an "individual" person. The dialectical has "additional qualifications" (CUP, 385) – namely, that "the subjective passion is to be joined together with something historical," without relinquishing the passion (576). Again, it is a question of a kind of joining-together – all of them, the ethical, Religiousness A, and Religiousness B, all involve a work that Climacus is at pains to distinguish from "mediation." The kinship of the Socratic with the eternal is broken through sin – one has to take history seriously. Religiousness A "does not base the relation to an eternal happiness upon one's existing but has the relation to an eternal happiness as the basis for the transformation of existence" (574). Christianity is pathos-filled because it involves "the passion in dialectically holding fast the distinction of incomprehensibility" (561); it will thereby generate a "new pathos" (555), indeed, "a sharpened pathos" (581) that expresses itself in the consciousness of sin, in the possibility of offense, and in painful sympathy (583–5).

One of the ironies of this "concluding" postscript is that Climacus has a hard time concluding. There are no less than three attempts at leave-taking. His "Conclusion" proper is a bit of an anti-climax. It begins: "The present work has made it difficult to become a Christian" (CUP, 587), but this is old news; already midway through the book he had emphasized the much more shocking claim that *"it is easier to become a Christian if I am not a Christian than to become a Christian if I am one"* (366). Following the conclusion, we find a leave-taking signed by Climacus, his "Understanding with the Reader." This is in some ways a fourth perspective on his authorship. In this appendix, signed by J. C., we hear again that he is a "humorist" (617) who writes for his own "enjoyment" (617, 621, 623). He writes that he "does not make himself out to be a Christian" (617, 619), but lest this be thought to allow that he might still be a Christian (albeit a modest one), we should remember that he has several times before stated clearly that he is not religious ("I am not a religious person but simply and solely a humorist" (501, see 511),[11] and "not" Christian (597, see 466). He is "an imaginatively constructing humorist" (619). The book is an "imaginary construction" in which he asks the question "How do I become a Christian?" (617). He is looking for a "teacher of the ambiguous art of thinking about existence and existing" (622).

Climacus presumably intends to be shocking when he suggests that the entire book is to be "revoked": "What I write contains the notice that everything is to be understood in such a way that it is revoked, that the book has not only an end but has a revocation to boot" (CUP, 619). But this is anti-climactic too since the notion of revocation has been introduced much earlier when he wrote that "the imaginary construction is the conscious, teasing revocation of the communication, which is always of importance to an existing person who writes for existing persons" (263). The "one who appeals to it [the book] has *eo ipso* misunderstood it" (618). Rather than appealing to the book, the reader must appropriate it and apply it to his own life, but "the application, when it is understood, is a revocation" of the book *as book* (567). The "revocation is the jest" (448, 448n), but this is in the service of earnestness.

This is followed by yet another leave-taking, entitled "A First and Last Explanation." This is literarily a most unusual document of five pages that are separated from *Postscript* proper by not being numbered and by being signed by S. Kierkegaard. It is personal, even making reference to his deceased father. S. Kierkegaard gives his own version of an understanding with the reader, about the nature of his authorship. He acknowledges that he has "responsibility" in "a legal and in a literary sense" for the pseudonymous authorship going from *Either – Or* to some articles in *The Fatherland*, but he insists that "in the pseudonymous books there is not a single word by me" and he disavows any "knowledge of their meaning except as a reader" (CUP, 626). He has an even more remote relation to these authors he has created than usual, because he allows them to take charge of their own prefaces and introductions.

He contrasts this relation to his pseudonymous books with his relation to his "upbuilding discourses," for he is "very literally and directly the author of . . . every word in them" (627). The pseudonymous authors have "the light, doubly reflected ideality of a poetically actual author" (628) whereas Kierkegaard has the role of "secretary, and quite ironically, the dialectically reduplicated author of the author or the authors" (627). His "distancing ideality" (628) represents the absolute indifference of S. Kierkegaard to the production, and all that is appropriate is a "forgetful remembrance" of him as indifferent to the authorship. He is not, he says, "an author in the usual sense," but is rather "one who has cooperated so that the pseudonyms could become authors" (628). In this way, "at a remove that is the distance of double-reflection, [he tries] once again to read through solo, if possible in a more inward way, the original text of individual human existence-relationships, the old familiar text handed down from the fathers" (629–30).

In sum, the supplement to *Fragments* elaborates the discussion of Socratic subjectivity in *Fragments* and in the process makes a new claim – that such pathos-filled and dialectical relation to an eternal happiness it itself a *sine qua non* for being aware of the Christian paradox. Socratic subjectivity, ethical actuality, is the task of a lifetime and has absolute validity as the relation to an eternal happiness (immortality and eternal life) that one can have outside Christianity – i.e., Religiousness A is enough of a task for a lifetime. If, as in Denmark, one is faced by the Absolute Paradox, this pathos is rendered decisively dialectical – but Christianity will always have a pathos-filled heart at its center.

II *A Literary Review: Two Ages*

In 1940, the English-speaking world was presented with a translation of one of Kierkegaard's writings, entitled *The Present Age*.[12] This, it turns out, was only the third part of a book commonly known as *Two Ages*, but the form of the book is better shown by the title under which Kierkegaard published it – namely, *A Literary Review*, with the subtitle *Two Ages*, "a Novel by the Author of 'A Story of Everyday Life'." Kierkegaard undertook to review the novel *Two Ages* soon after its publication (October 1845) because of his admiration for the earlier writing by the same anonymous author, but he set aside his draft of it in order to complete his *Postscript*. He began work on it again in the early months of 1846, publishing it on March 30, 1846.

This has long been an inspirational book of sorts. Although it is a critique of the particular age in which Kierkegaard lived, it has often been seen by later generations as eminently applicable to their own "present age." It is a work of social criticism masquerading as a literary review, and it focuses on ways in which the individual is "quantified" or, as we would say today, "commodified," the ways in which the press (or the media) form public opinion, and the ways in which "instant" communication and transportation affect our lives. What was symbolically true then has become literally true now – the citizen is "a spectator computing the problem" (TA, 79). In this book we find important statements of Kierkegaard's view of the normative relation between the part and the whole – the individual and the community, the particular and the general. It is also the site of another of Kierkegaard's attempts to negotiate the tension between immediacy and reflection.

After a brief "survey" of the novel, which in its two pictures of domestic life reflects the Age of Revolution (the late decades of the eighteenth century) and the Present Age (the first part of the nineteenth century), Kierkegaard offers "an esthetic interpretation" of the novel. The third section, "Conclusions from a Consideration of the Two Ages" serves basically as an occasion for Kierkegaard's own analysis of the characteristics of the age in which he lived – Denmark in the 1830s and 1840s. Writing in what has been called the "Golden Age" of Denmark, with its astounding renaissance of literature, the visual arts, and the sciences, Kierkegaard nevertheless worried about a social, cultural, and spiritual crisis. He was, at this point in time, part of a Danish "conservative mainstream" – he supported the monarchy; he was not advocating political change or democratic institutions. This need not mean that his critique was insipid – in fact scholars have compared *Two Ages* to the thought of Max Weber, Emile Durkheim, George Simmel, and even Marx.[13] In any case, although Kierkegaard did not advocate revolution in any external form, he hoped for a revolution from within, and echoed Climacus's claim in *Postscript* that the age is "essentially poverty-stricken ethically and is essentially a bankrupt generation" (CUP, 546, see also 363, 543). Kierkegaard was not unique in his concern about his age; others too decried the shortcomings of Danish society. But his critique has lasted and is popularly read today, whereas theirs are not – one can assume it has something of value worth exploring. What is clear is that *Two Ages* offers us his signed picture of his times, not as radical as it would later become, but still a challenge that may have import for our own time.

Kierkegaard undertakes a description of the novel's view of how the domestic life of each period reflects its context – the novel is a "reflexion" of each age (TA, 65, 112). The "age of revolution is essentially passionate" and all its traits (form, culture, propriety) flow from that foundation (61–8); most importantly, it was an age of action: "decision is the little magic word that existence respects" (66). The age was clearly a relative improvement on what preceded it.

The "present age," by contrast, is "essentially a *sensible, reflecting age*" (TA, 68), but its sensible reflection is "*devoid of passion, flaring up in superficial, short-lived enthusiasm and prudentially relaxing in indo-lence"* (68). Unlike the earlier "passion," tied to action and decision, the "reflection" that marks the present age is tied to "doing nothing" (69). In other words, reflection or thinking as such is not the problem – the problem is the age's "spinelessness" (67) in giving in to the "temptations of reflection" (77). The danger is the particular use of reflection to pro-vide "clever ways of avoiding decision" (76). The only force at work is the force of inertia – indeed, "not even a suicide these days does away with himself in desperation but deliberates on this step so long and so sensibly that he is strangled by calculation, making it a moot point whether or not he can really be called a suicide, inasmuch as it was in fact the deliberating that took his life" (69). The "suicide by means of premeditation" is found more commonly in the "stay-abed" who "has big dreams, then torpor, followed by a witty or ingenious inspiration to excuse staying in bed" (69). It is an "age of publicity, the age of mis-cellaneous announcements: nothing happens but still there is instant publicity" (70). Although there are "flashes of enthusiasm alternating with apathetic indolence" (74), reflection amounts to a "sort of slouch-ing, semi-somnolent, non-cessation" (80). It is, in sum, the opposite of self-awareness – it is "equivocating cowardice and vacillation" (83).

Kierkegaard's sociological analysis has an ethical motivation. He has an idea of the normative relation between the part and the whole: "when individuals (each one individually) are essentially and passionately related to an idea and together are essentially related to the same idea, the relation is optimal and normative. Individually the relation separates them (each one has himself for himself), and ideally it unites them" (TA, 62). When, however, people are not passionately related to an idea, either each one individually or together, reflection is used by people to turn inward in such a way that "gossip and rumor" (63) and "censorious envy" (82) fill the vacuum. Reflection leads to "ethical envy" (82), and the envy is "two-sided, a selfishness in the individual and then again the selfishness of associates toward him" (81). A perversion of inwardness occurs when people turn to each other, but with "suspicious, aggressive, leveling reciprocity" (63): "Envy in the process of *establishing* itself takes the form of *leveling*, and whereas a passionate age *accelerates*, *raises up and overthrows, elevates and debases*, a reflective apathetic age does the opposite, *it stifles and impedes, it levels*" (84). Leveling quantifies: it is a "mathematical, abstract enterprise" (84). Leveling is "abstraction's victory over individuals" (84), over "the individual" (86). Leveling is the negative version of equality, the distortion of equality – it is an abuse that confuses equality with the computing of numbers (85). In Kierkegaard's view, a troubling connection exists between procrastinating, apathetic reflection and cowardly, envious, leveling reflection.

Lack of passion leads to leveling, because it leads to a loss of individuality. Our passion, our enthusiasm, our interests, are what particularize us. The common fear of venturing reduces everyone to the lowest common "denominator" (TA, 96). Thus, whereas *Postscript* affirmed passionate ethical reflection and the subjective individual, the review of *Two Ages* is a warning against passionless reflection and the loss of the individual.

But Kierkegaard's protest against loss of individuality is ultimately in the service of community. The affirmation of the individual is the other side of the warning against the "idolized positive principle of sociality" (TA, 86) that amounts to "the herd" (62), the "crowd" (94), and "chatter" (97). It is not a warning against sociality as such. More specifically, what is put in question is "the public" – that "phantom" created by "the press," told what it thinks by "the press" (90–93). In an age of reflection, "the existence of a public creates no situation and no community" (91). What Kierkegaard rejects is a certain understanding of quantifiable and abstract "sociality" and "association" (106) composed of sheep who unthinkingly conform to "public opinion."

Two Ages is a book about intersubjective relation, or the lack or distortion of it. It is about walking the fine line between submergence in the group and selfish isolation from the group. In "the coiled springs of life-relationships," inwardness is lacking (TA, 78). The result is that "instead of the relation of inwardness another relation supervenes: the opposites do not relate to each other but stand, as it were, and carefully watch each other, *and this tension is actually the termination of the relation*" (78). Instead of relation, there is "inert cohesion" (78); the "tension of reflection" (81, 82) is not a vital dynamic tension, but rather, an "enervating tension" (80).

This book review is Kierkegaard's reflection on the reflection that is reflected in the novel. Despite cutting remarks, it is not an unrestrained diatribe. It targets a very specific misuse of reflection. A volume of essays on *Two Ages* published in 1984 by eminent Kierkegaard scholars begins with the editor's suggestion that "with the publication of this volume of essays on Kierkegaard's *Two Ages* a myth should die . . . The myth is to the effect that Kierkegaard presents his concept of the individual in a social and political vacuum."[14]

Here we do not see subjectivity as the point of departure for Christian religiousness (as we did in *Postscript*), rather we see that leveling can be the "point of departure" for religiousness (TA, 88). It can "be genuinely educative to live in an age of leveling" because it can constitute an "offense" (88), prompting a thorough reorientation. In a sense, the "crudeness" of a life without passion (62) and the "cruelty of abstraction" can expose "the vanity of the finite in itself" (108). Leveling is itself an evil, but a good can be drawn out of it, so long as there are people who are willing "in suffering to serve, to help indirectly" (109), people like Socrates who was an "authentic ironist" and a "hidden enthusiast" (81). The art of indirection must be employed to "unsettle" us (as Climacus suggested); in this way the alternative to debilitating, stagnating, and cowardly reflection will be seen to be "religious inwardness" (81).

In a sense, *Two Ages*, slight as it is, portends great things. It is a kind of originating spring flowing into two works that will appear in 1847. The first part of the *Discourses in Various Spirits* seems to follow naturally on *Two Ages*, perhaps because it was being worked on at the same time. Moreover, the practical import of his challenge to the authority of the "the crowd" is revealed in a note that Kierkegaard wrote in 1846, where his claim that "'the crowd' is untruth" (PV, 107) implies that "the crowd is unloving": that is, "*the neighbor* is the absolute true expression for human equality. If everyone in truth loved the neighbor as himself, then perfect human equality would be achieved unconditionally" (PV, 106, 111). The "crowd" sets the task of uncritical conformity as the means to "temporal and worldly advantage," but "the task is to love the neighbor" and "to love the neighbor is, of course, self-denial" (111). These are the threads that are taken up and elaborated in *Works of Love*.

notes

1 S. Kierkegaard presented himself as the editor.
2 G. W. F. Hegel, *The Encyclopedia Logic*, trans. T. F. Geraets, W. A. Suchting, and H. S. Harris (Indianapolis, IN: Hackett Publishing Co.), p. 128.
3 For example, "the truth is only in the becoming, in the process of appropriation" (CUP, p. 78) and "the contradiction is to base one's eternal happiness on an approximation" (CUP, p. 574).
4 See this chapter's further reading list.
5 In eight pages (CUP, pp. 98–106) the word "leap" (*Spring*) is found in almost every other sentence.
6 It is also found in CUP, pp. 278, 281, 282, 300, 313.
7 Climacus begins §1 "What It Means to Exist; Actuality," by explicitly referring to Hegel's *Logic* and criticizing "everything" Hegel says "about process and becoming" (CUP, pp. 301n, 307n).
8 Climacus's description appears continuous with Judge William's formulation of ethical transformation through the perception of actual and ideal self in tension, but Climacus makes the role of imagination in the process even more explicit than does Judge William.
9 The difficulty is to accept the demand that "with God [one is] capable of it" (CUP, p. 486).
10 This was against the background of a general "qualitative dialectic of the spheres" (CUP, p. 562).
11 This, however, seems at odds with his claim that he has his existence "within the boundaries of" Religiousness A (CUP, p. 557).

12 Trans. Alexander Dru (New York: Harper and Row, 1940, 1962).
13 Articles in IKC, vol. 14, by Michael Plekon ("Towards Apocalypse: Kierkegaard's *Two Ages* in Golden Age Denmark"), James L. Marsh ("Marx and Kierkegaard on Alienation"), and John M. Hobermann ("Kierkegaard's *Two Ages* and Heidegger's Critique of Modernity") provide detailed information about the historical and political situation. So too does Bruce Kirmmse's *Kierkegaard in Golden Age Denmark* (Bloomington, IN; Indiana University Press, 1990).
14 IKC, vol. 14, xiii.

further reading

Evans, C. Stephen, *Kierkegaard's "Fragments" and "Postscript": The Religious Philosophy of Johannes Climacus* (Atlantic Highlands, NJ: Humanities Press, 1983).

Ferreira, M. Jamie, *Transforming Vision: Imagination and Will in Kierkegaardian Faith* (Oxford: Oxford University Press, 1996).

IKC, CUP, vol. 12 (1997).

IKC, TA, vol. 14 (1984).

Kirmmse, Bruce, *Kierkegaard in Golden Age Denmark*, (Bloomington, IN: Indiana University Press, 1990).

KSY, 2005.

Lippitt, John, *Humour and Irony in Kierkegaard's Thought* (Basingstoke [UK]: Palgrave Macmillan, 2000).

Sarkar, Husain, *The Toils of Understanding: An Essay on Kierkegaard's "The Present Age,"* (Macon, GA: Mercer University Press, 2000).

Westphal, Merold, *Becoming a Self: A Reading of Kierkegaard's "Concluding Unscientific Postscript"* (Ashland, OH: Purdue University Press, 1996).

chapter 6

Works of Love, Discourses, and Other Writings

I *Upbuilding Discourses in Various Spirits*

*U*pbuilding Discourses in Various Spirits was published March 13, 1847, a full year after Kierkegaard's previous writing (*Postscript* and *Two Ages*). For this reason it is sometimes seen as a new beginning, the beginning of Kierkegaard's "second authorship." While it is true that there had been a notable cessation of publishing,[1] the first part of *Discourses in Various Spirits* seems to follow naturally on *Two Ages*, and he had worked on it in 1846. One could argue, then, that this second authorship does not begin a totally new direction, but rather develops the ideas of Climacus that Kierkegaard had radicalized in *Two Ages*.

A "Purity of Heart"

Part one, a discourse "on the occasion of a confession," is one many people have heard of, under the title "Purity of Heart is to Will One Thing." This discourse asks the listener: *"Are you living in such a way that you are conscious of being a single individual?"* (UDVS, 127). To be a "single individual"[2] is to take up eternity's standpoint here and now, apart from "the crowd," "the restlessness," "the noise," "the crush," "the jungle of evasions" (128). The echoes of *Two Ages* are clear ("the single individual" versus "the crowd") and the requirement of "purity of heart" is tied to "conscience," "accounting," and "responsibility."

Conscience is the mark of the "single individual," and "everyone must make an accounting to God as an individual" (UDVS, 128). Not surprisingly, conscience is between you and God. A shift to the language of "responsibility" permeates the following pages – the "crowd" is the place where responsibility is easily abdicated (130–38). The substance, however, is the same – "the awareness of being a single individual with eternal responsibility before God is the one thing needful" (137). But, when Kierkegaard affirms responsibility "before God" (130), we still need to ask *toward whom* the responsibility is directed, and the first answer we find in the discourse is that it is a responsibility to your conscience (your knowing with God). This responsibility does not, however, set itself against the notion of responsibility to and for another: Kierkegaard *assumes* we have responsibility to and for others when he assumes that we turn our "attention outward, [and] sympathetically give heed to people and events" (131), and when he says "You are not asked to withdraw from life, from an honorable occupation, from a happy domestic life – on the contrary, that awareness will support and transfigure and illuminate your conduct in the relationships of life" (137). Such a "transfigured one" is in "unity with oneself" (19), not "double-minded . . . divided in himself" (27), wholeheartedly willing what he wills – such a person becomes "more humanly involved with every human being" (138).

What is at stake for him is shown, as usual, by his examples. The person aware of being a "single individual" is "slow to form judgments," because something "may be a lie and deception and mirage and vanity, but it also may be the truth" (UDVS, 133). He also contrasts "the person who is aware of himself as a single individual" with "the angry person, the vengeful person" (135): our responsibility is to avoid being angry or taking revenge. Our non-preferential responsibility to and for others and the notion of unconditional equality are implied in the question "Do you want a different law for yourself and for yours than for others" (144). Moreover, he twice claims that "all alliances are divisiveness" – first, because they exclude people (whether commoner or king, Kierkegaard says, is irrelevant), and second, because they are "in opposition to the universally human" (144).

He says repeatedly that the "purpose" of the discourse is to prepare us for confession (UDVS, 150, 152, 154). In other words, the purpose is to remind us of our accountability for what we have done – not primarily to remind us of what we should do. The discourse is most directly, then, an examination of the *formal* requirement for confession. It illuminates a *how*, a way of always referring ourselves to what we know with God. It is a question of "integrity" (139) and "sincerity" (141) – that is, "purity of heart."

B "The Lilies"

The three discourses on "What We Learn from the Lilies in the Field and from the Birds of the Air" use the jest about flowers and birds teaching humans what they need to know. They teach us about equality and cre-atedness. The injunction to "Look at the lilies in the field" is used in the service of denying "that there could be any distinction among the lilies" (UDVS, 166). Just as a lily is a lily, so a human being is a human being – what is at stake here is our equality. Attention to "apparent diversity"

(181) leads us to forget "the essentially equal glory among all human beings" (171). To be contented with being a human being amounts, therefore, to recognizing that one is a "created being who can no more support himself than create himself" (177). Rich or poor, we are equal and equally dependent, even if the dependence of the poor might be more readily apparent.

In the third discourse on the lilies and the birds, they are no longer presented as teachers of confidence in God's solicitude. The call to attend to the lilies and the birds is understood, rather, as a way of getting someone who is "unwilling to accept comfort from another person" "to enter into someone else's suffering," "to share in another's cares" (UDVS, 201); the expectation is that to "worry" or to "suffer" or to "grieve" with another can take one's mind off one's own struggle (202). The transient beauty of nature reminds us that all passes away, that living is a way of dying: that the life of nature is "short, full of song, flowering, but at every moment death's prey, and death is the stronger" (203). But, the good news is that we are human beings, not lilies or birds. We are comforted by the contrast, for we are promised a "blessed happiness" (206) impossible for their nature.

This discourse, however, is the site of one of Kierkegaard's most troubling claims: namely, that one must choose "between God and the world" (UDVS, 206) since "love of God is hatred of the world and love of the world hatred of God" (205). Choosing the world is not a function of wanting extravagant material goods – "Whether the struggle is over millions or a penny, the struggle is a matter of someone's loving and preferring it to God" (205). If we insist on having anything at all without reference to God, as if it were simply ours, we have chosen against God.

These discourses are reminders to the listener – they do not endorse our judging others. Still, they are stern reminders, and they illustrate one of Kierkegaard's understandings of his maieutic goal. Although there is, in the discourses themselves, a subtle dialectical account of responsibility, as both unconditionally private and yet directed toward others, there is an undialectical emphasis on the choice between God and the world. While he often works a given theme dialectically within a given work, occasionally he allows another work of his to be the necessary supplement to something he presents one-sidedly. In this case, his next writing, *Works of Love*, will provide more nuance on the theme of the choice between God and world.

C "The Gospel of Sufferings, Christian Discourses"

The third part of *Discourses in Various Spirits* represents the first use of the phrase "Christian discourses" in the authorship. The tension between the overall title and the particular titles of the seven discourses is striking – instead of discourses about suffering as such, these discourses are all variations on the theme of the "joy" there is "in the thought of following Christ." Indeed, "each discourse drinks deeply enough to find the joy"; that a "single sufferer" will "find a heavy moment lighter" will fulfill the author's intentions (UDVS, 215).

II *Works Of Love: Some Christian Deliberations in the Form of Discourses*

Works of Love presents a Christian ethic, through 15 deliberations (in two series) on the commandment to love the neighbor as oneself; it was written by Kierkegaard in his own name and published in 1847. In it, Kierkegaard faces head-on the issue of the status of interpersonal relationships, intersubjectivity, and human needs. He classifies the book as "Christian deliberations in the form of discourses," and this makes it unique in his authorship – these are not upbuilding discourses or Christian discourses in his own name, nor are they pseudonymous writings. They are his only work in this genre. They are "deliberations" in the sense that he mentioned in *Discourses in Various Spirits* – namely, reflective weighings (UDVS, 306–7) – but their message is that "love is a revolution" (WL, 265). In particular, he is suggesting that the love commandment, "You shall love your neighbor as yourself," is revolutionary. He is not arguing in favor of the commandment to love the neighbor as oneself; he is speaking to people who already accept it, but who have, he thinks, failed to see the breadth and depth of its demand on them and therefore need to be awakened and provoked.[3] That provocation will be achieved by both a formal analysis (a formal statement of the law) and a material analysis (a description of concrete love, fulfilled duty). Moreover, *Works of Love* will be a remarkable display of his ongoing attention to doing things in the "right way" – the importance of the "how."

Just as important as the radicality of the demand placed on us by the love command, and the sensitivity required to fulfill it, however, is Kierkegaard's commitment to the importance of the human need for love. In the light of much that he has said in his discourses about being "alone before God," it may well be surprising to see in *Works of Love* such an unequivocal affirmation of human love: "Life without loving is not worth living" (WL, 38); "to love people is the only thing worth living for, and without this love you are not really living" (375). When he writes, "How deeply the need of love is rooted in human nature!" (154), he is not talking about the love of God. He is talking about our "innate need for companionship," a "need rooted in human nature" so "deeply" and "essentially" that even Jesus Christ "humanly felt this need to love and be loved by an individual human being" (154–5).

If we look back at *Either – Or* as an exploration of kinds of love and of the suggestion that to live rightly is to love rightly, we can see that *Works of Love* comes full circle. If we look back at *Fear and Trembling* and *Repetition* as inquiries into the relation between love of God and love of those human beings who are especially important to us, and if we look back at *Concluding Unscientific Postscript* as raising the question of the solitariness of the ethical subject and of interiority without outwardness, then we will find in *Works of Love* a place for the dialectical development of all these previous possibilities. Having been sensitized to the relevance of the pseudonyms in Kierkegaard's earlier forays into the ethical, we will not look to them for a Kierkegaardian ethic, but, rather, we will expect that this religious ethic in his own name will qualify and/or complete earlier and more limited perspectives on the ethical.

Kierkegaard's emphasis here on "works of love" – that is, fruits of love, love in its outward direction – is a radical response to a prevalent misappropriation of Luther's affirmation of "faith alone." Luther's theological position was itself a corrective to a theological over-emphasis on human ways to "merit" God's grace, but, in Kierkegaard's view, the Danish church had taken faith as an excuse for not striving, for ignoring the importance of action in relation to faith. Ironically, however, the irresponsible inwardness that Kierkegaard wants to correct walks hand in hand with an exaggerated emphasis on "externals" and "reciprocity." *Works of Love* thus perfectly exemplifies the way in which a given text of Kierkegaard's will revisit a particular place of tension in a radically new way: now a reconsideration of the tension between inner and outer reveals a variety of things that can count as outer – works, fruits, consequences, externals, and reciprocity. In this way, one can see *Works of Love* as a qualification of *Postscript*'s bold claims that "the less externality, the more inwardness" and "true inwardness does not demand any sign at all in externals" (CUP, 382, 414).[4]

As a book about love and its works, *Works of Love* is about relationship in two senses: it speaks about our relation to other persons, in the sense of our responsibility *to* and *for* them, and it speaks about our concrete relation *with* another person. It takes seriously the "as yourself" clause in the love commandment, as it addresses questions about the extent of our responsibility, as well as notions of self-esteem and self-sacrifice and mutuality. Thus, it is a reworking of the notion of the individual in relation to the greater whole insofar as the love commandment expresses the radical sociality of our human nature.

The task is a difficult one: namely, to suggest an understanding of Christian love which embodies a tension between an outwardness that appropriately understands the contingency of external achievements and an inwardness that is committed to striving and practical responsibility to and for others. Kierkegaard does this by maintaining a dual commitment to striving and gift, works and grace, law and love, and this leads to a re-visioning of both "transcendence" and "the individual." This re-visioning undermines common criticisms of Kierkegaard's thought as otherworldly and asocial.

Works of Love is even more important because it speaks to a more general question about the ethical relation to the "other" that is part of contemporary discussions of moral philosophy by pressing for a reconsideration of the notions of both impartiality and partiality, or, some would now say, sameness and difference. This dimension of *Works of Love* is actually a reworking of the contested concept of "equality." This concept of equality cannot be dismissed, as it was in the *Discourses in Various Spirits* as the "tyranny of the equal, this evil spirit" because of its tendency to slide into the irresponsibility of the "crowd."[5] It must be re-visioned, as a *sine qua non* for a Christian ethic. But at the same time, the dangers of an equality that issues in abstract substitutable individuals must be avoided, and attention to the concreteness and distinctiveness of each individual must be guaranteed. Kierkegaard here explores the way in which one becomes a self and maintains oneself as an individual before God, in the context of a God-given commandment to love the neighbor as oneself – which is, at the same time, the way in which one responds to other selves, building them up as individuals. The issues are important in their own right, and Kierkegaard offers a provocative account that contains resources for an understanding of impartiality which allows moral attention to concrete difference.

A A dialectical corrective

Works of Love is often spoken about or taught as if it began with the second deliberation, the three-part study of the unconditionality of the commandment's obligation. But this second deliberation needs to be seen in the context of the whole book, and the first contextualization is provided by what precedes it, namely Kierkegaard's opening prayer and his first deliberation.

The prayer is important (although it is seldom part of any assigned reading for students) because it embodies crucial assumptions which inform all the analyses and recommendations which constitute *Works of Love*. Kierkegaard opens extravagantly: "How could one speak properly about love if you were forgotten, you God of love, source of all love in heaven and on earth; you who spared nothing but gave everything; you who are love, so that one who loves is what he is only by being in you!" He repeats this refrain, completing his address to the Trinity of Love:

> How could one speak properly about love if you were forgotten, you who revealed what love is, you our Savior and Redeemer, who gave yourself in

order to save all. How could one speak properly about love if you were forgotten, you Spirit of love, who take nothing of your own but remind us of that love-sacrifice, remind the believer to love as he is loved and his neighbor as himself! (WL, 3)

Implied in this refrain is a question for the reader: how could one speak properly about these deliberations on love if this prayer were forgotten – that is, if one lost sight of the theological commitments embedded in this prayer and assumed throughout the entire work?

One of those commitments is a wholehearted embrace of the Lutheran principle of the priority of grace: Kierkegaard calls on God, "Eternal Love," to witness that "no work can be pleasing unless it is a work of love: sincere in self-renunciation, a need in love itself, and for that very reason without any claim of meritoriousness!" This sets the standard by which we are to interpret any and all references to "works" of love.

Even more important is his commitment to God as the source of love. When he says to God in prayer that the "one who loves is what he is only by being in you," he is assuming what he elsewhere expresses as the claim that "God loved us first" (WL, 336, 101, 126). We are given love by God (or better, love is the presence of God in us) and we are thereby empowered to love. The theme of grace as God's gift of Godself, the gift of enabling love, underlies all the deliberations. The prayer places the whole set of deliberations within a great parenthesis of "gift" and "striving," gifted love and grateful works.

The title of the first deliberation, "Love's Hidden Life and Its Recognizability by Its Fruits," makes clear that Kierkegaard is addressing a question that underlies all of his writings – namely, the question of the relation between inner and outer, here the relation between love's "hidden" life and its "fruits." More broadly, it is the question about the commensurability or incommensurability between inner and outer, and it is the culmination of all his concern with inwardness and interiority. In this deliberation, the tension is presented in visual metaphors: unseen and seen, invisible and visible, hidden and revealed. Moreover, in very Lutheran fashion Kierkegaard presents the contrast as a condition of simultaneity – hidden yet revealed – rather than a mutually exclusive either/or.

First, love is hidden because its source is God, who is hidden; God is even hidden in the Incarnation of God. Second, human love is hidden because there are no guarantees which can infallibly attest to the presence of love – it is "not unconditionally and directly to be known by any particular expression of it" (WL, 13). He insists that "there is no work, not one single one, not even the best, about which we unconditionally dare to say: The one who does this unconditionally demonstrates love by it," for "it depends on *how* the work is done" (13). After all, "one can do works of love in an unloving, yes, even in a self-loving way, and if this is so the work of love is no work of love at all" (13). Kierkegaard is suggesting that at least in one respect there is a kind of dissociation between inner and outer, and his point is commonsensical. He is reminding us of something we have all experienced – namely, that it is often difficult to tell from observation of externals (the outer) what is really going on. For example, it is hard to tell just from observing external behavior whether what is being handed to someone is a gift, a bribe, or a payment on a debt. This is an important point to which Kierkegaard returns repeatedly, and it is often the explanation for his emphasis on the irrelevance of externals.

Despite the inevitable uncertainty that comes from the fact that there are no necessary and sufficient conditions which certify that love is at work, Kierkegaard nonetheless appeals to the Scriptural verse that "every tree is known by its own fruit" (WL, 18). So too, love is known by its fruits. There are, he insists, two thoughts in one: "when we say that love is known by its fruits, we are also saying that in a certain sense love itself is hidden and therefore is known only by its revealing fruits" (8). Love is known by its fruits; but this manifest thought contains the hidden one that Love is *only* known by its fruits. Kierkegaard's double thought in fact contains a further hidden thought, which is that Love is *knowable* by its fruits, for as he notes later "*to be able to be known* by its fruits is a need in love" (10, my emphasis). Fruits are necessary and sufficient conditions of being "recognizable" (11) – the point is to work so that love "*could* be known by its fruits, whether or not these come to be known by others" (14). In an important sense the fruits of love cannot be hidden; they must be recognizable, they must allow grounds for determining, though not infallibly, whether love is our motivation. The requirement of fruits is not meant to encourage the practice of judging others: "the sacred words of that text are not said to encourage us to get busy judging one another; they are rather spoken admonishingly to the single individual, to you, my listener, and to me" (14). The importance of fruits is meant to preclude complacency with ourselves.

Moreover, Kierkegaard engages in the double-sided task of emphasizing the importance of fruits of love, while at the same time rejecting a consequentialist view of ethics. Love must have fruits which could in principle be recognized, love must express itself – but it will not invalidate the love which motivates an attitude or action if it is not recognized by others as loving or if it is not successful in what it attempts to achieve. "Fruits" must be active and "manifest" (WL, 16), as opposed to mere "words and platitudes" (12), yet "fruits" are not necessarily publicly observable external behaviors – it can equally be a work of love to forgive someone a wrong they have done you, to feed the hungry, or to "remain in love's debt." What is at stake in arguing that works of love are neither necessarily external nor able to be judged by observable results or achievements is that so-called works of love can be done unlovingly.[6]

What is also at stake in the resolute anti-consequentialism that Kierkegaard espouses is that loving works can be thwarted by nature or other people – they may not come to observable fruition. I may, for example, bind up the wounds of an injured person and convey him to the hospital for further care, only to find that he later died as a result of an intern's mistake in prescribing medication. However, nothing in this discussion emphasizing the limited relevance of consequences or observable results implies a cavalier attitude toward the concrete needs of other people. In fact, in this deliberation Kierkegaard anticipates his later comments on love as an outward task when he condemns the thoughtlessness involved in "thinking about [one's] own cares instead of thinking about the cares of the poor, perhaps seeking alleviation by giving to charity instead of wanting to alleviate poverty" (WL, 13–14). This simple distinction between "fruits" and consequences (or achievements) is important in responding to the criticism that in *Works of Love* Kierkegaard devalues this-worldly concrete needs or "externals."[7]

Kierkegaard's perennial concern with the relation and contrast between inner and outer will be explicitly retrieved and focused on in the two parts of the third deliberation, where he considers (1:III A) the importance of outer action (as opposed to simple inwardness), and (1:III B) the role of inner conscience (as opposed to what is external). In other words, the deliberation on the love commandment proper (1:II A, B, C) is surrounded on both sides by concern with inner and outer.

Before leaving this first deliberation it is important to note that it provides the first discussion of the theme of "need," which was alluded to in the opening prayer and which will play a crucial role in all the deliberations. Kierkegaard insists that "to be able to be known by its fruits is a need in love," yet this "signifies the greatest riches!" (WL, 10). The active force of such need is illustrated by his parallel with a plant's need to express its life; to insist on making love unrecognizable is as much against nature "as if the plant, which sensed the exuberant life and blessing within it, did not dare let it become recognizable and were to keep it to itself as if the blessing were a curse, keep it, alas, as a secret in its inexplicable withering!" (11). It is a devout person's riches that "he needs God" (11).

A second sense of need is found in Kierkegaard's recognition that love generates a claim on us by those we love. He tells us that we should not "hold back [our] words any more than [we] should hide visible emotion if it is genuine, because this can be the unloving committing of a wrong, just like withholding from someone what you owe him [because] your friend, your beloved, your child, or whoever is an object of your love has a claim upon an expression of it also in words if it actually moves you inwardly"; even more strongly, "the expression is your debt to him" (WL, 12). That is, others have a right to the expression of our love if we in fact love them. This has important ramifications for the question of the role of mutuality in his view of love of neighbor. In any case, from the opening prayer of *Works of Love* to its conclusion, the appreciation of the human need to love and be loved is front and center in his mind.

B The grammar of the commandment

Following the introductory clarification of the tension between inwardness and outwardness, between love's hiddenness and its fruits, we find the famous three chapters grouped together in a single "deliberation" (1:II A, B, C) which analyzes the commandment to love one's neighbor as oneself, focusing on the different elements of the commandment which Kierkegaard indicates by his typographical emphases as follows: (1:II A) "You *Shall* Love"; (1:II B) "You Shall Love *the Neighbor*; and (1:II C) "*You* shall love the Neighbor." The way it sets out the indispensable terms – the nature, object, and subject of obligation – suggests that it is a section intended for preliminary conceptual clarification. I propose that we take this discrete juridical discussion as providing a *formal* account of the *unconditionality of the obligation* – or, more precisely, the formal scope and bindingness of the commandment. That is, I propose that we take it as providing what Kierkegaard later refers to as a "sketch" as contrasted with its "fulfill[ment]" (WL, 104). A sketch is a skeletal structure of lines, outlines, and contours, as contrasted with its fulfillment in the form of a concretely fleshed-out, filled-in painting, with color, texture, and depth dimensions. That is, this second deliberation is the indispensable formal context in which the outlines are drawn and the rules given, while the work of illustrating love in practice is saved for later deliberations.

These rules are of the following kind. First, the term *"love of neighbor"* (*Kjerlighed*) is distinguished from preferential relationships like erotic love (*Elskov*) and friendship (*Venskab*) in ways that suggest that since it is not a feeling of attraction or inclination, it is better construed as a kind of "responsibility." Thus the obvious paradox of making a feeling a matter of duty is avoided. When Kierkegaard claims that *"erotic love and friendship are preferential love [Forkjerlighed]"* and "passionate preference is actually another form of self-love" (WL, 52–3), he is only repeating what Aristotle said – that "a friend is another self," based on feelings of attraction or inclination.[8] Since he later suggests that there is a proper self-love and a "selfish self-love" (151), it is clear that erotic love and friendship can be part of a proper self-love. The point is that erotic love and friendship, however good they are, are ways of being for oneself; neighbor-love, on the other hand, is a way of being for another. Being construed as responsibility rather than attraction guarantees that the fulfillment of the command is not seen as optional, or as in any way dependent on any preferential feelings we might have. This means that the commandment orders us to be responsible to those in need in front of us even if we are not naturally inclined to them or attracted to them; in other cases, where our love is preferential, the commandment orders us to be faithful because preference is contingent, changeable and unstable. We have responsibility to those we find likable and attractive, as well as those we do not. In both cases, the commandment asks that a person will never fail to be treated by us with the respect due an equal before God. The other's needs, not their attractiveness, are the determinant of our responsibility. To fulfill the love commandment is to refuse to exclude someone from my caring responsibility.

Second, the term "*neighbor*" is the expression of the "unconditional" equality of all people "before God" (WL, 60). The Christian doctrine is "to love the neighbor, to love the whole human race, all people, even the enemy, and not to make exceptions, neither of preference nor of aversion" (19). Kierkegaard labors the point that no one can be excluded, in virtue of the distinctions which constitute earthly life, from having a claim on us: "If in connection with Christian love one wants to make an exception of a single person whom one does not wish to love, then such a love is . . . unconditionally not Christian love" (49–50). The wife, the friend, the co-worker, the foreigner, the enemy, "the very first person you meet" (51) – any one who confronts you in need has a claim on your love and is your neighbor. The affirmation of equality is Kierkegaard's version of the general ethical quest for impartiality – an attempt to generate a more encompassing perspective and to avoid a reductive self-love ethic.

Third, in the service of equality, neighbor-love is normatively *blind to distinctions*: "equality is simply not to make distinctions" (WL, 58). Blindness, in the rhetorical context of clarifying the commandment as a rule of no exclusion, consists of eyes closed to dissimilarity and distinction. Distinctions (dissimilarities, differences) in one sense are neutral – they are necessary if we are even to pick out individuals. Kierkegaard concedes that "Just as little as the Christian lives or can live without his body, so little can he live without the dissimilarity of earthly life that belongs to every human being in particular by birth, by position, by circumstances, by education, etc. – none of us is pure humanity"(70). But some distinctions do more than particularize – they particularize in ways that disconnect us. Distinctions which merely particularize can thus be contrasted with distinctions that damage the soul (71), namely, those that "deny kinship" (74, 85). He emphasizes "the kinship of all human beings," a "kinship secured by each individual's equal kinship with and relation to God in Christ" (69). He speaks of the "inhumanity" of "wanting to deny kinship with all people" (74). A sense of kinship and solidarity or connectedness is not achieved by imagining an identity that does not actually exist, but, rather, by not making those distinctions which *alienate* one from another. It is not that any particular difference is innately alienating or morally relevant – what is at issue is the use to which the difference is put (either to disconnect or to build up). The differences that are used to divide us or alienate us from each other are the differences or distinctions that we must be blind to in order to love. This requirement of "blindness" or "closed eyes" can only be properly evaluated if one recognizes that it occurs in the particular context of clarifying the scope and unconditionality of the commandment. Such blindness guarantees that no one is excluded.

Fourth, this presentation of the commandment decisively orients us to the importance of the duty in terms of *action* or task – this is effective, engaged, responsive outwardness. This is clear from the early reference to action in 1:II A: "Christ does not speak about knowing the neighbor but about becoming a neighbor oneself, about showing oneself to be a neighbor just as the Samaritan showed it by his mercy" (WL, 22). This requirement of action is repeated in II B: "Go and do likewise" (46).

In sum, Kierkegaard's introductory deliberation on the love commandment, foundational as it is, provides an abstract model of equality – the abstractness of a formal clarifying sketch of the law rather than a description of its concrete fulfillment. The "closed eyes" which are required in this context are closed to all preferential or temporal distinctions that could be used as an argument for making an exception; they are closed to what would alienate or repudiate kinship. In this context, the neighbor is *potentially* every person – *therefore*, love ignores concrete differences that would be the basis for excluding any one. These chapters thus constitute the description of a *rule* for determining the category "neighbor" – "all" has the force of "no exceptions." The purpose is not to delineate a substantive response to the other, but to delimit a category by stipulating that no one can be excluded from this category on the basis of difference or dissimilarity (or included in it simply on the basis of similarity). This specification of the rule is not meant to describe its fulfillment. Moreover, the repeated refrain that "Christian love is sheer action" virtually takes over the third deliberation, "Love is the Fulfilling of the Law," with the important qualifications that such action is "as far from inaction as it is from busyness" (WL, 98) and that intellectual inquiry (the attempt to "define the concept 'neighbor' with absolute accuracy", 96) can be an escapist strategy, protracted so as to defer action. All of this suggests the formal requirement of practical response. The rules are in principle to be applied in action, but we need to see this in the concrete.

C The concrete application and vision

The fourth deliberation (on our "Duty to Love the People We See") turns us to concrete particularity, and for this reason it is the one I would begin with if I were assigning this book to students. Kierkegaard proposes that when one "goes with God," one is "compelled to see and to see in a unique way" (WL, 77). This is a decisive shift – it occurs within the first series (not between series) and it introduces a changed context that supports the claim that love appreciates, even cherishes, differences. Dialectically complementing the moral blindness that guarantees equality, it turns us to seeing the concreteness of "actuality" (159).

Kierkegaard signals a shift in focus by explicitly suggesting that this deliberation is a *different* discussion from that which precedes it: this duty, he says, is not to be construed "as if the discourse were about loving all the people we see, since that is love for the neighbor, which was discussed earlier"; rather, "the discourse is about the duty to find in the world of actuality the people we can love in particular and in loving them to love the people we see" (WL, 159). Coming after earlier clarifications concerning the unconditionality of the commandment and its formal requirement of expressing love in action, the fourth deliberation focuses on the character of those expressions of love. It begins to make concrete the earlier warning that "at a distance all recognize the neighbor. . . . But at a distance the neighbor is a figment of the imagination" (79). That is, while it is easy to affirm duty in the abstract, duty can only be fulfilled in relation to concrete humans in particular situations.

I suggest that the shift in context coincides with a shift to a different view of the moral relevance of concrete differences; the descriptions of love's fulfillment that begin here support the idea of an impartiality that includes loving the differences (even while it excludes "preference"). Kierkegaard insists that our duty is not to set about looking for some lovable persons to love; rather, "the task is to find the once given or chosen object – lovable" (WL, 159). This deliberation is concerned with our response to those who constitute our arena for moral action, those who constitute actuality *for us*. If our duty is to love the people we see, then we have to see them – we have to see their distinctive needs and the particular setting in which they live.

He makes his point by a striking and repeated contrast between loving someone "just as you see him" (WL, 174) and seeing him as you want him to be (which is a way of not seeing him, 162). He notes that we are prone to love the self-generated image of the other person, but this is not loving the actual other person at all – on the contrary (and the emphasis is all Kierkegaard's own) *"in loving the actual individual person it is important that one does not substitute an imaginary idea of how we think or could wish that this person should be.* The one who does this does not love the person he sees but again something unseen, his own idea or something similar" (164). Loving must be a kind of seeing. The moral focus here is on loving "precisely the person one sees" (173).

This fourth deliberation has a particularly apt complement in the fourth deliberation in the second series. "Love Seeks Not Its Own" (2:IV) makes especially clear love's appreciation of detail: we are to love *"every human being according to his distinctiveness; but 'his distinctiveness' is what for him is **his own**; that is, the loving one does not seek his own; quite the opposite, he loves what is the other's own"* (WL, 269, Kierkegaard's emphases). Kierkegaard illuminates the character of true human love as that which focuses on concrete differences when he describes God's generous love, which is to be our model:

> There is no difference in the love, no, none – yet what a difference in the flowers! Even the least, the most insignificant, the most unimpressive . . . it is as if this, too, had said to love: Let me become something in myself, something distinctive. And then love has helped it to become its own distinctiveness, but far more beautiful than the poor little flower had ever dared to hope for. What love! First, it makes no distinction, none at all; next, which is just like the first, it infinitely distinguishes itself in loving the diverse. (270)

Although "for God there is no preference" (63), there is an appreciation (even celebration) of differences. Kierkegaard unapologetically affirms differentially expressed love, distinctive in its response, when he says that love aids in the process in which one becomes "something distinctive." Divine love "makes no distinction" yet it builds up differentially, responding to need. Thus, genuine human love, emulating divine love, should love the differences.

Our commonsense connection between concreteness and difference is thus affirmed by him when he implies that we do need to pay attention to distinctions in one important sense – the concrete distinctiveness of the other person. Equality as sameness needs to be complemented by dialectical difference, or else the emphasis on equality can assimilate the other to oneself. A loving person is flexible, has a liberating awareness of others; the one who fails to love others according to their distinctiveness "wants everyone to be transformed in his image, to be trimmed according to his pattern for human beings," that is, demands that others fulfill his or her ideas of them (WL, 270). Whatever distinctions are ingredient in differential expressions of love, suited to each recipient, are differences allowed to be morally relevant.

The compelling question the reader faces is whether Kierkegaard's emphasis on difference is compatible with his emphasis on equality.

Readings of *Works of Love* have tended to do one of the following: (a) criticize its focus on the abstract category of "human being," ignoring its attention to distinctiveness/difference; (b) defend it from the charge of abstraction by indicating its emphases on distinctiveness and difference, de-emphasizing its reliance on assumptions about the "essentially" human; (c) admit emphases on both essence and difference, arguing that they are finally incompatible and irreconcilable. It is possible, however, to see at work a dialectical tension between equality and concrete distinctiveness in the form of the two different contexts – the context of the rule that indicates the scope and bindingness and then the context of the practical expression of love in a given case. That is, a formal context of *commandment* and a material context of *fulfillment*, or, alternatively, a context which focuses on (formal) *unconditionality* and a context which focuses on (material) *actuality*. This difference in contexts accommodates the contrasting emphases on equality and concrete distinctiveness. A recognition of the two rhetorical contexts does not obviate the difficulty of fulfilling the commandment, but it may dissolve a perceived inconsistency in the love ethic itself.

The fifth deliberation, "Our Duty to Remain in Love's Debt to One Another" (1:V) is highly provocative – in effect, it describes the love commandment as an infinite debt. Kierkegaard admits that his formulation is perhaps counterintuitive at first, when he writes that *"the one who loves by giving, infinitely, runs into infinite debt,"* and adds that it is *"our duty to remain in love's debt to one another"* (WL, 177). The point is to reject any economic model of love; the alternative to wanting to remain in love's debt is a kind of "bookkeeping arrangement" (178) that is at odds with love. The duty to remain in love's debt is the duty *not* to try to remove oneself from debt by an "installment payment" (178) – it is to recognize that nothing will lessen the debt. There will always be more to do – I can never say I am finished. Moreover, the debt is a function of our "kinship" (69),[9] and this is a fact about us, something not even God could change at some future date.

Saying that love of others is a debt we owe to them is not original – Kierkegaard is following in a long Christian tradition.[10] But what is the rationale for construing the commandment to love the neighbor as declaring an "infinite" demand? However egoistic we may be, we may not in fact want to be loved infinitely, so loving others as we want to be loved by them does not necessarily imply an infinite task. The rationale for an *infinite* task is found in the fact that Kierkegaard construes the commandment's "as yourself" in two different ways: it means to love your neighbor *as you yourself want to be loved*, but it also means that you are asked to love your neighbor *as you yourself have been loved*. Because we have been loved infinitely by God, an infinite task is embedded in the injunction to love others as we have been loved.

The presentation of such a demand should shock us! Is such a task fulfillable – can one live an ethic of infinite love? Kierkegaard knows that a task must be achievable for us to have an obligation to achieve it, yet he answers without hesitation: "eternity . . . calmly assumes that every person can do it and therefore asks only if he did it" (WL, 79). An example Kierkegaard likes to use to indicate both that we can love and why we can love is found in one of his earliest discourses, where he writes of the "child's gift" to its parents, purchased with what it has received from them.[11] I am loved, so I can love; I can love because I am already filled with love. For Kierkegaard, because we have been loved infinitely, we are *enabled* to love as the commandment directs.

But how can we fulfill such a task? The word "fulfill" is ambiguous – it can mean two quite different things. Kierkegaard assumes that I can fulfill the love commandment whenever I act in the appropriate way: love can be shown "in the least little triviality as well as in the greatest sacrifice" (WL, 181). There is nothing that cannot be done lovingly, with a sense of responsible caring – for this reason, Kierkegaard thinks fulfillment of the commandment is something of which everyone is capable (with grace). If I can at a given point in time perform a loving action, then I am capable of fulfilling the duty to love.

But this is different from *completing* the duty to love – there will always be more I can do. I can never finish the task, but that does not mean that I can never fulfill the duty. So we can fulfill the command to love or take infinite responsibility even though we cannot complete it. Even if the duty is never completed, we can express genuine love at a given time, whether it is helping someone who is starving, opening the door lovingly for another person, or forgiving someone without humiliating them.

Another way to understand how the commandment can be fulfilled even if it is infinite is to make a distinction between "helping everyone" and "not excluding anyone." The commandment is unconditional in scope – no one is excluded. But, the commandment cannot oblige us to help "everyone" "everywhere." That is an impossible task – we cannot affect everyone, we cannot be everywhere, and for each one we help there is another we cannot help at the same time or with the same resources. For Kierkegaard, the tendency to focus the question on whether I can help "everyone" is a way of trying to defer action – a way of construing it as an impossible task so that one can say one is not obligated to what one cannot perform. Once we realize that we cannot help "all" of them, we are tempted to give up and not help anyone. But to inflate the demand so that it will be unreasonable, and therefore not binding, is an escapist maneuver. It ignores the fact that there is a practical moral arena for our help – the "next one" we see. Remember the invocation of the Good Samaritan story (WL, 22) – we are never allowed to exclude anyone, to say of them that they are excluded from my responsibility. We are supposed to help the person in the ditch, not pass by with the excuse that he is not like me or the excuse that there are other people in need somewhere else. Moreover, the duty of response is directed to the distinctive needs of one who makes a claim on us – the Samaritan provides what *this* stranger needs at *this* moment. Although I cannot help "everyone," if I help the "next one" in the right way, I have fulfilled the task – so it is not an impossible command.

The fourth and fifth deliberations are the crescendo of the first series. Although the focus on infinite debt in the fifth deliberation might appear to turn away from the concrete particularity emphasized in the fourth, it could be seen as emphasizing the particular – the particular moment of fulfilling a particular task. This particularity is continued in the second series of deliberations, which provides examples of how love works in our day-to-day relationships.[12]

The majority of the deliberations in the second series show two things – (1) that the content of our debt is the welfare of others, and (2) the particular "how" of our giving. The title of the first deliberation – "Love Builds Up" (2:I) – could well serve as the overarching rubric for the first four deliberations. The content of the debt is a building up of others, rather than judging and criticizing them. Love is inherently social: "Love is not a being-for-itself quality but a quality by which or in which you are for others" (WL, 223). You are "for others" when you build them up, and one way is by presupposing love in them: "to have love is to presuppose love in others" (223). Other ways are by believing in them and hoping for them: "Love Believes All Things – and Yet is Never Deceived" (2:II) and "Love Hopes All Things – and Yet is Never Put to Shame" (2:III) illustrate how the loving person "continually holds possibility open with an infinite partiality for the possibility of the good" (253). A loving person is imaginatively creative in looking for the best rather than the worst in people; a loving person does not "unlovingly give up on any human being" (254). The point is to minimize "anger" and "bitterness" and "small-mindedness" in our relationships with others (257).

"Love Does Not Seek Its Own" (2:IV), we saw above, urges us to build up others by loving what is distinctively their own, rather than trying to trim them to our measure. Kierkegaard sees human welfare as follows: "to become one's own master is the highest – and in love to help someone toward that, to become himself, free, independent, his own master, to help him stand alone – that is the greatest beneficence" (WL, 274). This goal is not an abstract spiritual one – a person cannot be free or himself or his own master if he is oppressed, whether by poverty or by a particular political regime or by undue guilt. Kierkegaard does not give advice for public policy, and he is not into external revolutions, but we

works of love, discourses, and other writings

know that he is aware that people need sufficient food and adequate housing, as much as they need to be encouraged and forgiven. Building up is eminently practical – our debt to others is to promote their welfare. Kierkegaard's paradigmatic example, after all, is that of the Good Samaritan, and this should not be forgotten as we go along in the deliberations – it was said once, but it was said decisively, and it clearly goes against a spiritualist picture of helping others (22).

Promoting their welfare implies a direct relation to the neighbor, and the majority of the second series illustrates that. Although he sometimes refers to God as a "middle term" (WL, 67), his concept of God allows that we have a *direct* relation to the neighbor. In this his mature ethic, Kierkegaard's God is one who is "continually pointing away from himself," a God who tells us: "If you want to love me, then love the people you see; what you do for them, you do for me" (160).[13]

It is perhaps strange to say that a debt should be given as a gift, but it is stranger still to say that it should be given "as if" it were not a gift. Still, this is what Kierkegaard says: in a passage that has become important in the light of contemporary anthropological and philosophical discussion about "gifts," he tells us that *"love . . . gives in such a way that the gift looks as if it were the recipient's property"* (WL, 274). This prompts us as readers to ask both "how can we do this?" and "why should we do this?"

Kierkegaard calls our attention both to the *hiddenness of the giver* and to the *hiddenness of the gift*. When he speaks about the hiddenness of the giver, he means that we should keep attention away from ourselves and act out of concern for the other's self-respect. This is how to give compassionately. Kierkegaard is incredibly sensitive to the ways in which we can do good things for people in unloving ways – we can give to others in ways that demean them or humiliate them; we can give condescendingly, or in ways that make the other feel indebted to us; we can give a gift in a way that burdens another. Compassionate giving is concerned with what will happen to the other person as a result of the giving as well as with how the other person views himself or herself. This is an important way in which the "as yourself" of the commandment functions as an index for Kierkegaard as to "how" we should treat others.

He also speaks about the hiddenness of the gift – that is, what we do for others should not seem like a "gift" because in fact, for him, it is not technically a gift – it is something we owe others. This is because whatever we give to another has already been given to us (at the very least by our parents and our society). So, we are like the child who *gives* his parents a gift out of the allowance they give the child – we can see why we would still want to call it a "gift" and why someone might not want to. We can give to others good things that they need – in that sense, of course we can give gifts. And we can give them compassionately, with concern about their self-respect. But when we give such a gift, we do well to remember that it is not original with us – it was first a gift to us. All of this is what he means when he tells us that "*love . . . gives in such a way that the gift looks as if it were the recipient's property*" (274).

The fifth deliberation, "Love Hides a Multitude of Sins" (2:V) repeats a theme that we have already seen twice in Kierkegaard's 1843 discourses, and will see again after *Works of Love*. Both this discourse, and "Love Abides" (2:VI) and "The Victory of the Conciliatory Spirit in Love, which Wins the One Overcome" (2:VIII) offer a variety of perspectives on love's forgiving relation to others, and its aim of reconciliation. Love's ability to abide is love's faithfulness: it is expressed in "the moment of forgiveness" (WL, 314), as well as in its continued openness to reconciliation with the other. All three deliberations offer recommendations for cultivating loving relationships – ways that minimize divisiveness and maximize reconciliation. All three, like the earlier deliberations on presupposing love, believing in the other, and hoping for the other, work against mistrust and give indisputable evidence of Kierkegaard's concern with interpersonal relationships.

Kierkegaard adds a deliberation that is both provocative and reassuring when he suggests that "Mercifulness [is] A Work of Love Even if It Can Give Nothing and is Able to Do Nothing" (2:VII). This deliberation suggests that mercifulness is distinct from financial generosity – "mercifulness is infinitely unrelated to money" (WL, 319). Public displays of financial generosity may not actually be expressions of mercifulness – they may be ways of gratifying our ego or obtaining a tax advantage. Even if we have little or nothing, we can be merciful, because "mercifulness is *how* it is given" (193). Lest this give an excuse to people for not being generous to those in need if they have the means, he makes clear that he assumes that those who are able to will be generous – "it follows of itself that if the merciful person has something to give he gives it more than willingly" (317). Here his point is that the virtue of mercifulness can be fulfilled by all – it is not dependent on their means. The poor are not deprived of ways to be merciful to others. Again, as is his custom, Kierkegaard is highlighting our equal obligation and ability to be loving.

"The Work of Love in Recollecting One Who is Dead" (2:IX) emphasizes the faithfulness and unselfish devotion required for recollecting the dead, but also suggests that "from this work of love you will also have the best guidance for rightly understanding life" (WL, 358). Although this has seemed to some critics to imply the advice that we should love the living as we love the dead, it is more plausible to read it in the light of Kierkegaard's suggestion that love of the dead provides a "test" or "criterion" (358) of genuine love insofar as it is clearly a love in which we can demand no reciprocity. We cannot love the dead in a way that involves expecting "tit for tat" – and we should not love the living in this way. But excluding the demand for reciprocity does not itself entail excluding the hope of mutuality in relationship. Since he had early on noted that those we love have a right to our expression of love for them, it seems unlikely that he would be proposing that the ideal of love is one in which there is no mutuality.

Its curious title notwithstanding, the burden of the deliberation entitled "The Work of Love in Praising Love" (2:X) is to reformulate the dimension of love's inwardness and outwardness by suggesting that love implies a kind of "transparency" (WL, 361). This theme, found early on in Judge William's account of love, here means a kind of "self-denial" (360). But even the notion of "self-denial" as the way to express love has interpersonal import – we are never asked to deny ourselves for the sake of self-denial or to sacrifice ourselves for the sake of self-sacrifice. Rather, in the process of helping others we will be called on to forget ourselves, but the forgetting of the self will be in the cause of remembering *them*. Forgiving others will entail a denial of ourselves. The "purpose" of the unselfishness is to "reconcile" people in a "community of the highest" (365). The "as yourself" of the love commandment precludes self-sacrifice for its own sake. In fact, Kierkegaard often suggests that it is not a zero-sum game – he affirms the principle that "the one who loves receives what he gives" (281). That is, he highlights the Scriptural promise that we save our life (only) when we give it. This is but one of the many meanings of the "Christian like for like" – a thought so important that he says he would like to end all of his books with it (376).

The conclusion reminds us again of the principle of Lutheran simultaneity. Love is "simultaneously the highest comfort and the greatest strenuousness, the greatest leniency and the greatest rigorousness" (WL, 377). Love is dialectical – it should not be understood one-sidedly. This is true of some potentially disturbing claims in *Works of Love*, like the claim that "love of God is hatred of the world" (370). Hatred of the world, like the Scriptural injunction of hating mother and father which often preoccupied Kierkegaard, needs to be interpreted in relation to the commandment to love without exception. This illustrates an important aspect of reading *Works of Love* – namely, that the deliberations are meant to be read as a whole. Phrases taken out of the larger context may well misrepresent the tenor of the whole. Qualifications are made in certain deliberations that apply to others, though they will not be repeated there. The deliberations are interrelated, so that a given one is often qualified by something that went before or will be addressed later. It is all of a piece, but everything cannot be said at the same time; we are expected to remember as we go on from one deliberation to the next.

Note that Kierkegaard ends as he begins, with a provocative claim about inner and outer. He writes: "what love does, that it is; what it is, that it does – at one and the same moment" (WL, 280). This sounds like the Hegelian tenet he was often out to challenge, but here he complicates the relation, proposing a simultaneity.

III *Christian Discourses*

Even before *Works of Love* was delivered to the printer (August 1847), Kierkegaard had begun sketches for what would become part of *Christian Discourses*. These were addressed to a different audience from that of *Works of Love*, since he saw a distinction between Christian discourses and the "deliberations" in *Works of Love* which were meant to turn things topsy-turvy. These 28 discourses, however, do echo many themes from earlier discourses. The very title is retrieved from the final part of *Discourses in Various Spirits*, the "Gospel of Sufferings, Christian Discourses." Despite that somber title, the "Gospel of Sufferings" had really sounded a joyous note – all the discourses spoke of joy in suffering and the lightness of the burden. Parts two and four of this new set of Christian discourses carry on that note of joy. Part two consists of seven discourses, each of whose titles begins "The Joy of It" – the joy of it that some Christian paradox is true: the joy of it – that hardship procures hope, that poverty is wealth, that the weaker you become the stronger God becomes in you, that what you lose temporally you gain eternally. The discourses all address words of comfort and encouragement to "you poor sufferer." Part four is likewise meant to bring "joyful news to all the heavy-minded" (CD, 255). These "discourses at the Communion on Fridays," two of which Kierkegaard delivered in Our Lady's Church, are a "confessional address" rather than a sermon (270). They are not meant to instruct, but to provide a pause before the Communion service in which we are reminded to "rejoice (what infinite joy of love!) in his love" (284). The message is that "even if our hearts condemn us, God is greater than our hearts" (289); indeed, "language seems to burst and break in order to describe God's greatness in showing mercy" (292).[14]

By contrast, parts one and three, which were written last, sound a more somber note. Part one, "The Cares of the Pagans," is a polemic against "care": it does not "speak against poverty or abundance, lowliness or loftiness, but against the care" (CD, 60) – that is, the anxious concern that implicitly denies both our equality with others and our common dependence on God. The birds and the lilies again find a role – they are the middle term between the Christian and the pagan. The pagan is the one who has all these cares, the Christian is the one who does not, and the birds and lilies are the "assistant teachers" (9). The task is to learn from the birds and the lilies what paganism is – namely, "presumptuousness and rebellion against God" (66). Three kinds of presumptuousness are described.[15] First the presumption of "spiritlessness" (of being ignorant of God in Christendom), then the presumptuousness of wanting to do without God in rebellious denial (disbelief), and finally the presumptuousness of wanting God's help in a forbidden, rebellious way (superstition) (66–7). The "pagan" is a type who calls down "the wrath of God" (68), but still, we are not called to be their judges (10). Our task is to "learn to be satisfied with God's grace" (65) and to know that "to need God is a human being's perfection" (64).

Part three, which was added at the last minute, consists of calls to "awakening" (CD, 164) and polemics against "security" (163, 202) and "pernicious sureness" (211): "Watch your step when you go up to the house of God" – "take care with fire, it burns" (169–70). They are warnings about the need for "honesty before God" – namely, "that your life expresses what you say" (167); such honesty (185–7) should issue in "fear and trembling" (212). These discourses "prompt [people] to come closer to themselves" (215); the intention is not to judge others, but "to give the listener occasion to become aware of where *he* is, to test himself, his life, his Christianity" (215). They are (unlike the earlier upbuilding discourses) discourses for people who know the Bible passages "by heart" (234), meant to call their attention to the part that is the "question to *you personally*" (236). They aim to pose a question in a "penetrating" and "gripping way" so that "it becomes a question the person must answer for himself, so that this question . . . gives him no rest until he answers it for himself before God" (235). Kierkegaard actually announces his method: you tell someone a story and thus put him at ease (because this story is not about him); in the process you "place a question on someone's conscience" – it comes back to haunt him (235). Such is Kierkegaard's attack "from behind" (162).

A good example of what these Christian discourses are meant to do is found in the fourth discourse in part three, "There Will Be the Resurrection of the Dead, of the Righteous – and the Unrighteous." This discourse is not concerned to *demonstrate* the doctrine of immortality – but rather to "disturb peace of mind" (CD, 202), to generate an indirect "assault" (203) by not speaking directly about immortality, but about the distinction between the righteous and the unrighteous. A discourse like this, he says, will do what the demonstrators will never do – it will ask you whether you are righteous or unrighteous. He explains: "It certainly never occurred to any of the demonstrators to make this division or to raise this question – that would be pressing too closely to the listener or reader; one is afraid of pressing too closely to the listener or reader – that would be unscholarly and uncultured" (203). But pressing the reader is precisely what needs to be done. A Christian discourse presses the reader by addressing the matter of immortality this way – "tremble, because you are immortal" (203); it seeks to "abandon the scholarly to go over to the personal" because "truly, the one who never had his immortality decided in such a way that he became anxious and afraid has never really believed in his immortality" (204). Immortality is not about a "continued life as such in perpetuity" – "immortality is judgment"; "the question ought to be whether I am living in such a way as my immortality requires of me" (205). In sum, "*Immortality is judgment, and this pertains to* **me**; *in* **my** *view it pertains to* **me** *most of all, just as in* **your** *view it pertains to* **you** *most of all*" (209, all emphases are Kierkegaard's). In this discourse, Kierkegaard insists, "I cannot understand you in any other way, I do not wish to understand you in any other way, and I do not wish to be understood by you in any other way" (212). He is not preaching, because he says: "I know nothing concerning *my* salvation, because what I know I know only with God in fear and trembling, and therefore I cannot speak about it" (212). This explains the following prayer he offers:

> Save me, O God, from ever becoming completely sure, keep me unsure until the end so that then, if I receive eternal blessedness, I might be completely sure that I have it by grace! It is empty shadowboxing to give assurances that one believes that it is by grace – and then to be completely sure. The true, the essential expression of its being by grace is the very fear and trembling of unsureness. *There* lies faith – as far, just as far, from despair and from sureness. (211)

Still, despite the polemics, these discourses should help us "become aware of the comfort, or rather, the joy, that Christianity proclaims, because these discourses are for upbuilding even if they, as is said, wound from behind" (223).

IV *The Crisis and a Crisis in the Life of an Actress*

This work (July 1848) was Kierkegaard's second attempt to end his authorship (the first time being with *Postscript* and *Two Ages*). On the one hand, it was a tribute to an actress he admired; on the other hand, it was another attempt to raise the question (though this time solely in the confines of the esthetic) of a second immediacy – "a more intensive return to the beginning" (C, 324), a "second time" that brings with it the "distance" of "consciousness and transparency" (321). *Crisis* was the esthetic piece that would appropriately parallel the *Christian Discourses*, and bring to a conclusion a significant amount of signed religious writing.

V *The Point of View for My Work as an Author*

By the end of 1848, however, as he contemplated having a second edition of *Either – Or*, Kierkegaard was prompted to think about how his authorship to date would be viewed, and wrote what he called *The Point of View for My Work as an Author*.[16] His journals reveal a great deal of agitation and second-guessing about whether to publish it and he eventually decided against its publication at that time. It was published after his death by his brother in 1859. But he did not let go of the idea of explaining himself or his authorship, and would soon bring forth an abbreviated version of the retrospective.

VI Three Godly Discourses

The most immediate thing on his mind was providing something religious to parallel the re-issuing of *Either – Or*, and he arranged for *The Lily in the Field and the Bird of the Air* (three "godly" discourses) to be published on the same day, May 14, 1849. Redoing one of his favorite themes (from *Discourses in Various Spirits*), he proposes that we learn silence and obedience from the lily and the bird. The "jest" or comic nature of humans being taught by lilies and birds is now informed, however, by an emphasis on "unconditional obedience" (WA, 24) that is premised on the impossibility of serving two masters: "either love God *or* hate him"; "either be devoted to God *or* despise him" (22). But it ends with a call to learn "joy" as well, the joy of being truly "present to oneself" in the present (39).

The years 1848 and 1849 were very full years for Kierkegaard – he seems to have had lots of different possibilities in mind at the same time. During this period, the material for the books we would come to know as *Sickness unto Death* and *Practice in Christianity* was being refigured; he kept changing his plans, imagining different ways of dividing up the material.

notes

1 The series of attacks on him by a local paper, *The Corsair*, influenced his decision to resume writing and not become a pastor.
2 He says that this category "essentially" contains his "entire thinking" (UDVS, Supp., p. 395).
3 Kierkegaard made an explicit contrast in his 1847 journals between a "deliberation" (*Overveielse*) and an "upbuilding discourse" which can shed light on *Works of Love*: "A deliberation does not presuppose the definitions as

given and understood; therefore, it must not so much move, mollify, reassure, persuade, as *awaken* and provoke people and sharpen thought"; whereas an upbuilding discourse "presupposes that people know essentially what love is," a deliberation "must first fetch them up out of the cellar" and "turn their comfortable way of thinking topsy-turvy with the dialectic of truth" (WL, Supp., pp. 469–70).

4 Pathos must not be "directly expressed by any direct or distinctive outwardness" (CUP, p. 406) (as with monasticism). But he does recognize it is not black and white: "the less externality, the greater the possibility that the inwardness will entirely fail to come" (CUP, p. 382).

5 "Bold Confidence in Suffering Has Power" (UDVS, p. 327).

6 Kierkegaard contrasts genuine and non-genuine works of love. If this is appreciated early on, it should not produce confusion. Both in the opening prayer and in this deliberation Kierkegaard distinguishes between what we traditionally term "works of love" (acts of charity like feeding the hungry and clothing the naked) and works actually done in love: "But even giving to charity, visiting the widow, and clothing the naked do not truly demonstrate or make known a person's love, inasmuch as one can do works of love [acts of charity, *Kjerlighedsgjerninger*] in an unloving way, yes, even in a self-loving way, and if this is so the work of love [*Kjerlighedsgjerningen*] is no work of love [*Kjerlighedens Gjerning*] at all" (WL, p. 13). Thus, the physical behavior may be the same, but the "work" is different.

7 Luther too identifies "good works" with "fruits of faith" ("The Judgment of Martin Luther on Monastic Vows," in *Luther's Works*, vol. 44, ed. James Atkinson (Philadelphia: Fortress Press, 1966), p. 279.

8 Aristotle, *The Nichomachean Ethics*, trans. Sir David Ross (London: Oxford University Press, 1954), pp. 228, 238, 241.

9 See also WL, pp. 75, 85.

10 Martin Luther cites St Ambrose to this effect ("Treatise on Good Works," in *Luther's Works*, vol. 44, ed. James Atkinson, Philadelphia: Fortress Press, 1966, p. 109).

11 "Every Good and Every Perfect Gift," (1843), EUD, p. 46. Also "It is like a child's giving his parents a present, purchased, however, with what the child has received from his parents" (JP, 1: 1121 [1847], p. 10).

12 When first thinking about this project, Kierkegaard noted his intention to produce a single series of 12 lectures on love: erotic love, friendship, and neighbor-love (WL, Supp., p. 374 [JP, 5:5996, 1847]). Moreover, since there is only one "Conclusion" to the deliberations, it seems appropriate to treat the whole as a single work.

13 This contrasts with de Silentio's understanding that in the ethical we do "not enter into any private relationship to the divine" (FT, p. 60), which is to say that in ethical duty "I enter into relation not to God but to the neighbor I love" (FT, p. 68). The implication is that the private relation to God in religiousness excludes the direct relation to the neighbor.

14 Two of these discourses anticipate *Practice in Christianity*, with their emphasis on Christ's utterances about drawing all to himself and about not being offended by him.

15 These foreshadow themes to be developed in *The Sickness unto Death*.
16 I return to this in chapter 9.

further reading

Evans, C. Stephen, *Kierkegaard's Ethic of Love: Divine Command and Moral Obligations* (Oxford and New York: Oxford University Press, 2006).
Ferreira, M. Jamie, *Love's Grateful Striving: A Commentary on Kierkegaard's Works of Love* (Oxford and New York: Oxford University Press, 2001).
IKC, UDVS, vol. 15 (2005).
IKC, WL, vol. 16 (1999).
KSY, 1998.
KSY, 2000.

chapter 7

The Sickness unto Death and *Discourses*

After the publication of *Christian Discourses*, Kierkegaard seems to have been quite torn between the pros and cons of what and how to publish. He was amazingly prolific during the year 1848, and played with many possibilities for what he thought would be his "final" conclusion to the authorship. The possibility of a new book entitled "Thoughts that Cure Radically, Christian Healing," dealing with the doctrine of atonement, was, after much consideration, divided up into two discrete works, both written during 1848: *The Sickness unto Death* (1849) and *Practice in Christianity* (1850).

I *The Sickness unto Death*

The Sickness unto Death was written between March and May, 1848, although Kierkegaard delayed its publication until July of the following year. At the very last minute he made changes to the title, and he changed the author from S. Kierkegaard to Anti-Climacus, putting himself as the editor.

The very title of the book, *The Sickness unto Death,* tends to repel as many potential readers as it attracts. Some find it a somber and disheartening topic, while others feel a pang of recognition because the phrase resonates with something in their own experience. In any case, for all those who find the idea of a book about "the sickness unto death" less than appealing, the subtitle, *A Christian Psychological Exposition for Upbuilding and Awakening*, provides an important counterweight by focusing on the positive goals of "upbuilding and awakening." As the preface announces, "From the Christian point of view, everything, indeed everything, ought to serve for upbuilding," and we find that the book is written by a "physician" for use at "the bedside of a sick person" (SUD, 5). This diagnostician of sicknesses of the spirit addresses "despair" (6) as a sickness and promises to build up the suffering sick.

The book purports to have a universal audience:

> there is not one single living human being who does not despair a little, who does not secretly harbor an unrest, an inner strife, a disharmony, an anxiety about an unknown something or a something he does not even dare to try to know, an anxiety about some possibility in existence or an anxiety about himself. . . . a sickness of the spirit that signals its presence at rare intervals in and through an anxiety he cannot explain. (SUD, 22)

To such people the book offers a diagnosis that promises hope – it is ultimately a strong reminder of the possibility of forgiveness and grace. Of course, it also intends to awaken those who think they are not sick at all – and this will be a rude awakening.

The subtitle also reveals the first time that Kierkegaard has used a pseudonymous author to be "upbuilding" in a specifically "Christian" way. Anti-Climacus is a new and different kind of pseudonym, marking another shift in the authorship. In this respect, the phrase "for upbuilding" in the subtitle is significant. In the prefaces to the upbuilding discourses which Kierkegaard had been writing up until now, he had noted a distinction between "upbuilding discourses" and "discourses for upbuilding," implying that the latter relied on a teaching relationship which he did not take on; this should lead us to expect that Anti-Climacus, by proposing a Christian exposition "for upbuilding," assumes the role of an authoritative teacher. References to what is or is not "Christian" pervade the preface and introduction. Moreover, Anti-Climacus's assumption in the preface that he can present "the Christian point of view" and speak about what is "essentially Christian" (SUD, 5) reinforces the expectation of didactic and dogmatic teaching.[1] The preface ends with a determined instruction: "once and for all may I point out that in the whole book, as the title indeed declares, despair is interpreted as a sickness, not as a cure" (6). He ends, as if with authority: the "cure is simply to die, to die to the world" (6), but this will presumably be a topic for another book.

The table of contents tells us, through its simple division into part one and part two, that "The Sickness unto Death is Despair" and that "Despair is Sin." The book certainly is provocative – it makes the counterintuitive suggestion that despair is something we are responsible for and can be blamed for. One wonders immediately how the successive focus, first on despair and then on sin, fits with the apparent claim that they are identical (despair is sin). That is, it is part of the reader's task to struggle with the relation between parts one and two.

It is quite common to associate *The Sickness unto Death* with the earlier book, *The Concept of Anxiety* by Vigilius Haufniensis, and there are some good reasons for doing so, including two explicit indications of agreement with Haufniensis (SUD, 44, 47) and explorations of "inclosing reserve" and the "demonic." Both books detail an anthropology of the self and focus on psychological experiences (in the one case, anxiety, in the other, despair). But the difference between the pseudonymous authors should lead us to expect a significantly new dimension in this new book.

I propose that it makes three main contributions. The first is as a theological account of sin. Although the discussion of sin in *The Concept of Anxiety* was important, it concentrated on the formal character of sin as a qualitative leap; *The Sickness unto Death* will explore, instead, sin's distinctive theological substance – its character as a particular kind of disobedience. Related to this is the new emphasis on the import of our createdness, our dependence on what established us. While not denying our freedom, it importantly qualifies it. It is possible to see this emphasis on dependence as a development of a theme we have found repeatedly in Kierkegaard's writings, namely, that we are "nothing before God." This continues to be decisive, but this book will solidify the good news (which we have seen intermittently before) that we can be "co-creators."[2]

Finally, *The Sickness unto Death* develops the suggestive but very underdeveloped notions of "despair" and the "demonic" found in *Either – Or* and *Fear and Trembling*. Even the notions of "inclosing reserve" and the "demonic" found in *The Concept of Anxiety* receive important inflections. This shows how the same topic can receive different treatments depending on the purpose of the book; they are probably also categories in which Kierkegaard's own thought developed over time.

Unlike *The Concept of Anxiety* with its daunting table of contents, this book seems to be simpler, since it has only two parts. But this promise of simplicity is belied almost immediately. Anti-Climacus takes his teaching role seriously and uses a laboriously detailed outline, with numerous levels and sublevels, to guide us through each part. For example, the first section of part one is outlined not only in terms of three forms of despair, but also in terms of both possibility and actuality, and in terms of the relation between despair and two pairs of opposites: the opposites of infinitude and finitude, and possibility and necessity. It looks like a complex matrix is in the works, but this extremely elaborate outline may well simplify the enormous amount of information Anti-Climacus is presenting about the features of despair; just as in the case of a musical instrument, sometimes the more keys or openings it has, the easier it is to play – the less work there is to do in generating the variety of sounds. There is, however, an important way in which the book is straightforward – namely, the first one or two pages in each part lay out the fundamentals at the heart of each part. There are no real surprises to come – the rest of each part simply fleshes out the first one or two pages.

A Part one – the essential categories of despair

1 The dialectical
The preface gives us Anti-Climacus's most important piece of guidance when he announces that despair is "dialectical" (SUD, 6). The category of the "dialectical" has been weaving in and out of the entire authorship thus far, but it could be said that *The Sickness unto Death* provides some of the best examples of what it means. So it may be useful to begin examining this "exposition" about despair from this vantage point.

He asks, "Is despair an excellence or a defect?" and answers immediately, "Purely dialectically, it is both" (SUD, 14). He suggests what dialectical means here in several ways. The first is somewhat abstract, in relation to possibility and actuality. He puts before us a picture of a strange thing – something whose possibility is a good thing and whose actuality is a bad thing! Despair in the abstract is "a surpassing excellence" – that is, "the possibility of this sickness is man's superiority over the animal" (15). Despair in the concrete, however, is a problem, because "with respect to despair . . . to be is like a descent when compared with being able to be" (15) – that is, actual despair is the sickness in which one experiences "the hopelessness of not even being able to die," an "impotent self-consuming" (18). Despair is a dialectical category because its possibility is a good thing, yet its actuality is a bad thing.

Another example of despair's dialectical nature is found in the repeated use of analogies and disanalogies with sickness in general. Despair is like a sickness, but is also unlike a sickness. For example, to have a fever does not show that one has always had a fever; despair, however, has something of the eternal about it – if you are ever in that condition, you always were. Moreover, the one in despair is "responsible" for getting sick and for remaining sick (SUD, 16). Despair is a "dialectical" indisposition (25), "totally dialectical" (26), since it is bad never to have it and it is bad not to be cured of it.

The most thematized and the best example of the dialectical is located in the final section of part one, but before considering it in detail, it is important to have an introduction to the relevant terms or categories as a background. These – the most crucial of which are "spirit," "synthesis," "self," "relation," and "transparency" – are found in the first two pages of part one.

2 The relating self
Part one begins with a short programmatic statement of what will follow – a definition of the self, definitions of different forms of despair, as well as a formulation of the opposite of despair. In the first two pages we learn the basics about the structure of this strange sickness and its cure. More importantly, we have a preview of the way in which the discussion

of despair is at the same time an account of the implications of divine creation and our task as co-creators.

The first section, A, opens with a description of "the self" that has often been parodied as an example of the "gibberish" that continental philosophy speaks; Anti-Climacus writes:

> A human being is spirit. But what is spirit? Spirit is the self. But what is the self? The self is a relation that relates itself to itself or is the relation's relating itself to itself in the relation; the self is not the relation but is the relation's relating itself to itself. A human being is a synthesis of the infinite and the finite, of the temporal and the eternal, of freedom and necessity, in short, a synthesis. A synthesis is a relation between two. Considered in this way, a human being is still not a self. (SUD, 13)

The language is quite abstract, but a concrete image emerges. For example, (and it is so obvious it could be overlooked), the focus is on a description of "spirit" that is conceived of individually (and thus is a radical modification of the Hegelian concept of "spirit"). The focus is on a "self" – a single individual.[3] Moreover, we get an image of movement, of activity: "the self is the relation's relating itself to itself." Becoming a human self is an activity; "self" is an achievement word.

The "relation between the psychical and the physical" (SUD, 13) is the structural relationship of the sets of polarities: infinite and finite, eternal and temporal, and freedom and necessity. That is, the synthesis of soul and body in space and time is a relation, analyzable into the tensions between its dynamic opposing tendencies. This "synthesis" is not yet a "self," but it has the potential to relate itself to itself – to become aware of itself and to take charge of itself. The synthesis of soul and body has the potential to guide itself in the activity of negotiating the polarities that constitute it so that they are in the most fruitful tension. The synthesis is the locus of becoming a self, with ever-deepening consciousness of itself – self or spirit are contrasted with mere body or mere psyche. In saying that "the self is a relation that relates itself to itself" (13), Anti-Climacus is suggesting that the self is a reflexive relation – the self is a relation to the second power.

Moreover, when he introduces the possibility that the relation "must either have established itself or have been established by another" (SUD, 13), he adds further depth to the idea of the self as a relating. While *The Concept of Anxiety* put the accent on the self as freedom, *The Sickness unto Death* is a reminder that the self is grounded in a necessary finitude. A human being is a potential dynamic synthesis that guides itself in achieving a particular kind of synthesis, the character of which should be determined by its optimal relation to its ground (whatever that ground may be, even if it is itself). When Anti-Climacus considers the hypothesis that the self is "established by another" he points to the relation to the third power, so to speak – that is, he says that the relation "is yet again a relation" (13). Already we can see that that there are three distinguishable aspects to the self – the potential relation within the synthesis, the specific actual relation of the synthesis to itself, and the relation of the synthesis to itself in relation to the power that established it. The task of relating is a task of increasing self-consciousness, increasing awareness of the way in which the relating needs to be guided. If a synthesis is grounded by another, then the optimal relation a synthesis can have to itself is simultaneously a relation informed by the character of what grounded it.

It is important to note that already in the second page of the book, the author reveals a normative account of what it is to be a self, the state of health, as it were – "the formula that describes the state of the self when despair is completely rooted out is this: in relating itself to itself and in willing to be itself, the self rests *transparently* in the power that established it" (SUD, 14, my emphasis). The task is to become a self by becoming conscious of oneself. The antidote to despair is interpreted as a kind of self-knowledge, a transparency of the self to the ground of its being. The notion of "transparency" is an echo from many earlier works (e.g., *Either – Or, The Concept of Anxiety*) – namely, increase in consciousness is increase in clarity or transparency. Thus, becoming a self, working through despair, involves both a kind of clarity and a kind of contentment (lack of restlessness). This will later be termed "faith" – "the formula for faith: in relating itself to itself and in willing to be itself, the self rests transparently in the power that established it" (49).

3 The dialectical synthesis

The idea that becoming a self is a progressive taking-responsibility for the way in which the synthesis is maintained leads us ahead to what I consider the best example in this book of how despair is dialectical. Johannes Climacus had contrasted the dialectical with the one-sided. Anti-Climacus goes into detail on this through a lengthy illustration of what a dialectical tension between opposites looks like. Before considering despair in relation to consciousness, Anti-Climacus examines the "concept" of despair in relation to "the constituents of which the self as a synthesis is composed" (SUD, 29).

The meaning of the dialectical here is shown through a definition and then examples. To define something dialectically is to see it indirectly, through its opposite: "No form of despair can be defined directly (that is, undialectically), but only by reflecting upon its opposite" (SUD, 30). There is a "dialectic inherent in the self as a synthesis, and therefore each constituent is its opposite" (30).

With respect to the first pair of opposites (finitude and infinitude), "the self is the synthesis of which the finite is the limiting and the infinite the extending constituent" (SUD, 30). Infinitude's despair, therefore, is "the fantastic, the unlimited" (30). Feeling, knowing, and willing can all become "fantastic," with the result that "the self is squandered" and fails to become concrete (31); "the self, then, leads a fantasized existence in abstract infinitizing or in abstract isolation, continually lacking its self, from which it only moves further and further away" (32).

On the other hand, "to lack infinitude is despairing reductionism, narrowness," where one loses oneself "not by being volatilized in the infinite, but by becoming completely finitized, by becoming a number instead of a self" (SUD, 33). Such people have "no self before God" (35). This kind of despair is a constriction of the self in which a person "does not dare to believe in himself, finding it too hazardous to be himself and far easier and safer to be like the others, to become a copy, a number, a mass man" – and such despair goes "practically unnoticed" (34).

The goal is to become a concrete self and "to become concrete is neither to become finite nor to become infinite, for that which is to become concrete is indeed a synthesis. Consequently, the progress of the becoming must be an infinite moving away from itself in the infinitizing of the self, and an infinite coming back to itself in the finitizing process" (SUD, 30). These two movements echo the two movements considered in *Fear and Trembling* – the resignation and the reception that constitute faith. Moreover, they show the importance of imagination as well. Only imagination can do anything infinitely, and the double movement described here is one in which there is an infinite infinitizing and an infinite finitizing.

Moreover, the role of imagination in the synthetic activity is here shown as dialectical. "Imagination is infinitizing reflection" (SUD, 31), but it can be used badly or well. When untethered, it can lead to "the fantastic" – it can lead a person out into the infinite in such a way that he cannot return home to actuality (31). But without imagination we cannot deal with possibility at all. Imagination is the only medium for rendering the self's possibility – it is the "capacity *instar omnium* [for all capacities]" and "when all is said and done, whatever of feeling, knowing, and willing a person has depends upon what imagination he has" (31). The importance of imagination in achieving and maintaining this dialectical synthesis is clear: "inasmuch as the self as a synthesis of finitude and infinitude is established . . . in order to become itself it reflects itself in the medium of imagination, and thereby the infinite possibility becomes manifest" (35).

Anti-Climacus represents the second set of opposites (necessity and possibility) in an ideal tension: "Insofar as it is itself, it is the necessary, and insofar as it has the task of becoming itself, it is a possibility" (SUD,

35). On the one hand, necessity is part of our concreteness – the "necessity of this particular self" is what "defines it more specifically" (37). Necessity refers here to our concrete embeddedness in a context, most of which we cannot change (e.g., where and to whom we are born, the particularities of our physical and intellectual constitution). So if "possibility outruns necessity so that the self runs away from itself in possibility, it has no necessity to which it is to return; this is possibility's despair" (35–6).

On the other hand, necessity is by itself the lack of possibility (fatalism or determinism), and he suggests that "possibility is the only salvation" (SUD, 38). A one-sided instantiation of necessity is the imprisonment of the self's possibility – this is necessity's despair. Therefore, imagination is absolutely indispensable to becoming a self: "In order for a person to become aware of his self and of God, imagination must raise him higher than the miasma of probability, it must tear him out of this and teach him to hope and to fear – or to fear and to hope – by rendering possible that which surpasses the *quantum satis* [sufficient standard] of any experience" (41). With no appreciation of possibility, one can have no conception of what the self can become, and that entails that one can have no conception of God, for God is that all things are possible – "the being of God means that everything is possible, or that everything is possible means the being of God" (40) or equivalently, "since everything is possible for God, then God is this – that everything is possible" (40). The refrain is constant: "What is decisive is that with God everything is possible" (38).

In sum, the dialectical nature of maintaining the synthesis is expressed by showing how each constituent exercised undialectically (one-sidedly) is a kind of despair. Despair is a misrelation. There is despair (misrelation) when finitude and necessity are our only horizon, just as there is despair when we lose ourselves in the fantastic, abstracted from actuality. Moreover, Anti-Climacus suggests that imagination is indispensable to the achievement of selfhood, insofar as it is used both to cultivate a concrete and realistic sense of our embeddedness in culture as well as to preclude fatalism and the "spiritlessness" of the "philistine-bourgeois mentality" (SUD, 41).

Before leaving these forms of despair (with their exemplary illustration of dialectical structure) and seeing how Anti-Climacus connects them with the forms of despair in relation to consciousness, we should reconsider the notion of freedom that is raised by the second set of dialectical opposites – namely, possibility and necessity. To say that "freedom is the dialectical aspect of the categories of possibility and necessity" (SUD, 29) is to say that freedom is only able to be exercised when the categories of possibility and necessity are maintained in the appropriate tension with each other – not too much, not too little. Freedom must be possible since it is the goal: "to have a self, to be a self . . . is eternity's claim" upon us (21) and "the self is freedom" (29), "the self has the task of becoming itself in freedom" (35). But "the self is freedom" only by exercising freedom, and Anti-Climacus correlates freedom with self-awareness. Our greatest freedom comes only with our deepest appreciation of our actual condition in life, and he proposes that our true status is dependency – "the human self is such a derived, established relation, a relation that relates itself to itself and in relating to itself relates itself to another" (13–14). This exposition intends to awaken us to the ethical demand to build-up oneself and to be built-up, and (from a particular Christian perspective) it offers guidance for freedom. Since we are in fact derived, our project normatively has to be worked out in relation with what has established us; in particular, the project of becoming a self is a difficult task because it means working through the tensions between freedom and necessity, eternal and temporal, infinite and finite, and working through them in relation to what has established us.

The bad news is that "there is no immediate health of the spirit" (SUD, 25); to become a self we must work through a misrelation in which we have gotten ourselves: "The misrelation of despair is not a simple misrelation but a misrelation in a relation that relates itself to itself and has been established by another, so that the misrelation in that relation which is *for itself* also reflects itself infinitely in the relation to the power that established it" (14, my emphasis). Despair is a misrelation or imbalance – it occurs when a being that is dependent sees itself as being "for itself." Another way of expressing this misrelation is in terms of a being that sees itself as "for itself" at the same time as it "reflects itself infinitely in the relation to the power that established it" (14). This focuses both on our status as dependent and on how the exercise of our freedom puts us at risk for misrelating to our dependence.

4 The misrelation: two forms of conscious despair

Despair is the failure to maintain the relation of the synthesis to itself and hence to whatever ground it might have. How does the misrelation express itself? The first definitions of the forms of despair (after the ones in the table of contents) come in the title of the first section of part one. Three forms are presented, although the first, an unconscious form, is qualified as "not despair in the strict sense" (SUD, 13). All three will be considered in greater detail in the final section of part one yet to come, entitled "The Forms of this Sickness (Despair)," but the two conscious forms are given a preliminary explanation at this early stage.

The "two forms of despair in the strict sense" are (a) "Not to will to be oneself, to will to do away with oneself" and (b) "in despair to will to be oneself" (SUD, 14). One almost misses how remarkable this is – despair is defined in both cases as a kind of willing, an active posture, rather than something passive. Whereas we might have thought of despair as if it were a kind of depression that sweeps over us, willy-nilly, as "something that is happening" to us (14), we find instead that it is presented to us as a kind of deliberate willing on our part.

More importantly, the two definitions raise a crucial question. The reader begins to wonder about these two forms – to will despairingly to do away with oneself, and to will despairingly to be oneself. Since they seem to be opposites (if one wills to be himself, he cannot at the same time be willing to do away with himself), how can they both be despair? If willing not to be oneself is bad, then surely willing to be oneself should be good. If not, why not? It is important, therefore, to get a sense of what is at stake in the difference between the two forms. Some light is shed when he explains that "the inability of the self to arrive at or be in equilibrium and rest by itself" (SUD, 14) reveals our dependence. But the difference between the two forms only becomes clearer at the end of part one when he reconsiders the two kinds of despair – one "either in despair does not will to be itself or in despair wills to be itself" (47) – in terms of the categories of weakness and defiance, and feminine and masculine.

The first kind, the despair of not willing to be oneself is the despair of weakness or feminine despair. The second, the despair of willing to be oneself, is the despair of defiance or the masculine despair. Anti-Climacus tries to qualify the sexism of this contrast by affirming that they are not essentially gender characterizations (each can occur in either gender – SUD, 49n), and he admits that they are ideal types (in actuality neither is found without something of the other in it – 49).

The despair of weakness is despair over something – illustrated by an ambitious man who wants to be Caesar and a girl in love who loses her beloved. They despair either in not willing to take on the project of being any self, or not willing to be the self they are because they will to be another self. This is not difficult to imagine. We see people every day who are not satisfied with themselves. For some it is so overwhelming that they simply want to get rid of themselves – they want to be no self. Others want to get rid of themselves by being someone else: "If only I had X" . . . or "If only I were Y." They want to be another self. In other words, such people admit themselves to be inadequate or even hateful to themselves, and so want to be rid of themselves or be another self.

By contrast, the despair of defiance is one in which one wills to *be* one's self – the very self one is, in contrast to any other selves. I want to be my self – "You're not the boss of me!" The defiant despairer insists on his freedom to be himself even if it harms him. This "demonic" mutiny against God is "inclosing reserve," it is "an inwardness with a jammed lock" (SUD, 72). It is what children do out of spite – the defiance of refusing to open your mouth so you can continue to blame someone for your hunger, refusing to be nourished so you can still insist that you are mistreated.

These are thus two distinctive ways of rejecting the task of becoming oneself, of becoming spirit – one accentuates passivity and one accentuates activity. Yet Anti-Climacus also says that the "opposites are only relative" since "no despair is entirely free of defiance" and "even despair's most extreme defiance is never really free of some weakness" (SUD, 49). In both cases of despair, the upshot is the same – it is a quest for the self one dreams of, either the form of another self, or the fictionalized perfect form of oneself. In both cases, there is a rejection of the task of becoming. One thereby gives up on the work of becoming the self one is created to be – one refuses the challenge to continue the creation begun by God. One gives up on *the task of freely crafting a dependent self*, and so one refuses to be a co-creator with God.

5 The misrelation: unconscious despair
Although part one ends by describing the highest pitch of intensity of despair, Anti-Climacus's challenge of "awakening" is directed to the by far larger number of people who do not realize that they are sick. He admits that the most intense despair is the rarest form, and that despair is increasingly less common the more intensely self-conscious and rebellious it is. In order to defend his claim that despair is universal he will have to make plausible the idea that unconscious despair counts as despair.

He unapologetically claims that there is a "qualitative distinction" between despair that is conscious and despair that is not (SUD, 29).[4] But it is difficult to know how to speak of unconscious despair at all – since he has already claimed it is something we do freely. From the beginning there is a vacillation about whether unconscious despair is despair "in the strict sense" (13). Although he initially seemed to present despair undialectically, as if it is merely active (14), something we bring on ourselves (17), he repeatedly enacts the difficulty of drawing a clear line between conscious and unconscious despair, by going back and forth on whether unconscious despair is justifiably called despair (42).[5] He mirrors the ambiguity of "actual life" which embodies no cases of despair in which one is "completely aware" or "completely unaware" of the despair (48). In actuality, there will be a spectrum of degrees of consciousness, beginning with what is intermittent and obscure and ending with what is clear and deliberate defiance.

In any case, Anti-Climacus's view is that the most conscious despair is the most dangerous, and the least conscious despair is the most common. What is at stake here is that this condition – "not to be conscious of oneself as spirit" (SUD, 44) – is the one in which most people are. That is, the person who is ignorant of his possibility and destiny as spirit is still in despair, and it "can in fact be the most dangerous form of despair" because it secures the person against becoming aware (44). The picture of "spiritlessness," also found in many of Kierkegaard's books, is here presented with an unusual abundance of building or house metaphors (SUD, 55). Of course, this makes the discussion more concrete, more graphic, but it is also interesting given that the book is supposed to be an exposition "for upbuilding." The first picture of someone in despair appeals to our common sense:

> Imagine a house with a basement, first floor, and second floor planned so that there is or is supposed to be a social distinction between the occupants according to floor. Now, if what it means to be a human being is compared with such a house, then all too regrettably the sad and ludicrous truth about the majority of people is that in their own house they prefer to live in the basement. . . . Moreover, he not only prefers to live in the basement – no, he loves it so much that he is indignant if anyone suggests that he move to the superb upper floor that stands vacant and at his disposal, for he is, after all, living in his own house. (43)

This is a typical strategy in this book and others – namely, presenting a picture and asking the reader to decide what is wrong with the picture.

Anti-Climacus then targets philosophical spiritlessness. Imagine, he says: "A thinker erects a huge building, a system, a system embracing the whole of existence, worldly history, etc., and if his personal life is considered, to our amazement the appalling and ludicrous discovery is made that he himself does not personally live in this huge, domed palace but in a shed alongside it, or in a doghouse, or at best in the janitor's quarters" (SUD, 43–4). What would you, the reader, think of such a person?

He reproaches this spiritlessness sarcastically: "Ideally understood, it is extremely comical that underlying the worldly wisdom that is so celebrated in the world, underlying all that diabolical profusion of good advice and clever clichés – 'Wait and see,' 'Don't worry,' 'Forget it' – there is utter stupidity about where and what the danger actually is. Again, it is this ethical stupidity that is appalling" (SUD, 56). He is more satirical than passionate when he wonders out loud why people seem to think that wisdom and faith come with age, the way teeth and a beard come (58).

It is as if such spiritlessness has actually weighed Anti-Climacus down. There is more compassion than passion:

> Every human existence that is not conscious of itself as spirit or conscious of itself before God as spirit, every human existence that does not rest transparently in God but vaguely rests in and merges in some abstract universality (state, nation, etc.), or, in the dark about his self, regards his

capacities merely as powers to produce without becoming deeply aware of their source, regards his self . . . as an indefinable something – every such existence, whatever it achieves, be it most amazing, whatever it explains, be it the whole of existence, however intensively it enjoys life esthetically – every such existence is nevertheless despair. (SUD, 46)

It is only a problem for him because he cares so much.

Unconscious and conscious despair thus are the psychological correlates of the abstract structural descriptions first posited by Anti-Climacus.[6] This means that despair is the failure to guide the constituents of the synthesis in an appropriate dialectic; in other words, despair is the failure to maintain the negative in each constituent. Insofar as not willing to be a self or willing defiantly to be a self are ways of rejecting possibility, imagination is a necessary element in avoiding despair.

B Part two – the qualitative intensification of sin

Part one culminates in a picture of the most intense defiant despair – "the demonic." It is clear that there is something absolutely new in part two, "Despair is Sin," insofar as the category of "sin" is introduced for the first time. Sin is said to be despair under a certain condition – namely, "Sin is, *before God, or with the conception of God, in despair not to will to be oneself, or in despair to will to be oneself*" (SUD, 77). This definition of sin is unexpected since reference to God had been made many times in part one, including times at which Anti-Climacus specifically referred to despair as failing to be "conscious of itself before God as spirit" (46).[7] But if conscious despair is possible only when a person is aware of being "before God" (48), then how is part two different?[8] It seems that if we look back, despairing before God, which is now called "sin," was already described in part one. Is part two simply a redescription of the latter part of part one? But he alerts us to the fact that "this whole deliberation must now dialectically take a new direction" (79). What is the relation between the two parts – how does the second "dialectically take a new direction"?

1 "Before God, having the conception of God"

Intensification   One way of construing the relation between parts one and two is strongly suggested by the author's initial claim that "sin is the intensification of despair" (SUD, 77) and by the title of chapter 1, "The Gradations in the Consciousness of the Self (the Qualification 'Before God')," which suggests that "before God" is to be understood in terms of gradations of consciousness. Since we have already seen the condition of being "before God" in part one's description of despair, the difference in part two is an intensification in being "before God, or with the conception of God." Part two looks back at part one, describing it as having pointed out a "gradation in the consciousness of the self" (79). By calling sin "the intensification of despair," Anti-Climacus suggests a continuum – a continued description of an escalation in gradations of despair until it reaches the highest intensity, sin. On this view part two continues the description of the psychological malaise which anyone can experience in varying degrees, now putting the spotlight on the highest gradation in consciousness, corresponding to the most intense way of being "before God." For such a project, the appropriate question is, where on the psychological continuum does the pitch of intensity worth calling "sin" emerge?

This reading is supported by the fact that although he does mention God and even uses the phrase "before God" in part one, the particular phrase, "with the conception of God," is (like "sin") new to part two. Moreover, the Danish expression Anti-Climacus uses for "conception of God" (*Forestilling om Gud*) is much more concrete than the English translation suggests. A "conception" of God sounds like a vague idea or thought of God. The word Anti-Climacus uses – *Forestilling* – has important connotations of performance or presentation or introduction – for example, the mime show in Tivoli Park is advertised as a *Forestilling* at a particular time. The mime show is not an abstract idea one has, but a performance, an active presencing.

The introduction or presentation of a person can engage me; a performance can engage me. The other can be before me, over against me, in such a way as to preclude mere observation on my part. Some presentations so engage us as to demand a response; one may embrace or reject them, but they are compelling in a way that precludes indifference. To have a "conception of God," in part two, is not just to have a thought of God, or a notion, in some abstract conceptual sense, but to have a deep and engaging appropriation of the presence of God. Like the imaginative apprehension of love or of "eternity in a grain of sand," this need involve no visual images. The phrase "before God" fruitfully trades on the way in which when I am before another person, that other is before me, as well, and when I place another before me, I am placed before the other. Having a conception of God, on this reading, means that I am radically engaged, confronted by God. That is, there is a dynamic relation – we are "before" God in a very real way because God is "before" us in a very real way. Although it might look like in part two (by contrast with part one) the focus shifts to willing and the imagination is forgotten in any positive sense, the notion of the conception (*Forestilling*) of God actually is an imaginative category.

This would mean that the intensification of despair would be appropriately considered "sin" or "disobedience" only when one has a conception of God strong enough to be able not to will as God wills (SUD, 81). It could in fact be the case that a person did not will what God willed, without the person's knowledge that he was not willing what God wills. The latter degree of self-consciousness – of clarity about despair and the self – is a condition for the application of the theological term "sin." One could then say that being "before God" is when God is most intensely present to one, when "God is not some externality in the sense that a policeman is" and that "what really makes human guilt into sin is that the guilty one has the [heightened] consciousness of existing before God" (80). This would be taking a new direction, and it would apparently do justice to the suggestion that a qualitative difference in intensification of consciousness of God marks "sin." We would be left with the idea that what is distinctive about sin is a function of our psychologically intensified conception of God, a deeper imaginative appropriation.

But Anti-Climacus goes further when he says that part two will address the self "whose criterion is God" (SUD, 79); the fuller account of how a "self directly before God" takes on "a new quality and qualification" (79) suggests a different way of understanding the transition to part two – one which involves a new idea of the *kind of God* one is "before."

The criterion of the qualification   Anti-Climacus suggests that the concept of sin is marked decisively in two ways: first, by the "crucial Christian qualification" that is the qualification of being "before God," and second, by "Christianity's crucial criterion: *the absurd, the paradox, the possibility of offense*" (SUD, 83). The "criterion" is the criterion of paradoxicality. This "qualification" and this "criterion" are both necessary – indeed, he says that the qualification "*has* Christianity's crucial criterion" (83, my emphasis). Hence, the qualification "before God, or with the conception of God" cannot be treated in isolation; any reference to it must imply reference to its criterion of paradoxicality. When he claims that "sin is now despair qualitatively intensified once again" (100), he suggests that the *qualitative intensification* is achieved through the way the qualification has the criterion of paradoxicality. The criterion provides the prism of paradox through which God is before us, and we are "before God"; the explication of God as the "criterion" in the four-page appendix to chapter 1 thus qualifies the conception of God more radically than by intensification of appropriation.

"Christianity's crucial criterion" includes "the possibility of offense" in the definition of sin (SUD, 83) – that is, what is at issue is a conception of God at whom one can take "offense." The possibility of such offense is tied to a revelation: "there has to be a revelation from God to show what sin is" (89). He implies that a self whose "criterion" is God is in a different situation from one who is simply "before God," because the revelation of what sin is becomes expressed in the Incarnation of God. In this sense, being "before God" takes on the particular characteristic of us being before an Incarnate God. "Offense" is (as it was in *Fragments* and *Postscript*) correlated with "the absurd, the paradox," but this book has a remarkable way of construing it. Appendix 1 describes the possibility of offense as follows: "it lies in this . . . that as an *individual* human being a person is directly before God and consequently, as a corollary, that a person's sin should be of concern to God" (83). This is what it means to be "before God" and it involves specifically the idea of the "individual human being" – an individual about whom God cares. It requires "humble courage to dare to believe" what Christianity teaches – namely, that "this individual human being – and thus every single individual human being, no matter whether man, woman, servant girl, cabinet minister, merchant, barber, student, or whatever – this individual human being exists *before God*" (85). More specifically, the possibility of offense lies in the idea that "this person is invited to live on the most intimate terms with God!" (85). He asks us to imagine the scenario of a "poor day laborer" offered an extravagant favor by "the mightiest emperor" – if the laborer told anyone of this "favor," he might become the "laughing-stock of the whole city" and "there would be cartoons of him in the newspapers" (84). (Kierkegaard's personal life and suffering is never very far from the mind of his pseudonyms). The revelation provided by an Incarnate God is that "for this very person's sake, God comes to the world, allows himself to be born, to suffer, to die, and this suffering God – he almost implores and beseeches this person to accept the help that is offered to him!" (85). Such a thought could make one lose one's mind – it seems to make "too much of being human" (87). Sin is despairing in the face of such a revelation: "sin is – after being taught by a revelation from God what sin is – before God in despair not to will to be oneself or in despair to will to be oneself" (96).

Sin takes on a different character depending on the defied God's character. Anti-Climacus suggests that the concept of God a human can have without revelation is not sufficient to make the term "sin" appropriate. The conception of God which aggravates the notion of despair into something qualitatively different (namely, sin) is one that can be gained only through a revelation of the way in which God is the criterion. The character of what or whom you defy changes the character of the defiance. Rebellion, or "disobedience" (SUD, 81), against this paradoxical God is so terrible precisely because this paradoxical God represents the absolute offer of love and forgiveness. One cannot be guilty of rejecting forgiveness until one knows that it is offered and what it is like. One can *be* without love or forgiveness without knowing it, but one cannot reject or rebel against it without knowing it. There has to be a certain level of awareness. Only the person aware of the revelation can truly rebel against it (although if there has been such a revelation then even the person who is not aware of it will be deprived of what it offers). Only the person who knows he has been invited to live on the most intimate terms with God and that this suffering God-Man implores him to accept the help God offers – only such a person can "sin" in the Christian sense.

Here again the dialectic of imagination is brought in – it requires imagination to see the depth of the offense involved, but "the more passion and imagination a person has," the closer he is to the possibility of believing (SUD, 86). The possibility of offense must be maintained, and this requires excluding any and all attempts at "defending" Christianity (87). Defending Christianity is defrauding it, leaving nothing to the imagination, so to speak.

In sum, part two begins with a grammar of the concept of sin that locates the qualitative intensification in "the conception of God" by highlighting the qualitative intensification of the *object* of our consciousness (paradox) as well as the qualitative intensification of our *consciousness* (imaginative appropriation) of the object. It illustrates how sin is despair "before God and with the conception of God." Chapters 2 and 3 then draw out the implication of despair's defiance by contrasting sin (as something positive, a position taken) with ignorance, or weakness, or sensuousness. Thus, despite the claim that we need another Socrates in our age, Anti-Climacus criticizes the Greek position that sin is ignorance insofar as Christianity completes the Socratic position by uncovering the hidden willfulness behind ignorance (SUD, 95). The opposite of sin is not virtue, but faith – the faith of affirming "the gulf of qualitative difference between God and man" (99) that renders not only God's presence on earth, but sin itself, a paradox that cannot be understood (98). The God we are before is the paradoxical tension of both our unlikeness with God and our likeness with the God-Man, the paradoxical tension of both judgment and forgiveness.

The appendix to the whole of the first section (A) of part two offers itself as "The Moral." It addresses the apparent peculiarity of the outcome that, given the strictures on the application of the word "sin," sin is not possible to pagans outside of Christendom and only seldom found in Judeo-Christendom. That is, sin seems to be a rarity. But even if sin, strictly speaking, is a rarity, that does not mean that all is well in Christendom. The loss of "sin-consciousness" (SUD, 101) is the problem: "most men are characterized by a dialectic of indifference and live a life so far from the good (faith) that it is almost too spiritless to be called sin – indeed, almost too spiritless to be called despair" (101). But, and here's the rub, spiritlessness is one's "own fault" – "no one is born devoid of spirit" (102). Foreshadowing the explicit attack on Christendom that is in the making, he writes: "it has to be said, and as frankly as possible, that so-called Christendom (in which all are Christians by the millions as a matter of course . . .) is not merely a shabby edition of the essentially Christian . . . but is also a misuse of it, a profanation and prostitution of Christianity" (102). He connects the lack of spirit to the spiritless way Christianity is presented to people: when pastors " 'defend 'Christianity' or transpose it into 'reasons,' " they inform against themselves that they do not know what Christianity is (104). This challenge is grounded on an analogy between faith and love, precisely in terms of the ludicrousness of a lover trying to defend the idea that he is in love (103–4). Concluding section A with the admission that Christendom is full of people whose lives "are far too spiritless to be called sin in the strictly Christian sense," (104), he turns to section B, which will be a study of sin, strictly speaking, because, even if it is rare, it needs to be shown how sin is "despair qualitatively intensified once again" (100).

2 The continuance of sin
Section B is entitled "The Continuance of Sin" and its introduction makes the strong claim that remaining in sin is itself a new sin (SUD, 105). Earlier passing references to despair as the condition of "repentance" (59, 61n) are continued here in the claim that every moment a sin is "unrepented is also a new sin" (105). This stress on sin as the "state of sin" (108) has an unusual implication. It is a re-visioning of the notion of continuity and discontinuity, de-emphasizing the notion of sin as a qualitative leap (found in *The Concept of Anxiety*). Here, he emphasizes that "the continuity of sin" (105) is the decisive characteristic of the defiance of sin.

The three short chapters of section B consider "The Sin of Despairing Over One's Sin," "The Sin of Despairing of the Forgiveness of Sins (Offense)," and "The Sin of Dismissing Christianity *Modo Ponendo* [Positively], of Declaring it to be Untruth." They make up a Christian psychology of sin, in which levels of sin-consciousness are described.

Anti-Climacus suggests that sin is "intensified in a new consciousness" when one despairs "over one's sin" (SUD, 109). "Despair over sin is the second severance," the break with "repentance and grace" (109). Despair over sin is "a heightening of the demonic" (110); it is despair to the second power because it is despair over one's despair. There is psychological insight in suggesting the self-deception that can occur in cases of despair over sin: the phenomenon of despairing over one's sin, telling oneself that "I will never forgive myself," or even, "God can never forgive me for what I did," is really an arrogant kind of defiance, a choice to remain in sin by refusing the possibility of repentance and forgiveness. It barricades oneself against the demands of repentance and ultimately against the good. Such an attitude of demonic defiance is not sorrow over sin – it is "exactly the opposite of the brokenhearted contrition that prays God to forgive" (111). It is often the attempt to make oneself look better, since it is supposed to be "the mark of a deep nature" to be "so sensitive" about sin (111). On the contrary, Anti-Climacus, the diagnostician of the sickness of spirit, judges that this is just the pride of wanting to be without sin, the pride of not wanting to repent because that would mean an admission of a sinfulness one cannot bear.

Despair "over one's sin" (SUD, 109) becomes a despair "of the forgiveness of sins" insofar as "the intensification of the consciousness of the self is the knowledge of Christ, a self directly before Christ" (113). The awareness of Christ is a deepening of the awareness of God because "only in Christ is it true that God is man's goal and criterion" (114). Our access to God is through the Christ "before us," through our "conception of Christ." To despair of the forgiveness of sins is to reject the specific promise of forgiveness and reconciliation that came in Christ. It is taking offense at the promise and the one who promises: "The sin of despairing of the forgiveness of sins is *offense*" (116). In offense one either does not dare to believe or one refuses to believe; one is defiant either by not wanting to be a sinner or by insisting on being a sinner (by not wanting there to be forgiveness) (113). To despair of the forgiveness of sins is to walk up to God in Christ and say, "No . . . it is impossible" (114). Sin is to despair while being aware of a God who paradoxically announces our sinful distance from him while offering forgiveness and reconciliation, and despair is the failure of imagination to conceive that such love and forgiveness is possible for oneself. In order to sin, in the strict sense, one has to have the conception of a God whose Incarnation offers absolute forgiveness. In paganism such sin was not a possibility (116).[9]

Finally, the book ends with the highest intensity of sin – the sin of declaring Christianity to be untruth goes further than the despair of the "offer of God's mercy" in Christ. Sin goes on "the offensive" rather than the "defensive" (SUD, 125). It is an explicit rejection of Christ's plea: "Blessed is he who takes no offense at me" (126).

Anti-Climacus finds it astonishing that Christ should have "so repeatedly and fervently warned against offense," while "thousands upon thousands" live in Christendom "without having noticed the slightest possibility of offense" (SUD, 128n). Whenever these words, "Blessed is he who takes no offense at me," are not part of the essential proclamation of Christianity, "Christianity is blasphemy" (128). The complement to *The Sickness unto Death*[10] will take up this thread, in its thoughts on radical healing.

On the one hand, *The Sickness unto Death* puts selfhood forth as a task or project, but it is at the same time a polemic against the notions of self-creation and absolute autonomy that have become a part of secular existentialist accounts of the self as a task or project. *The Sickness unto Death* rethinks the notion of what selfhood means – contextualizing our freedom. But it is also, in the end, a book "for upbuilding" precisely in the sense that it is a book about Christian forgiveness. It is a book "for awakening" insofar as it provokes the reader to reflect on the Christian revelation she ostensibly already accepts and its relation to her life experience. The Christian revelation calls for obedience and an offer of forgiveness. *The Sickness unto Death* suggests that we are deeply at risk because it is difficult to accept our ultimate dependence. If we recognize ourselves in his descriptions of the despairing person, we may come to see in his descriptions a reason for connecting our experience with the notion of absolute dependence, and thus be built up for the obedience that it calls for.

II *Three Discourses at the Communion on Fridays*

On November 14, 1849, three and a half months after *The Sickness unto Death* was published, Kierkegaard published *Three Discourses at the Communion on Fridays*. These continue a concern with preparation for confession, as a condition for communion. The most intriguing is the discourse on the "woman who was a sinner," another theme Kierkegaard liked. Going into the festive dinner, where she knew she would be judged and scorned, she nevertheless loved "her saviour more than her sin" (WA, 143), forgetting herself completely because "she loved much." We learn about Christ's love: "you are love of such a kind that you yourself love forth the love that loves you" (137). Going to the dinner was going to confession, indicating her need for God, which Kierkegaard says was a legitimate kind of "self-loving" (142) despite the fact that he says that her lack of leniency for herself meant "she hated herself" (139). This dialectic of self-love and hatred of self is an important ingredient in any assessment of Kierkegaard's many references to hatred of self. Moreover, it is very striking that Kierkegaard would go on to write two more discourses on this same woman.[11]

notes

1 Kierkegaard corroborates this when he suggests that the relation between the two pseudonyms is best seen as referring to the way in which Anti-Climacus is portrayed as "higher, a Christian on an extraordinarily high level," whereas "Climacus is lower, denies he is a Christian" (SUD, Supp., p. 140 [JP, 6:6439, p. 177]).
2 A theme found repeatedly in the discourses.
3 Although *The Sickness unto Death*'s account of the complex relating that is a self does not thematize any need for intersubjective relations, the construal of despair as a kind of defiance does have implications for the ways in which we relate to each other. Defiance against God expresses itself as violence against

others. A world of people who are either spiritless or who want to be someone other than themselves or who desperately insist on their own self-definition at all costs is a world ripe for violence because it is a world of apathy, envy, and anger.

4 It is unclear how this is to be reconciled with talk about degrees or gradations ("despair a little," SUD, p. 22).

5 The vacillation is crystallized when, on a single page, despair is called "universal" and its absence is said to be "very rare" (SUD, p. 26).

6 The fact that unconscious despair has striking affinities with what Anti-Climacus called finitude's despair and possibility's despair – the number, the copy, mass man, the bourgeois-philistine (SUD, pp. 33, 41) – suggests that the other misrelations of the synthesis could be correlated with other forms of despair.

7 He fails to have "the impression that there is a God and that 'he,' he himself, his self, exists before this God" (SUD, p. 27), or has "no self before God" (SUD, p. 35).

8 Presumably, one cannot despair at all without some consciousness of being before God – although the lesser gradations of that consciousness are dim and obscure and intermittent, a "dialectical interplay between knowing and willing" (SUD, p. 48).

9 He writes: "from another point of view it is true that in the strictest sense the pagan did not sin, for he did not sin before God, and all sin is before God" (SUD, p. 81).

10 *Practice in Christianity.*

11 *An Upbuilding Discourse*, December 20, 1850, and then again *Two Discourses at Communion* (1851).

further reading

IKC, SUD, vol. 19 (1987).

KSY, 1997.

Mooney, Edward, *Selves in Discord and Resolve: Kierkegaard's Moral-Religious Psychology from Either/Or to Sickness unto Death* (New York: Routledge, 1996).

chapter 8

Practice in Christianity, *Discourses*, and the "Attack"

I n Kierkegaard's next work, *Practice in Christianity* (begun in 1848 and published in 1850), we find the most polemical stance thus far in the authorship, a veritable diatribe against the "calamity" (PC, 35) that had occurred: "Christendom has abolished Christianity without really knowing it itself," and "to be a Christian has become a nothing, a silly game, something that everyone is as a matter of course" (36, 67). Anti-Climacus sees his task as follows: "one must attempt again to introduce Christianity into Christendom" (36). The distinction is between Christian faith ("Christianity") and so-called Christian civilization ("Christendom"). One could say that *Works of Love* had already tried to introduce Christianity, but Kierkegaard saw the need for a stronger polemic; the delicate tension between "leniency" and "rigor" that was explored in *Works of Love* needed to be violently upset before it could be restored. *The Sickness unto Death*'s reinterpretation of the notion of sin also sounded a rigorous note, but even there judgment was surrounded by forgiveness. *Practice in Christianity* presents what Kierkegaard had not attempted before. Whereas he presented *Works of Love* in his own name, "without authority," and *The Sickness unto Death* was by a restrained Anti-Climacus, now "truly it is high time for the requirements of ideality to be heard" (67). Many of Kierkegaard's later writings carry on this challenge, but this was the first explicit instance of Kierkegaard's strident call to "judge, then, for yourself," to "examine yourself, now" (38, 39) to end the "blasphemy" and "mockery of God" (29, 30, 33), the "everlasting Sunday babbling about Christianity's glorious and priceless truths, its gentle consolation" that had turned Christianity into "paganism" (35). The writings that followed illustrate the ever-present dialectic between comfort and critique.

I *Practice in Christianity*

Practice in Christianity (whose earlier translation was *Training in Christianity*) is a book about the imitation of Christ, who is the pattern or prototype of the Christian life. But if a new reader approaches it this way, she will be surprised to see that until the end the references to "imitation" or "prototype" are few and far between. Instead, it deeply explores the notion of "offense," which we have seen repeatedly in Kierkegaard's writings, and most recently in *The Sickness unto Death* where despair and defiance were related to offense. The connection between offense and imitation is not obvious, and the whole of *Practice in Christianity* is dedicated to revealing the connection between them in an ever-widening circle of inquiry. We cannot understand what we are to imitate until we are absolutely convinced that we have to take seriously the "situation of contemporaneity" – the physical conditions under which Jesus Christ lived. We should not pass too quickly to the Lord Jesus Christ – we must begin from below, recognizing what preceded that lordship and what it implies for the possibility of "offense" which conditions faith. Only then will we begin to see why the "practice" of Christianity involves "imitation."

Practice in Christianity has an unusual format. It is one book, insofar as it has one title (*Practice in Christianity*), one author (Anti-Climacus), and one editor (S. Kierkegaard), but it is made up of three books, each of which repeats the title and author and editor's preface. So we have *Practice in Christianity I*, *Practice in Christianity II*, and *Practice in Christianity III*, each by Anti-Climacus. When the book was reissued in 1855, Kierkegaard noted some regrets about the initial publication form, suggesting that were he to do it again, he would have used his own name (as he had done initially when writing each of the three parts).[1]

The editor's preface by S. Kierkegaard, which introduces the three writings or parts of *Practice in Christianity*, announces that the author, Anti-Climacus, has forced "the requirement for being a Christian" up to its "supreme ideality." Here "ideality" refers to the positive notion of the ideal – i.e., unconditionality or stringency, what Anti-Climacus later calls its "infinitude" (PC, 67). The preface is striking in the way the editor, S. Kierkegaard, emphasizes the strictness of the requirement while insisting that he is nevertheless not judging others – this message of the requirement is spoken to him alone, reminding him of his need both for grace and for an understanding of how to relate to grace. The message is addressed to him as much as to everyone else, and the way to guarantee that readers understand this is to distinguish the editor from the pseudonymous author.

The three numbered writings are studies based on three of Christ's utterances in the New Testament. The first is an invitation: "Come

Here to Me, All You Who Labor and Are Burdened, and I Will Give You Rest." The second is an affirmation: "Blessed is He Who is Not Offended at Me." Unlike these two first-person claims by Christ, the last writing is introduced as a third-person report, "From On High He will Draw All to Himself," that is based on Christ's prophetic utterance: "When I am lifted up, I will draw all men to myself." Moreover, each writing is subtitled to indicate a somewhat different genre: the first is "For Awakening and Spiritual Deepening," the second is "A Biblical Exposition and Christian Definition," and the third is described as "Christian Expositions." Given the editor's preface, he intends *Practice in Christianity* to teach "the requirement," so the question of what precisely is "the requirement" should always be kept in the background of our reading. We can expect either three approaches to "the requirement," or three elements of it, to be presented.

A The invitation and the halt

Practice in Christianity I (PC I), is headed by the Scriptural quotation, "Come Here, All You Who Labor and are Burdened, and I Will Give You Rest." Already we encounter something unexpected – having been led to expect discussion of the stringent requirement for being a Christian, we find it first approached in terms of a loving invitation to rest, a heartfelt offer of comfort. The infinite requirement is first addressed as a requirement to accept something that is offered – to find rest from our labor and our burden, i.e., to accept a gift. That the three-part study of the rigor of the Christian requirement begins with an encouraging offer of help alerts us to the fact that it must be difficult to accept such help from Christ.

PC I has two main subdivisions – "The Invitation" and "The Halt." The first begins with a concise and passionate encapsulation of the impulse behind the invitation: "How amazing . . . What love! . . . To offer it, no, to shout it out, as if the helper himself were the one who needed help . . . that he feels need, and thus needs to help, needs those who suffer in order to help them" (PC, 11). The appreciation of love's need to love echoes the message of *Works of Love*, and the word-by-word exegesis of the invitation that follows resembles the word-by-word exegesis of the love commandment found there. Anti-Climacus finds each part of the utterance "Amazing!" It is "amazing" that the invitation to "come here" is offered by one who takes the initiative and "seeks" us, calls to us "almost pleading" (12). It is "amazing" that the offer includes everyone – "all you"; the Giver of the Gift seeks us out without "the slightest partiality" (13). Nevertheless the Giver, the Inviter, attends to us in our uniqueness: in a way that echoes the central tension of *Works of Love*, Anti-Climacus suggests that the one who helps is "completely blind to who it is that one is helping, seeing with infinite clarity that, whoever that person may be, he is a sufferer" (13). Our equality is not at odds with our distinctiveness – the clarity of vision *sees* us as if we were the only "patient" (15). The analogy of the physician and patient suggests the way in which this work complements *The Sickness unto Death*. It is "amazing" that the invitation, come "to me," is not an impersonal offer of help from a distance; it is an invitation to intimacy that can only be offered by "sharing the very same condition" (13) as those needy persons it wants to help. It is "amazing" that the object of the invitation is so general – "all you who labor and are burdened"; there is no "specific definition" (15), no restriction that can allow anyone even to wonder if they are excluded. It is "amazing" that the offer, "I will give you rest," is an offer of intimacy in that the "rest" we will be given is being close to Christ – "the helper is the help" (15).

Following this rendition of "Amazing Grace," the second part of the exegesis of "The Invitation" offers a lengthy litany of human sorrows. The list details the "enormous variety" and "almost limitless differences" of our "temporal and earthly suffering" (PC, 16) – e.g., poverty, pain, unfair treatment, and insult. But it also suggests that our essential poverty or neediness is our sinfulness: "if you are conscious of yourself as a sinner, he will . . . raise you up when you accept him," he will "hide your sins" (20).

The third part of the exegesis of "The Invitation" escalates the encouragement found in the earlier parts and begs us not to despair, noting that the inviter seeks us before we call to him – he takes "the first step" (PC, 21). Although the invitation is extended only to seekers (there is no invitation to those who cease "to seek and to sorrow" – 20), still, Anti-Climacus poignantly notes that even a "sigh" will satisfy the condition – even if pain were to render us speechless, a "sigh is enough" (22). In effect, Christ shouts at us to get our attention, but he hears even a silent sigh in response.

Thus, in this intriguing tripartite exegesis of "The Invitation," the requirement is addressed in terms of an offer of comfort and help, punctuated by attention to our earthly suffering and our sinfulness, and culminates in encouragement. This is immediately followed by a section with the jarring title, "The Halt." We are abruptly stopped, forcing us to consider the price or "penalty" (PC, 37, 39) we pay for such comfort, the "risk" we run (52) in allowing ourselves to be helped by Christ: "there is a prodigious halt, the halt that is the condition for faith to be able to come into existence: you are halted by the possibility of offense" (39). "The Halt" turns the focus from the invitation as such to the character of the inviter; it accounts for why the invitation is not accepted eagerly by all (23) – namely, we are *offended* by the one who issues the invitation. The shock here is that it is not the Christ of glory who is offering rest and comfort, but Christ in his "abasement" (24). Although the previous discussion of the invitation inevitably revealed some characteristics of the inviter (that he sacrificed himself, that he was as poor as the poorest – 12, 13), this section develops the kind of sacrifice Christ made and suggests the practical implications of following Christ. It is difficult to accept this gift because with it we have to accept this particular Giver, this abased, lowly, poor man.

"The Halt" thus contrasts with the comfort of "The Invitation,"[2] and it delineates the way in which the possibility of "offense" (PC, 23, 24, 56) is the necessary condition for the decision of faith, and its relation to abasement and paradox.[3] "The Halt" develops the notion of the "situation of contemporaneity" with Christ (41) as the hallmark of faith because the possibility of offense is revealed only in this situation: "one cannot become a believer except by coming to him in his state of abasement, to him, the sign of offense and the object of faith" (24). It calls on us to "examine" ourselves: what would you feel at the sound of these words of invitation to comfort from someone who "looks like this" (38)?

Anti-Climacus elaborates a Christology that goes beyond the sketch of the "sign of offense" found in *Philosophical Fragments* (PF, 23–4). It develops a kenotic Christology, a theology of Christ that emphasizes the emptying out (*kenosis*) of God in Christ, and it seems to locate the *kenosis* of God in the physical conditions of Christ's poverty and suffering (PC, 40). The requirement in its ideality is "becoming contemporary with Christ" (63) – to hear the invitation of faith you have to be facing Christ "as he has existed," indeed, in the only way he has ever existed (24). We do not have the right to appropriate any of Christ's words until we face full on the radical character of the Inviter – that is, until we have "become so contemporary with him in his abasement" that we become aware of his "admonition: Blessed is he who is not offended at me!" (37).

PC I goes further than *Fragments* by developing the practical implications of contemporaneity: that embracing this abased Christ means suffering with him and because of him. Only "that with which you are living simultaneously is actuality – for you" (PC, 64), and to be contemporaneous with Christ means to be present to him in such a way that one risks insult, persecution from others. Even in the invitation it was easy to see why one would prefer to say "No, thanks, then I would still rather go on being deaf and blind, etc. than to be helped in this way" (38). To be contemporaneous with Christ is to embrace Christ in his abasement, but to do that is to refuse to take offense at the condition in which he offers help. Paying attention to the abasement means we follow a poor and persecuted Christ. It means we suffer, and the irony is that to accept this invitation of rest and healing comfort is to *become burdened* with the specific sufferings and persecution that will befall anyone who tries to be Christian. Come to me all you who are burdened and be further burdened. This is offensive.

Even more burdensome than the insult and persecution that are heaped on one who chooses to become a Christian, is the news we receive from the abased Christ – the news that we are sinful human beings. The offense is that "the inviter's real meaning was that *sin is a human being's corruption*" (PC, 61). The healing we are offered abases us. This is offensive.

Offense and imitation are connected because only in the offensive situation of contemporaneity are we aware of what to imitate. We are to imitate Christ's obedience to God and the abasement that involved. But Anti-Climacus suggests another kind of imitation in his references to daily life in Copenhagen, to "the market on Amagertorv" (PC, 59), as well as in much of his discussion about compassion "in actuality" rather than from a distance, as in sharing a common situation with the poorest. That is to say, one can also imitate Christ by imitating his compassion to the poor, his concern with the suffering of others rather than his own self, his compassion for all without exclusion (by contrast with "the compassion of sausage peddlers [which] is trapped in . . . consideration for other sausage peddlers" and a few others) (59). Imitation of divine compassion means to "in earnest seek the company of, completely live with, the poor and lowly of the people, the workers, the manual laborers, the cement mixers, etc.!" (58). He contrasts the superior philanthropy which maintains its own comfortable lifestyle, with actually living with the poor; of course this may invite further suffering, because anyone who actually does what Christ did is accused of pride or vanity or eccentricity or madness (58). The requirement to imitate Christ by doing what he did puts you in the position of being laughed at, criticized, and persecuted by those who have a different notion of compassion.

"The Halt" thus presents us with what seem to be two conditions for faith: (a) the possibility of offense and (b) the consciousness of sin. But they are actually two formulations of the same condition, insofar as one is offended by the attribution of sin. It also suggests two kinds of imitation – imitation of Christ's obedient abasement and imitation of Christ's compassion for others. This section also strongly echoes the claims in Climacus's *Fragments* that the "object of faith" is a "paradox" (PC, 25, 30) and that there is an "infinite qualitative difference" between God and man (28–9).

This emphasis on the "situation of contemporaneity" with the abased Christ raises the question of the relevance of history that Climacus raised in *Fragments*. Now the problem is exacerbated precisely to the extent that the condition of the "abased" Christ is seen to be decisive. *Fragments* wanted to marginalize historical detail, yet *Practice in Christianity* requires it for the determination of the abasement of the man who said he was God, for the description of the "situation of contemporaneity." "The Halt" offers a deeper theological and philosophical inquiry into the philosophical question embedded in *Fragments* – namely, it explicitly asks what kind of results would demonstrate "God"? He distinguishes between "world history" and "sacred history" (PC, 23, 25n): "knowledge annihilates Jesus Christ" (33), even though Christ's "historical actuality" must be attended to for him to be known as abased (37). History could at most show that he was "a great man," not that he was God (27); history could at most show that he was a poor man – but it could not show that this poverty was God's abasement. The notion of abasement entails an appreciation of the distance between what ought to be and what is, and history cannot help in this determination. But although it affirms and fills out Climacus's sketch of the relation between faith and history, there is a decided difference in the tone. An absoluteness and authoritative inflexibility are evident here: "A historical Christianity is nonsense and un-Christian muddled thinking, because whatever true Christians there are in any generation are contemporary with Christ" (64). The detached tone of a thought-experimenter is missing. The frustration and anger are evident: the attempt to approach Jesus Christ by what can be known of him historically is "blasphemy" (29, 30); it is a "mockery of God" (30, 32); it is "blindness" and "impiety" (33). The "either – or" is repeatedly put bluntly: "Jesus Christ is the object of faith; one must either believe in him or be offended" (33).

What then is the requirement for becoming a Christian according to PC I? Is the "requirement" to let oneself be helped by Christ, to find rest and comfort in him, or is the "requirement" to become contemporaneous with Christ in his abasement, and so suffer with him. What is the role of suffering? Interestingly, "The Moral" that concludes PC I puts suffering in a slightly different perspective. The requirement is

> that each individual in quiet inwardness before God is to humble himself under what it means in the strictest sense to be a Christian, is to confess honestly before God where he is so that he still might worthily accept the grace that is offered to every imperfect person – that is, to everyone. And then nothing further; then, as for the rest, let him do his work and rejoice in it, love his wife and rejoice in her, joyfully bring up his children, love his fellow beings, rejoice in life. (PC, 67)

It is not all about suffering, it seems, but also about rejoicing in life. "The Halt" had emphasized the inevitability of suffering if one chooses to be Christian and had insisted that God's notion of human misery differed from the human notion, so that only sin was considered human misery. "The Moral," on the contrary, implies that the requirement is to live joyfully, except when some self-denial is part of a humble consciousness of personally being a sinner, "a contrite conscience" (68), and duties to one's fellow beings. It rejects the notion of self-denial for its own sake, and it rejects the notion that being a Christian is only about suffering.

"The Moral" is thus slightly out of keeping with the tone of what immediately precedes it: "The Halt" had emphasized that we need humble honesty and "fear and trembling" (PC, 65) before the "task" (66). "The Moral," on the other hand, opens with a reference to "grace" (this is the first mention of grace since the editor's preface). The muscular and purely active tone of the task is softened: "the terrible language of the Law" sounds "so terrible" because one thinks one has to hold on to Christ, whereas "it is Christ who holds on to him" (67).[4]

But in the end, it is always a case of simultaneity – rigor and comfort. "The Moral" repeats the double-edged character of what precedes it: the abased Christ offers to comfort us, yet the abased Christ requires imitation of Him in his abasement. The rigor is that "admittance is only through the consciousness of sin; to want to enter by any other road is high treason against Christianity" (PC, 67–8), and the comfort is that nevertheless "at that very same moment the essentially Christian transforms itself into and is sheer leniency, grace, love, mercy" (67).

B The sign of offense

The title of PC II, "Blessed is He Who Is Not Offended At Me," as well as a quick glance at its table of contents, leads the reader to expect a continuation of the discussion of offense already seen in PC I. There is repetition, but we will also see something new.

The initial section approaches the notion of offense from a different perspective, focusing on the emotions that Jesus feels – both sadness and joy. Anti-Climacus emphasizes the "infinite abyss of sadness" (PC, 77) that Jesus feels because his love causes us to be in a situation that can be our undoing, the "infinite sadness" that we can refuse to let ourselves be helped by love (78). But it ends on a high note – the joy Jesus feels over the one who overcomes offense. The ultimate irony is that Christ has "to be the sign of offense in order to be the object of faith!" (98).

PC II's first major section, "The Exposition," goes beyond what was done in "The Halt" in several ways. First, it immediately lays out a schema of three versions of offense: "essential offense" (PC, 83), whether in the form of offense in relation to Christ's "loftiness" or offense in relation to Christ's "lowliness" (82), is distinguished from another kind of offense that Jesus incurred when he came into "collision" with the established order of his day (83). Second, it fleshes out this brief summary in a way that illustrates an important feature of Kierkegaard's writing – his deep reliance on Scripture. "The Exposition" makes reference to at least 18 New Testament passages, and includes detailed exegesis of at least six passages – all in the service of illustrating differences between three kinds of offense. The first set of textual exegeses illustrates the ways in which Christ came into collision with the Pharisees – and interestingly it is in this discussion of conflict with the "established" order that Anti-Climacus brings up the question of "inwardness" and the relation between inner and outer that so fascinates Kierkegaard (89, 92). Fear and trembling are impossible when the established order is deified, when there is commensurability between inner and outer, when piety guarantees esteem, when "inwardness" and hiddenness are feared (86–90).[5] The two forms taken by "essential offense" (83) are illuminated by reference to two more sets of scriptural exegeses of Jesus' claims: the first is offense at a human being's claims to be God (the offense of "loftiness"), and the second is offense at God's appearance as a human being (the offense of "lowliness").

"The Exposition" also adds to the message of "The Halt" insofar as it presents "offense" as intellectual. Although "The Halt" had suggested that historical knowledge is irrelevant because God assumes an "incognito" in the form of a lowly servant (PC, 25), as well as how the same "signs and wonders" can either repel or attract (41), it had emphasized that the source of the offense was that "the inviter's real meaning was that *sin is a human being's corruption*" (61), suggesting the offensiveness of having to have a "contrite conscience" (68). This affronts our sense of ourselves as righteous rather than our intellectual understanding as such. "The Exposition" in PC II, however, places more of an accent on how "all human *understanding* must come to a halt in one way or another, must take umbrage" (105, my emphasis), must come to a "standstill" (82, 120).[6] Here the point is distinctively theological – "the contradiction in which the possibility of offense lies is to be *an individual human being*, a lowly human being – and then to act in the character of being God" (97, my emphasis). Anti-Climacus had insisted in the summary of the exposition that the God-Man is "not the union of God and man," but rather "the unity of God and an individual human being" (82).[7] The former is the abstraction of divinity and humanity; the latter is the concretion of God and an *individual* human being. This constitutes the "paradox" on which "the understanding must come to a standstill" – i.e., "offense in the strictest sense" (82).

The very fact that Christ has to say "Blessed is He who is not offended at Me," when he is feeding the crowd and curing the sick, suggests that none of these things directly reveals who Christ is, indeed, that nothing could: Christ himself makes it clear that we do not come to him by means of demonstrations, and (echoing Climacus in the *Postscript*[8]) that "there is no *direct* transition to becoming Christian" because any purported demonstration remains "ambiguous" (PC, 96). The whole point is (again echoing Climacus) "how difficult it is to become a believer" (99). Another source of offense to the understanding is the issue of miracles. Anti-Climacus makes a philosophical point about the ambiguity of "miracle" as scientifically unexplained event: "In the situation of contemporaneity you are placed between this inexplicable thing (but from that it still does not follow that it is a miracle) and then an individual human being who looks like others – and it is he who does it" (97). Thus, in "The Halt" the offense is related to our sinfulness, whereas in PC II, the offense is either how this man can claim to be God, or how God can be this man.

PC II's second main section, "The Essential Categories of Offense," illustrates Kierkegaard's concern with communication, particularly in terms of linguistic "signs." The issues of "incognito" and epistemological indirection now assume a different form; the entire section serves as another place to revisit the theme that permeates the whole authorship – namely, the relation between inner and outer. Seven theses are presented, and their very titles provide a fairly good summary of the discussion: "1. The God Man is a Sign," "2. The Form of a Servant is Unrecognizability," "3. The Impossibility of Direct Communication," "4. In Christ the Secret of Suffering is the Impossibility of Direct Communication," "5. The Possibility of Offense is to Deny Direct Communication," "6. To Deny Direct Communication is to Require Faith," and "7. The Object of Faith is the God-Man Precisely Because the God-Man is the Possibility of Offense."

Anti-Climacus indulges in semiotics – the study of signs. He asks, "What is meant by a *sign*?" and he answers: "A sign is the denied immediacy . . . the sign is only for the one who knows that it is a sign and in the strictest sense only for the one who knows what it means; for everyone else the sign is that which it immediately is" (PC, 124). A sign is a strange thing – on the one hand, it does communicate something. The sign is needed. But what it communicates is not absolutely direct. For example, we all need to learn how to interpret traffic signs – there is the possibility that they can be misunderstood and the person who has not been trained in the practice of traffic signs will see only an indeterminate squiggle on a placard. What we might think of as the most obvious signs can be interpreted differently.

PC II suggests the notion of Christianity as a practice of learning how to interpret signs. Insisting on the "impossibility of direct communication" only makes sense if there is some communication, some revelation – a sign, after all, communicates something. If the God-Man is a sign, then God's hiddenness is not absolute. Whereas the earlier remarks on the relation between inner and outer concerned the relation between inner piety and external behavior, here the relation between inner and outer is explored in terms of God's hiddenness and God's revelation. A "sign of contradiction" must communicate something – "the contradictory parts must not annul each other in such a way that the sign comes to mean nothing. . . . an unconditional concealment" (PC, 125). We are supposed to notice something – "to justify the name of 'sign,' there must be something by which it draws attention to itself or to the contradiction" (125). But the communication is indirect.

The elaborate discussion of the divine incognito and the impossibility of direct recognizability of God in Christ is Anti-Climacus's response to the church that appeals to demonstrations and historical documentation. It is meant to unsettle the smug assurances of those who are certain they know they are Christians. But the discussion is perplexing – how, for example, is "unconditional concealment" (PC, 125), which precludes the possibility of faith, different from the "absolute unrecognizability" (127) that is constitutive of God being "an individual human being" (127)? The tension between the hidden and the revealed is a constant and ineradicable part of Christianity; it is an example of how the offensiveness of the paradox is raised to its highest level.

In the end, the "situation of contemporaneity" posits a direct connection between offense and imitation: "to be an imitator means that your life has as much similarity to his as is possible for a human life to have" (PC, 106). It ties together the two main versions of the "requirement" for being a Christian – namely, passing through the possibility of offense, and the requirement of imitation of Christ. The final part of *Practice in Christianity* focuses on this imitation.

C Imitation and love

In PC III, "From On High, He Will Draw All to Himself," we find seven discourses, each an elaborate exegesis of John 12:32 ("And I, when I am lifted up from the earth, will draw all to myself"), showing various ways in which the sacred words can be read, such that the differences reveal "the one and the same meaning" of the passage (PC, 259). The scriptural reference here trades on the ambiguity between being lifted up on the cross and being lifted up finally in triumph and glory. Anti-Climacus does not explicitly note this, but appeals exclusively to the "crucifixion" as providing "the right meaning" (259); however, each exegesis begins with a prayer addressed to the "Lord" Jesus Christ, which suggests the "loftiness" of the Christ who has been "transfigured" (152).

(1) The first exegesis is a sermon that "Magister Kierkegaard" gave at a communion service in Our Lady's Church, which (we learn in a footnote) Anti-Climacus prints with his consent, because it gave him the title for PC III as a whole. Magister Kierkegaard insists that Christ draws

us to himself "through the consciousness of sin" (PC, 155), but he gives a crucial warning not to be one-sided (154) because the emphasis on final glory and the emphasis on suffering in the world need to be corrected by each other. The person who feels drawn to Christ only in Christ's abasement "does not recognize Christ and therefore does not love him either" (154). This dialectical appreciation of the tension between both abasement and lordship probably accounts for what Anti-Climacus calls the milder tone of this sermon.

(2) The second exegesis is of the word "draw," and contrasts it with the situation of being drawn downward, through deception, delay, or seduction. To draw is to draw up. To draw up can only be done by what is "something in itself or . . . something that is in itself," not the "sensate, the secular, the momentary, the multiple" (PC, 158) – not by earthly things. And what is drawn up is a self, not an object. To draw a self to something higher means to help it to become itself, because Jesus Christ "first and foremost wants to help every human being to become a self" (160). And because the self is a "free being" (160) to draw the self is "to posit a choice" (159). Christ's words imply a contrast: "when I am lifted up" implies that I am not yet lifted up. Abasement is a residue in these words, even if they make us think of the loftiness: "you are not going to escape the abasement, for if these words remind you of the loftiness, the speaker reminds you of the abasement. You cannot choose one of the two without becoming guilty of an untruth" (166). Here the "either – or" that had such a prominent place in PC I and PC II – either believe or be offended – is recuperated in the idiom of a "choice," but ironically the choice is to take both of the two things in tension, not "either – or." It looks as if Anti-Climacus offers the same warning or reminder that Magister Kierkegaard did – namely, that Christ must be embraced in both his abasement and his loftiness.

(3) The prayer in the third discourse, again emphasizing the "Lordship" of Jesus Christ, in glory (Savior and Redeemer), asks for help: help us to "want to be like you" (PC, 167) in your abasement since we are not naturally drawn to suffering. This discourse repeats that Christ's life is the "story of suffering" (168), but it introduces a new accent – Christ's love for us becomes a leitmotif (170, 171, 175, 176, 178). "The point of the discourse" (176) (perhaps the point of the whole book) is that the loftiness does not erase the abasement, or, in other words, the world "crucifies love" (178). Practice in Christianity is practice in loving, as Christ loved (175–6).

(4) The fourth discourse, at the very center of the seven, serves several strategic purposes. First, it reveals the unity of the entire book by

looking back to the initial "Invitation," coming full circle in two respects. It looks back to the "Invitation," "Come to Me All You who Labor and are Burdened," to illustrate that Christ's desire to draw all to himself was always present ("come to me" equals "I want to draw you to myself"). Moreover, it makes the important qualification that although Christ called "all" to himself, wants to draw "all" to himself, not all will come or allow themselves to be drawn (PC, 184).

And this is the second strategic purpose – it deliberately makes the emphasis on suffering so great that it is likely to be criticized as an "un-Christian exaggeration" (PC, 197). That in this world "love is hated" and "truth is persecuted" (198) is a deep and constant refrain, and the stringency of the requirement to suffer reaches such a pitch that people will likely think (mistakenly) that Christianity is "cruel" (196). In this way, it intensifies the paradox that Christianity, which seems to be "cruel," is actually "leniency and love" (196). When Christ draws people to himself, he "does not take them out of the world in which they are living" (185) – the requirement is "to become and continue to be a Christian" "in this world" (196) and this will likely lead to the world's "opposition," even alienation, ostracization, or other forms of persecution by society (192). However, Anti-Climacus makes significant qualifications about suffering. He suggests that the likelihood or even the inevitability of suffering does not equal the recommendation to adopt suffering for its own sake. Suffering is not a goal in itself – "enough lowliness and abasement surely come of themselves" if we try to imitate Christ (185), enough suffering is "in store" for us without trying to make more (190). Suffering simply follows from holding fast to the prototype (193, 197).

The third strategic move made in this discourse is to refocus the notion of the abasement of Christ as an "image" (*Billede*) that becomes "prototype" (*Forbillede*) by placing a demand on us (PC, 184). Christ passed the "test" of life each of us is subject to, and he thereby "developed the prototype" for us (184). Although there is caution about the use of imagination here, there is also an appreciation of it. Imagination is the medium for a kind of "seeing-as" and it allows us to see an image of abasement as a demand on us – to make the conceptual leap from an "is" to an "ought." The language of being or feeling "drawn" is the language of captivation, imaginative engagement. Moreover, saying that the world will make you suffer if you are a Christian implies that the world can *see* that you are a Christian, and this raises a crucial question about the kind of "inwardness" involved. With sharp sarcasm he notes that in Christendom, when the "so called pastors" say that Christianity is only about God loving us, inwardness becomes an escapist excuse – inwardness is concealed, "perhaps so well concealed that it is not there at all" (197). This ironic inversion of the notion of "inwardness" (214–20) is also the subject of most of the fifth discourse.

(5) The fifth discourse serves to develop the image of Christ as "the truth" (PC, 202–9), offering us another understanding of "the require-ment" – the goal is "not to know the truth but to be the truth" and "when the requirement is to be truth, to know the truth is an untruth" (205). It strongly echoes the *Postscript* when it points to "the difference between truth and truth" (207): truth is expressed in the "striving for it" and "nobody knows more of the truth than what he is of the truth" (205–6). The truth is literally "the way" and the "life" (207, 206). The fallacy of regarding "truth in the sense of results" rather than "in the sense of *the way*" (207) is one of the sources of the confusion in the Danish church of Kierkegaard's day – it thinks it can benefit from the truth without living it. We are led directly to a critique of what he calls "Christendom." Anti-Climacus introduces three terms: the "Church militant," the "Church triumphant," and "established Christendom." The first two terms are part of a long Christian tradition, and assume their traditional meanings – the church militant is the church on earth that is "struggling . . . battling to endure" (212), and the church tri-umphant is the victorious church in heaven. The third term, "estab-lished Christendom," means two different things; the discussion is complicated, and while at first we seem to have a single kind of criticism of the Danish church, it turns out that there are two (almost opposite) kinds of things wrong with it.

First, the "task of the discourse," Anti-Climacus says, is to dispel "the illusion of a Church triumphant" (PC, 209). That is, the Danish church's self-understanding implies that it confuses itself with a church tri-umphant, a church that is victorious already here on earth. The church militant, on earth today, should resemble the original situation of Christianity: one of striving to be Christian "within an environment that is the opposite of being Christian" (212). Instead, in the Danish church being a Christian is carried out in "an environment that is synonymous, homogeneous with being Christian" (212). It "pays" to be Christian in such a world; "being a Christian will as a necessary conse-quence . . . be *directly* recognizable by the favor, honor and esteem I win in this world" (212). In the original situation of Christianity, the situa-tion of contemporaneity with Christ, however, the church suffered from the world's "opposition" and "hostility"; there was a criterion of "inverse recognizability" – I am *inversely* recognizable" as a Christian "by the opposition I experience" (212). Thus, the issue of inner and outer, of commensurability, is re-engaged in the following way: in Christendom, there is direct recognizability ("being the true Christian is rewarded with distinction" – 213) in that the church and world are commensurate because the outer directly reflects the inner; in the church militant, direct recognizability is impossible (214–15) – the outer contradicts the inner because true piety is rewarded with persecution or scorn.

But Anti-Climacus complicates his criticism when he shifts to another, apparently opposite, way of viewing "established Christendom." He does this by accusing the Danish church of an ill-egitimate appeal to "hidden inwardness": "insofar as so-called *established Christendom* does not call itself the Church triumphant, it perhaps disdains this externality but produces the same confusion by means of *hidden inwardness*" (PC, 214). Now Christendom, established Christianity, has adopted a new relation to worldly esteem and reward – it tries to avoid them as a way of proving itself. It appeals to hidden inwardness as the mark of the Christian and claims that its Christianity is not to be expressed externally, but to remain hidden. The result is that everyone can claim to be Christian, inwardly. Anti-Climacus ironically commends the church on "such lofty piety!" when he writes: "What an infinite depth of piety, since the whole thing could so very easily be pretence" (217). There is no way to judge who is a Christian, because Christianity on this view does not express itself in the world. Anti-Climacus puts this forward as a false relation between Christendom and inwardness.[9] *Practice in Christianity* thus indirectly insists on what *Works of Love* had directly insisted on – namely, fruits of love.

In sum, *Practice in Christianity* criticizes the commensurability between the world and the church that established Christendom holds, as well as the kind of incommensurability it holds. What should we think of as the normative relation between church and world? Anti-Climacus's performance suggests that one cannot put it simply without being misleading – there is no single answer. One needs to say both that a certain kind of commensurability is bad and that a certain kind of incommensurability is bad. It is a fine line to walk.[10]

The final insistence on the Christian church as a "militant" church (PC, 221) opens out into a normative account in which the notion of "single individual," a notion that "corresponds to struggling," is developed (223). And here we find such provocative claims as that " 'fellowship' is a lower category than 'the single individual' " (223) and that the Christian should be "so turned inward that it seems as if all the others do not exist at all" (225). This culminates in the apparently heartless claim that "love of God is hatred of the world" (224). The "heterogeneity" of the God-Man (221) seems to lead to a heart-wrenching collision between Christianity and indispensable values. This forces one to think about what "the world" means – insofar as "this world is Christendom," it is opposed to love of God; insofar as the world is the sensate, the multiple, it is opposed to love of God. This is not, of itself, a rejection of creation, of the natural.

(6) The sixth discourse finally puts the spotlight on "imitation" proper, and it develops the crucial contrast between an *imitator* of Christ and an *admirer* of Christ. Christians are supposed to be "imitators of a life" rather than "adherents of a teaching" (PC, 237). An imitator is or strives to be what he admires, whereas an admirer contrives to remain ignorant of the fact "that what is admired involves a claim upon him" (241). This is a barely disguised attack on the clergy – a reminder of the risk involved in putting oneself forward as a preacher because the preacher "himself should be what he proclaims" (235). The "prototype" is again front and center, not as the object of admiration, but as a *"requirement"* (239).

(7) The final discourse is technically one short page summarizing Christ's "life and works on earth as what he left for imitation" (PC, 259), and a recognition that each reader has to decide for himself what he wants to do with the book. But appended to this is a very long prayer to the "Lord Jesus Christ" that he will draw us all to himself. It is a prayer on behalf of everyone: infants, parents, lovers, husbands and wives, the fortunate and the suffering, but it is turned finally to those who are specially charged with drawing people to Christ – preachers. It reminds them of their duty and the dangerous consequences of their failure to do their duty. Kierkegaard will not drop this challenge, but will go on to intensify it.[11] Before he does so, however, he turns to the genre of religious discourse.

II Discourses (1850, 1851)

Two months after publishing *Practice in Christianity*, Kierkegaard published a single upbuilding discourse (December 20, 1850), his second one on the theme of "The Woman Who Was a Sinner." This woman is important to Kierkegaard because the only thing that was "unconditionally important" to her was to find forgiveness (WA, 154).

From 1851 on, Kierkegaard produced only signed works. The first of these (*Two Discourses at the Communion on Fridays*) was a set of discourses that was different from all those preceding it, in virtue of both its particularly poignant dedication and its preface. In place of the simple dedication to his father is the following: "To One Unnamed, Whose Name Will One Day Be Named, is dedicated, with this little work, the entire authorship, as it was from the beginning." The phrase "as it was from the beginning" suggests a kind of unity to the "entire authorship." Moreover, Kierkegaard speaks his heart, or so it seems, more directly and passionately than in any of the earlier prefaces. He expresses a view

which in a way is my life, the content of my life, its fullness, its bliss, its peace and satisfaction – this, or this view of life, which is the thought of humanity and of human equality: Christianly, every human being (the single individual), unconditionally every human being, once again, unconditionally every human being, is equally close to God – how close and equally close? – is loved by him. Thus there is equality, infinite equality, between human beings. (WA, 165)

This suggests a deep Christian impulse as the "content of [his] life."

The first of the discourses at the communion, "But One Who is Forgiven Little Loves Little," reinforces the comfort found in the upbuilding discourse that preceded it, which was also on "The Woman Who Was a Sinner." Admitting that literally these are "words of judgment," he works desperately to find the "comfort" in them (WA, 171) to share with the reader. First, he notes that nothing is said about God's love in this statement but only about human love, and from the absence of any comment on God's love, he takes comfort that "God is unchanged love"; second, he takes the little word, "loves," notes that it is in the present tense, and suggests that there is comfort there because it is not as if the accounts are closed – it is now, there is still time to change (175).

In the second discourse, "Love Will Hide a Multitude of Sins" (the third on this theme), he notes that in contrast to his earlier discussion of this theme in *Works of Love*, where the hiding was human love's response to the neighbor, this time he is speaking about how "Christ's love hides a multitude of sins" (WA, 182). In other words, here at this period of his life, his deepest hope is the comfort of God's forgiving love, expressed through Christ.

The concern expressed in these discourses, to dedicate the "entire authorship, as it was from the beginning," probably revived memories of his earlier attempts in 1848 to provide a retrospective account of his authorship. Although he chose not to publish the longer account, entitled *The Point of View for My Work as an Author*, in his lifetime, now (in August 1851) he decided to bring out his abbreviated version of *The Point of View*, entitled *On My Work as An Author*. In a mere 14 pages he describes what he saw as the direction his authorship had taken. This brief account and the original fuller version have the peculiar status of being *published* retrospectives, and I will briefly consider the matter of Kierkegaard's point of view in chapter 9.

III The "Attack"

A *For Self-Examination*

As if to provide a dialectical counterweight to the comfort in the last discourses, Kierkegaard decided to upset people again, shoving on them an "opportunity" – *For Self-Examination* – in 1851. (He also wrote at the same time a sequel to this, entitled *Judge for Yourself*, but held it back from publication during his lifetime.) In the course of recommending self-examination to the present age, Kierkegaard put forth a possibility that Anti-Climacus could not have: although he agreed with Anti-Climacus's account of the rigor of the requirement, Kierkegaard here offered a "lower form of the religious," one suited for all those "pampered" and "average" people among whom he included himself (FSE, 11, 21). His counsel was: "let us at least be honest and admit it" (12). This "lower form" is a "restlessness oriented toward inward deepening" and, however mild a form of "godly piety" it is, we still need to work for it (24). This goal of "restlessness oriented toward inward deepening" is in continuity with *Practice in Christianity*, although it is presented more modestly. The modesty does not, however, preclude the biting satire, with which he mocks the scholars who think that they have read God's word when they have puzzled through a translation – "God's Word is given in order that you shall act according to it, not that you shall practice interpreting obscures passages" with "ten dictionaries, twenty-five commentaries" (29, 32). However important such scholarly work is, it is preliminary to "reading" God's word, and often used as a delaying tactic so that one need not act on God's word. It is part and parcel of the "secular mentality" of those who want "to become Christian as cheaply as possible," those who took Luther's corrective in vain and shouted "we are free from all works – long live Luther!" (16). This challenge to those who "applied *grace* in such a way that they freed themselves from works" (17) is Kierkegaard's corrective to the misuse of Luther's corrective. An appeal for honesty pervades this work (honesty is another way of talking about transparency, and commensurability between inner and outer), and he insists that our life "should express works as strenuously as possible," but the rigor is tempered by the further requirement: namely, gratitude for "grace" (17).

For *Self-Examination* was published in 1851, with the hope of obtaining an admission from the highest prelate of the church, Bishop Mynster, that he too saw the need for an inner reformation of the Danish state church. Not getting such an admission deeply disappointed Kierkegaard and there followed a three-year silence in his writing career.

B Late writings[12]

In 1854 Bishop Mynster died, and, prompted by Bishop Martensen's public praise for Mynster as a religious exemplar, Kierkegaard's defense/attack on the established church became unambiguously an attack. Utterly frustrated that his writings seemed to have had no effect on the leaders of the church and that his attempt to awaken people to the difference between cultural Christianity and the Christianity of the New Testament had failed, he turned to more public media. During 1854–5, he produced extremely outspoken, indeed, exasperated criticism in 21 articles in the newspaper *The Fatherland*, and then 10 more volumes of essays in his own series of pamphlets, *The Moment*. The tenor of those volumes is reflected in the two essays he published during this period: *This Must Be Said, So Let it Be Said*, and *What Christ Judges of Official Christianity*. On September 1, 1855, in a draft for *The Moment*, and in what appears to have been the last piece he penned before his death, he wrote: "I cannot serve these legions of huckstering knaves, I mean the pastors, who by falsifying the definition of Christianity have, for the sake of the business, gained millions and millions of Christians. I am not a Christian – and unfortunately I am able to make it manifest that the others are not either – indeed, even less than I, since they fancy themselves to be that" (TM, 340).

One can construe Kierkegaard's life as ending with an attack on his church, but one can also highlight another kind of ending: that is, on September 3, 1855, as if to enclose these polemical writings in the parentheses of comfort, Kierkegaard published a sermon on "The Changelessness of God." He turned back to this sermon (which he had preached in Citadel Church in 1851) to find the message he wanted to publish at this point. This prayer to the *"Father"* who "wants nothing else, thinks of nothing else than, unchanged, to send good and perfect gifts" is admittedly followed by a reminder that we must receive such gifts "worthily" (TM, 269, 270). Because God's will is changeless, we must "honestly" strive to align ourselves with it or be crushed by it, but there is also *"reassurance and blessedness in this thought"* of God's changelessness (272, 278). The other side of "unconditional obedience" is "sheer consolation, peace, joy, blessedness" (271).

Kierkegaard was only 42 years old when he died in a Copenhagen hospital on November 13, 1855. In keeping with his extravagant claim that he "would rather gamble, booze, wench, steal, and murder than take part in making a fool of God" by participating "in the kind of earnestness Bishop Martensen calls Christian earnestness" (TM, 21), he refused to receive a final communion from any official churchman.

notes

1 The change to the pseudonym had been a late one.
2 The offer of *"rest"* in "The Invitation" had already hinted at the notion of forgiveness from sin (PC, pp. 18–19), but "The Halt" replays in a deeper register the notions of offense and sin.

3 It echoes the *Fragments'* emphasis on offense and its claim that there is no follower at second-hand, and that we each individually have to embrace Christ.

4 Admittedly, "The Invitation" also spoke of the requirement in terms of letting oneself be helped by Christ, but this seems to get lost sight of until "The Moral."

5 This will be developed later in the third, fourth, and fifth discourses of the final part of *Practice in Christianity*.

6 The offense is, nevertheless, not at a "doctrine"(PC, p. 106).

7 Kierkegaard is not distinguishing here between unity and union – he uses the same Danish word for both.

8 Climacus uses this very phrase (CUP, p. 381).

9 This is a most interesting critique of Christendom because it anticipates the objection that Kierkegaard himself renders religion too inward; Anti-Climacus is, however, expressing Kierkegaard's awareness of the way in which such a criterion of inwardness can be pretense.

10 *Works of Love* makes this clearer in its contrast between "externals" and "fruits."

11 *For Self-Examination* and the articles that constitute what is called the "attack on Christendom."

12 These are collected in *The Moment* (TM).

further reading

Gouwens, David, *Kierkegaard as a Religious Thinker* (Cambridge: Cambridge University Press, 1996).

IKC, FSE/JFY, vol. 21 (2002).

IKC, PC, vol. 20 (2004).

KSY, 2001.

Walsh, Sylvia, *Living Christianity: Kierkegaard's Dialectic of Christian Existence* (University Park, PA: Penn State University Press, 2005).

chapter 9

Looking Back and Looking Ahead

Although a summary of general themes would go against the point of this introduction to Kierkegaard's work, which has been to attend to each of the texts as a particular provocative performance, it is still possible that a concluding (or unconcluding) comment on the authorship as a whole may be useful. There are several ways to do this.

I Looking Back – The Retrospectives

One way involves looking into the two retrospectives on his authorship written by Kierkegaard. In 1848, he felt it important to produce what he called *The Point of View for My Work as An Author*; when he decided against publishing this in his lifetime, he chose to do an abbreviated version, entitled *On My Work as an Author*, which he published in 1851. In this brief work, he describes his authorial intention as follows: "'*Without authority*' **to make aware** of the religious, the essentially Christian, is the category for my whole work as an author regarded as a totality" (OMWA, 12, Kierkegaard's emphases). In the fuller version, published after his death, he insisted that he had been "a religious author" and that "the esthetic in the works . . . is the incognito and the deception in the service of Christianity" (PV, 23–4). What should we make of this suggestion of a unity in the authorship – that all his writings, from the very beginning and including the pseudonymous work, were "in the service of Christianity"?

It has become fashionable in some quarters to dismiss any author's retrospectives as either self-serving, or at least revisionary, and certainly a caution is in order lest a reader think that a retrospective offers privileged information. Kierkegaard, however, evinced a healthy anxiety about his ability to understand or explain his authorship when he himself reminded the reader that this is a *retro*spective: "This is how I *now* understand the whole. From the beginning I could not quite see what has indeed also been my own development" (OMWA, 12, my emphasis). He refers to an experience many authors have themselves had: "In my case what I myself have planned, carried out, and said – I myself sometimes understand only afterward how correct it was, that there was something far deeper in it than I thought at first" (PV, 292). Moreover, Kierkegaard was not at all shy about revealing that a deep interest behind the authorship was the joy he took in writing: "Fundamentally to be an author has been my only possibility . . . my need to write was too great and writing satisfied me too much" (211–12).

More importantly, Kierkegaard never intended for us to take his word for what he did. He anticipated modern literary critics' insistence on the need for a very careful use of authorial commentary and retrospective accounts. He advises readers to exercise caution: "It might seem that a simple declaration by the author himself in this regard is more than adequate; after all, he must know best what is what. I do not, however, think much of declarations in connection with literary productions" and "if in the capacity of a third party, as a reader, I cannot substantiate from the writings that what I am saying is the case, that it cannot be otherwise, it could never occur to me to want to win what I thus consider as lost" (PV, 33).[1] He continues:

> *Qua* author it does not help very much that I *qua* human being declare that I have intended this and that. But presumably everyone will admit that if it can be shown that such and such a phenomenon cannot be explained in any other way, and that on the other hand it can in this way be explained at every point, or that this explanation fits at every point, then the correctness of this explanation is substantiated as clearly as the correctness of an explanation can ever be substantiated. (PV, 33)

He offers for our consideration the possibility that if we assume that the authorship is the work of an esthetic author, we are at a loss to explain the *Two Upbuilding Discourses*, whereas if we assume the authorship was by a religious author, "step by step it tallies at every point," and is plausible as "the explanation" of why a religious author would ever use the esthetic forms (PV, 33–4).

Kierkegaard's accounts of his authorship, whether in the published retrospectives or in his journals, do not provide definitive guidelines for reading the authorship, but they may still prove useful. Sometimes, they illuminatingly corroborate something in the texts; at other times, they may offer fruitful possibilities that can be tested in (and possibly corroborated by) the texts. For example, he writes: "Before God, religiously, when I speak with myself, I call my whole work as an author my own upbringing and development, but not in the sense as if I were now complete or completely finished with regard to needing upbringing and development" (OMWA, 12). An educational development is, I suggest, both initially plausible and a useful way of reading the developing treatment of themes like paradox, the demonic, second immediacy, despair, faith, and sin. In other words, I do not give Kierkegaard's retrospective accounts any privileged status, but the claims found in them deserve to be considered as possibilities about Kierkegaard's authorship; their validity will be a function of their value in illuminating and connecting the existing texts. So too with his journal entries – they are not privileged, but his comment that "On the whole, the very mark of my genius is that Governance broadens and radicalizes whatever concerns me personally"[2] seems a good way to make sense of the texts. If, however, I have even come close to what I set out to do in this introduction to Kierkegaard's writings, working through and evaluating the retrospectives is not necessary – the reader certainly has enough material to come to her own point(s) of view.

II Looking Back – The Attack

Kierkegaard's official retrospectives were written in 1848–9 – that is, years before the end of his (short) life. The final years of his very public and unconditional calls for awareness, first in the newspapers and then in his own pamphlet series, give us another perspective on his authorship. In 1855, the last year of his life, he claimed that his motivation for what has been called the "attack on Christendom" was "honesty": "What do I want? Very simply, I want honesty" (TM, 46). He goes so far as to say that he takes his risks for the sake of honesty *rather than* for the sake of Christianity (49). This is not a new theme, emerging under the pressure of criticism. The importance of honesty (transparency, earnestness) is stressed from *Either – Or* to the final writings. The length and breadth of the authorship corroborate that it was the ultimate requirement he placed on others, and on himself – "Honesty is preferable to half-measures" (CUP, 589).

Perhaps it is this emphasis on honesty that attracts those who would otherwise be turned off by Kierkegaard's Christianity. Kierkegaard insisted on the dialectical character of faith in order to protest the religious fanaticism of those who were sure they knew God's Truth and sought to impose it on others. His emphasis on the aloneness before God of religious faith makes him especially relevant in our time, when the politicization of religion is decidedly dangerous. His fight against the dangers of having a state church and the hypocrisy this can lead to prevent his own sense of the truth of Christianity from being exclusive, divisive, or condescending.

III Looking Back – Dialectical Tension

Although there are many ways to rehearse lessons learned from the authorship, I think it is more valuable at this point to reconsider one structure that informs the authorship from beginning to end – namely, the emphasis on a (Greek) dialectic (as opposed to a speculative, theoretical, or Hegelian one). Such a dialectic rejects one-sidededness, staticness, and closure in the name of a dynamic, ongoing, tension. Kierkegaard's name will probably always be linked to the phrase "either – or." Towards the end of his life (May 24, 1855), he tells his audience with some evident annoyance, he was "known even to children on the street by the name of Either – Or" (TM, 94). For better or worse, even those who never read the book *Either – Or* often locate Kierkegaard's legacy in this ultimatum. It is a catchword that seems to cover his challenge to Christendom, but it is important not to let this catchword misrepresent his work. Even the "either – or" is subject to the constraint of dialectical tension; even though the "either – or" is an indispensable part of the story, it is only a part of it. We have seen repeated attempts to emphasize a kind of joining together, holding together, a tension-filled "both–and."[3] Even the strategy of "indirect communication" (like trying to paint someone in the clothes that make him or her invisible) can be seen as a way of avoiding the dilemma of "either direct communication or no communication."

From the beginning to the end of his authorship, Kierkegaard engaged and re-engaged one particular question – whether it is possible to do justice to the qualitative difference between categories (like the esthetic, ethical, and religious) so that they are not confused with each other, at the same time as one does justice to the possibility that these are meant to be in a *lived* harmony. The contrast between qualitative and quantitative is never far from any important passage, but it is not the whole story. Keeping qualitative difference and dialectic in tension was always a thorn in his side. Since what can and must be separated conceptually often needs to be *lived together*, Kierkegaard had to hold open the possibility that an appreciation of qualitatively different ways of orienting oneself is congruent with a practical preservation of the lower in the higher that does not make the mistake of philosophical mediation. He engaged this concern first and foremost in *Either – Or*, but the same problem is addressed in *Fear and Trembling*, *Philosophical Fragments*, and *Concluding Unscientific Postscript*. Of course, this preservation is also a *transformation*. The normative lived harmony is not a case of the esthetic *per se* and the ethical *per se* and the religious *per se* sitting side by side; for example, insofar as the esthetic sphere highlights imagination and the concrete, it is preserved in the ethical and the religious, but it is no longer used for the same ends (to escape engagement and responsibility).

This concern is also at the heart of the upbuilding and the Christian writings, especially with respect to the tension between God and the world. The importance of the qualitative difference is front and center in claims about "hatred" of the world and "dying to self," yet the norm of *lived harmony* is apparent in his refusal to let go of the finite, the creation beloved by God. He reminds us that it is Christianity itself (not he, Søren Kierkegaard) that teaches that the Christian "must, if required, be able to hate father and mother and sister and the beloved" (WL, 108). But he immediately qualifies this requirement when he asks whether Christianity requires this "in the sense, I wonder, that he should actually hate them? *Oh, far be this abomination from Christianity!*" (108, my emphasis). As he makes clearer a few pages later, we cannot be asked to "refrain from loving them"; indeed "How unreasonable – how then could your love become the fulfilling of the Law" (129). Not only can God not ask us to actually "hate" father or mother or beloved or self, we cannot even be asked by God to refrain from loving them – after all, we are to exclude no one from our love. Even at his most polemical, he doesn't lose the dialectical. When he speaks about the apostles and their task of dying to the world, he asks:

> Did they indeed swear eternal enmity to this unloving world? Well, in a certain sense, yes, because love of God is hatred toward the world, but in another sense, no, no – by loving God, in order that they might continue in love, they joined with God, so to speak, in loving this unloving world – the life-giving Spirit brought them love. (FSE, 85)

His ever-present emphasis on a Greek dialectic should support the reader's effort to find the dialectical in his writings – that is, the effort to avoid stopping prematurely at any shocking claim without trying to find the counterweight to it, without patiently reading on and appreciating the context. Kierkegaard's claims are meant to provoke and awaken – all the more reason for them to be appreciated in their particular context. The dialectic of rigor and leniency and of requirement and encouragement is ubiquitous. The themes of gift, forgiveness, and reception of the finite inform the authorship, and it is important to look for what they imply about the question of how to live the good life, or how to love rightly.

The importance of the dialectical also bears on the much-discussed issue of Kierkegaard's radical "individualism." The category of "the single individual" contrasts with "the crowd," "the public," the "race," "humanity," precisely because loving and building up cannot be done *en masse*. But insofar as his emphasis on "the single individual" insists on individual responsibility in the social sphere, his fight against the "numerical" amounts to love for "the neighbor."

His commitment to the dialectical also reveals itself in the way in which he increasingly nuances the relation between "inner" and "outer" (within a single work, as well as throughout the authorship). Initial bold statements of contrast give way to the question of whether the relation is more complicated. For example, the range of what "inwardness" can mean depends on whether Kierkegaard wants to criticize a lack of passion (in the earlier works) or the way inwardness can be used as an excuse for not acting (in the later works).

When, near the end of his life, he suggested in a journal entry that his program was "Either – Or," he explained: "*either* our lives must express the requirement and we are then justified to call ourselves Christian, *or*, if our lives express something quite different, we must give up being called Christians, we must be satisfied with being an approximation of what it is to be a Christian."[4] An "either – or" may apply to being a Christian or not, but it does not justify reading the authorship as suggesting that we must be either esthetic or ethical or religious.

I have also pointed to the limits of an "either – or" as a way of interpreting the goal of a text or an authorship. In Kierkegaard's case, the literary, religious, philosophical, theological, psychological, and personal are not mutually exclusive. Here again a "both–and" is at work.

IV Looking Ahead

Are Kierkegaard's writings of lasting significance? Descriptively the question is answered positively by reference to the *numbers* of people who have cared and continue to care about these writings. A more interesting answer arises from the variety of different *audiences* his writings have sustained, and from the *reasons* people care.

It is not surprising that there are to be found academic scholars interested in Kierkegaard – if only because almost anything could be of interest to an academic researcher. The magnitude of the recent resurgence of such academic interest, however, is surprising. No doubt some of that is due to the new appreciation of the sophisticated intricacies of Kierkegaard's use of literary genres and his self-consciousness in the use of literary strategies like pseudonymity, humor, irony, and indirect communication. Indeed, in recent years we Kierkegaard scholars have become a chastened audience; provocative writers with literary sensibilities have shattered our naïveté about Kierkegaard's writings, pointing out how even prayers and letters may have been part of his literary projects. No introduction to Kierkegaard can be innocent again. But it is important to note that much of the lasting impact of Kierkegaard's writings is on readers who care little about the academic or scholarly assessment of Kierkegaard's thought, or his ingenious crafting of an authorship. Let me give you two examples.

On January 23, 1997, a young man named Jim Hernandez gave a talk at Seattle University, entitled "Kierkegaard Prevents Gang Violence."[5] This young man, later nominated for the Nobel Peace Prize, was not your run-of-the-mill lecturer – he wasn't a Kierkegaard scholar, or even a professional academic, but in his talk he referred to several of Søren Kierkegaard's writings (*The Present Age*, *The Sickness unto Death*, and "Purity of Heart") and to concepts associated with Kierkegaard, such as dialectic, passion, paradox, and indirect communication. Jim Hernandez had been, for 15 years, a high-ranking member of a Los Angeles street gang, but now he was speaking publicly both to young people at risk for gang involvement and to social care professionals who work with such people. In his talk, he spoke of the many deaths he had experienced because of gang violence, and the despair to which he had been led by living a life "without a conscience," and how the hopelessness of that life had been changed because he heard about and then read some works by Kierkegaard. He said he somehow "understood" what Kierkegaard was talking about, and that the category of "dialectic" was both central for his re-visioning of himself and useful in his work with young people. Kierkegaard has an audience that is philosophical in the broadest sense; they see in his writings explorations of the questions of "perennial philosophy": What is the "good life"? What is it to be fully human? What do guilt and anxiety reveal? This is a practical interest in Kierkegaard's writings, and there is a parallel practical impact on those who have been religiously edified or religiously challenged by various writings about the paradox and passion of faith, and Christianity in particular.

Another audience is quite new. On August 17, 2007, the Danish newspaper *Kristeligt Dagblad*, in its section on "culture," reported on the Søren Kierkegaard Research Seminar taking place at the Søren Kierkegaard Research Center in Copenhagen. That seminar hosted scholars from around the world, but the presence of an Iranian professor speaking on "Kierkegaard in Tehran" was what made the news. The headline was provocative: "Either Kierkegaard or Fundamentalism." In response to increasing student interest in Kierkegaard's works, this Iranian professor had invited Kierkegaard scholars to a gathering in 2004, and these scholars reported that they had audiences of more than a thousand students, who were anxious to learn more about Kierkegaard. Why? In great part, it seems, it was because they saw Kierkegaard's "attack on

Christendom" as an attack on a state church – an attack on the politi-cization of religion and on the religious "fundamentalism" often aligned with it.

An appreciation of the significance of Kierkegaard's writings will, therefore, have to include his reception by very different kinds of audi-ences. The literary character of Kierkegaard's writings is part of what distinguishes him among other thinkers about religious and philosoph-ical matters – but much of the lasting impact of Kierkegaard's writings will be on readers who find in these writings something that resonates with them, that provokes them in profound ways, that awakens them to something of value in themselves, and helps them revision and cope with their lives. In sum, the debate about the implications of Søren Aabye Kierkegaard's literary sensibility will go on – fortunately, it need not be resolved in order to see if there is anything of lasting significance in his writings.

notes

1 Climacus gives the same advice (CUP, p. 252).
2 JP, 6:6388 [1849], p. 144.
3 For more on this theme, see Michael Strawser, *Both/And: Reading Kier-kegaard from Irony to Edification* (New York: Fordham University Press, 1997).
4 JP, 6:6946 [1854], p. 556.
5 Tape #00-032-A, The Ernest Becker Foundation, Mercer Island, Washington 98040, and communication from Neil Elgee, (email July 5, 2005).

Index